The Advanced Guide to Meditation

by Goswami Kriyananda

BOOKS AND HOME STUDY COURSES
BY GOSWAMI KRIYANANDA

Books
    Spiritual Science of Kriya Yoga
    Beginner's Guide to Meditation
    Intermediate Guide to Meditation
    The Wisdom and Way of Astrology
    The Bhagavad Gita
    The Laws of Karma
    Extraordinary Spiritual Potential
    Kriya Yoga Upanishad and the Ten Mystical Yoga Upanishads
    Pathway to God-Consciousness
    Yoga Dictionary of Basic Sanskrit Terms
    Yoga Dictionary of Basic Astrological Terms
    Beginner's Guide to Meditation, A Talking Book
    Beginner's Guide to Meditation, Book-Tape Set
    Wisdom & Way of Astrology

Home Study Courses
    The Chakras: The Garden of God
    Kriology
    Sacred Apprenticeship: Guru-Disciple Relationship
    Philosophy and Methodology of Kriya Yoga
    Establishing a Firm Foundation for Your Spiritual Life
    The Yoga Sutras of Patanjali
    Hatha Yoga Teacher Training & Certification Home Study

In French
    La Science Spirituelle du Kriya Yoga
    Guide Pratique de Méditation
    Astrologie, voie de Sagesse
    Les Lois du Karma
    Le Kriya Bindu

In Spanish
    Su Primer Guía de Meditación

In Italian
    La scienza spirituale delle yoga di Kriya
    E.S.P.: tuoi eccezionali poteri spirituali
    Astrology: via e saggezza

In Dutch
    Kriya Yoga: Werk en Oefenboek

Goswami Kriyananda

PREFACE

This is a text on advanced meditation. It is assumed that the reader has had some training in meditation or has read the first two books in this series: *The Beginner's Guide to Meditation* and *The Intermediate Guide to Meditation.* What exactly is advanced meditation? Meditation is a continuous, effortless stream of consciousness. However, for the purpose of teaching the science of meditation, it is helpful to divide the process into three levels: beginning, intermediate, and advanced. This should not cause you to think that meditation consists of three separate and independent steps. It may be taught in three steps, but the practice of meditation is still one continuous flow of consciousness.

Advanced meditation is not a technique for getting something. Rather, it is a technique to remove things. It is a method used to dissolve negative and constrictive states of consciousness, limited mind-states, confining karma, and most importantly, false memories. As you let go of these states, clarity comes into your mind and therefore into your life. As constrictive thinking is removed from the various levels of your mind, positive thoughts and events flow in. Just as day follows night, the practice of advanced meditation brings about enlightenment.

Enlightenment is attained by the process of samadhi, which is the perfected tool from which all goodness flows. However, there is an intermediate stage between advanced meditation and samadhi, which I call the outer fringes of samadhi. It is attainable in this very lifetime by everyone. Few earthlings will attain samadhi in this lifetime, but everyone who practices the techniques from this text can and will attain the outer fringes of samadhi. The key difference between samadhi and the outer fringes of samadhi lies primarily in the intensity and the duration of the experience.

It is vital to attain and sustain the outer fringes of samadhi without losing sight of your essential daily responsibilities. One foot must be kept firmly rooted on earth while the rest of your being soars unto heaven. It is imperative that you attend to your worldly responsibilities because the earth life is the spiritual life. Only when you begin to balance your earth life will your spiritual life become balanced. To deny your earthly responsibilities is to fail to fulfill your spiritual responsibilities. Your spiritual obligation is to reach enlightenment so that you can serve others.

This text has been written with a continuous thread from beginning to end. Some readers will see this thread more easily than others. Study the text and practice the methods that are explained so that you can perceive that thread. It will lead you to the Door of Truth. Open that Door. Contact the Powers that Be. Be blessed. Be a greater blessing to others, for that is the goal of advanced meditation.

Goswami Kriyananda

TABLE OF CONTENTS

INTRODUCTION

This *Advanced Guide to Meditation* explains the psychology of overcoming karmic limitations and provides methods for creating positive karma in this lifetime as well as the next. These techniques will help you develop greater inner freedom and will assist you to attain your spiritual goals. At the same time, this process will help you discover your collective destiny. This text explains how to use meditation concepts and techniques to expand your consciousness, enhance your intellect and thereby improve your everyday life and your spiritual Life. These methods will also enhance your creative ability, enabling you to solve life problems for yourself and for others more harmoniously.

The practice of advanced meditation techniques will also enhance your emotional maturity, making life more meaningful and enjoyable. Experiencing joy is one goal of a healthy life. Most people are so preoccupied with everyday problems that they find very little joy in life; life has little or no meaning for them. Meditation is a way to overcome and remove this everyday struggle. The enemy is not external to us. Our adversary is our own constrictive and often subconscious thinking patterns, which cause the mind to develop a self-limiting and self-constricting personality. In this pattern, one experiences neither joy nor success and there is a lack of awareness of the possibilities for a better life. Meditation is a way to remove constrictive, limiting thinking. It liberates the cosmic mind that dwells within all of us and arises from the ego self.

There are many pathways to meditation. In my first two books on meditation, I emphasized Kriya Yoga techniques. In this text, I am branching out and discussing techniques from other schools of thought, both Eastern and Western. These comparative techniques will enhance your understanding and assist you in the mastery of this ancient wisdom.

A primary tenet of Kriya Yoga, common to all schools of mysticism, is that we are not to interfere in the lives of others. We should not tell others how to live their lives. It is we, ourselves, who must break free from our own karmic limitations. It is by example that we teach best.

The technical term for becoming free from our karmic limitations is called enlightenment. The path to enlightenment begins by watching the flow of your thoughts, softening the negative thought patterns, replacing them with positive thoughts, and finally manifesting expanded, balanced self-conscious awareness. In short, as you will find in the pages of this text, mysticism and Kriya Yoga are based on the spiritual psychology of the soul.

Om Shanti

CHAPTER ONE
Meditation and the Spiritual Journey

This text has three major goals:

• To introduce fundamental knowledge regarding advanced meditation procedures and to clarify misconceptions regarding advanced meditation.

• To answer general questions that are repeatedly asked by students interested in advanced meditation.

• To explain basic comparative meditation techniques from traditions that differ from yoga in their approach to meditation. By practicing these different approaches, you will gain a clearer understanding of meditation and a deeper awareness of your personality.

It is my hope that these three goals will merge into a meaningful study program that will shed light on the pattern that underlies all meditation practices. If a technique is a viable meditation technique, it is a meditation technique no matter who espouses it or who practices it. In mysticism we say, "No circle is more circular than any other circle." In other words, we should not engage in a categorical secularism, thinking that there is only one true school or technique.

No meditation technique is better than any other meditation technique. Because human personalities differ, a technique that is effective for one person may not work successfully for another. Nevertheless, any meditation technique that is practiced in a dedicated manner will, in time, result in intense self-awareness.

My purpose in writing this text is not to encourage you to think the way I think. Rather, it is to share with you many different techniques. It is my hope that you will practice the various methods explained and find the one best suited to you. As you practice them, look for the technique that works most effectively for you, the one that best quiets your mind and lifts your consciousness. Stay with that technique. Unfold by using it. Share what you have discovered with those who are interested in the deeper side of Life. Experience the beauty, wonderment, and joy that are your existence.

It will be helpful to begin this text with a discussion of the nature of the human being. Traditionally, we think of the human being as a body of clay that has some sort of spirit poured into it. Respectfully, this is a rather naive concept. Ancient civilizations, on the other hand, conceived the human being, or the true Self, to have three bodies surrounded by five fundamental vibrations referred to as *sheaths*. These three bodies are the gross body, the subtle body, and the super-subtle body. The sheaths occlude the celestial light of this primary Self and are the obstacles that hinder us from gaining a full realization of this Self (the *Atma*).

In Sanskrit these sheaths are called *koshas* and are referred to as the five *maya-koshas*. The word *maya* here means transitory. In other words, these sheaths are temporal. From their grossest to their subtlest form, the Sanskrit names of these sheaths are:

- The temporal food sheath (*anna-maya-kosha*).
- The temporal life-force sheath (*prana-maya-kosha*).
- The temporal mind sheath (*mana-maya-kosha*).
- The temporal knowledge sheath (*vijnana-maya-kosha).*
- The temporal bliss sheath (*ananda-maya-kosha*).

Running through these three bodies and the five sheaths are channels through which life-energy, called *prana*, flows. It is prana that vivifies and sustains these three bodies and five sheaths. The ancient texts say the numbers of channels are infinite, but most texts agree that there are some 72,000 existing throughout the astral body. These channels are called *nadis* and are pathways over which the life-energy flows. The three most significant nadis are the *ida*, the *pingala* and the *sushumna*. It will be much easier to think of these three nadis as the moon channel (*ida-nadi*), the sun channel (*pingala-nadi*), and the divine fire channel (*sushumna-nadi*). The moon channel runs along the left side of the spine and carries energy currents that activate the mental/emotional and imagination centers of the subtle body, also known as the astral body. The sun channel runs along the right side of the spine and carries energy currents that activate the mental/logical centers of the astral body. The divine fire channel runs exactly through the center of the spine and carries the energy currents that activate the spiritual centers existing in the super-subtle body, known as the causal body.

You might wish to refer to my home study course on the chakras for a very extensive discussion on the subject of the nadis, the chakras, and the subtle anatomy of the cerebro-spinal body. However, it is not necessary to do this for the purpose of reading this text on advanced meditation.

An awareness of these three channels will enable you to easily answer many different questions regarding various states of meditation. With an understanding of these three nadis, you can comprehend the nature of the mind/body complex. This, in turn, will help you to grasp the nature of meditation and to recognize that every technique is *not* a meditation technique.

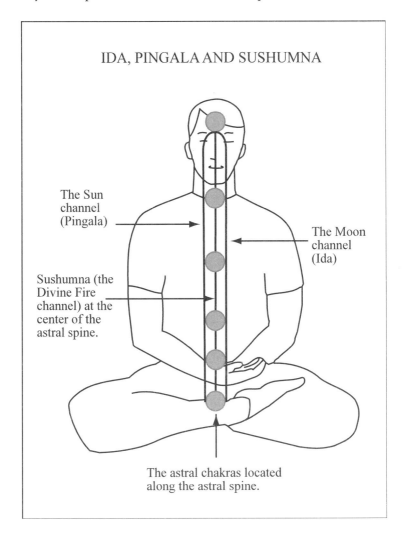

IDA, PINGALA AND SUSHUMNA

The Sun channel (Pingala)

The Moon channel (Ida)

Sushumna (the Divine Fire channel) at the center of the astral spine.

The astral chakras located along the astral spine.

Exoterically, it does not really matter what you use as the object of your meditation. You can meditate upon a beautiful flower, a person, a jewel, a candle, a mantra, the Grand Canyon, or something more subtle. However, esoterically, what you meditate upon *does* make a difference. What you focus on has a very powerful effect on your mind and thus on the states of consciousness you experience. Each object (gross, subtle, or super-subtle) is a symbol recognized by the mind and, esoterically, will have a very powerful effect on your moods and therefore on the states of consciousness that you can summon forth.

A man can meditate on a beautiful woman. A woman can meditate on a diamond ring. However, as objects of meditation, these are not wise choices because they are emotional symbols and usually evoke passionate or emotional states. These emotions hinder the attainment of a state of meditation. When you choose an object to meditate upon, it is very important that you select a neutral object—one that does not produce emotionality. Do not select an object that evokes even the smallest degree of emotion. In the early practice of deep meditation, you should even be cautious about choosing religious symbols because they all evoke emotionality. We are seeking to transcend thought. In order to do this, we must quell all emotions. It is only after the emotions have been quelled that we are able to transcend thought and move to a transcendental state of consciousness.

Before we can attain a state of meditation, we must reach a state of concentration. Concentration simply means focusing the mind *effortfully* upon a single object. We can concentrate upon anything and produce a given state of mind. By concentrating on a given object (mental or physical), that object-as-symbol will produce a very specific state of consciousness. Meditation simply means focusing the mind *effortlessly* upon a single object. Concentration must precede meditation.

You can meditate upon anything, and within that meditation a singular mind state will manifest esoterically in your consciousness. Meditation is an effortless movement of the mind from its surface thoughts and emotions into its depths, past deeper thoughts, until it turns its awareness back upon itself. Meditation is turning away from the thought of the object and the thoughts that the object invokes, back to the "thinker of thoughts." Meditation is transcending thought. Meditation releases your awareness from thought, allowing it to focus upon the true Self, the Reality of which you are a part and not apart from.

When one attains a state of meditation, independent of the object, it produces a neutralization of the energies existing in the solar (pingala) and the lunar (ida) channels of your astral body. When these two force-fields collapse, the divine fire (sushumna) channel is revealed. When these two force-fields neutralize each other, your consciousness ascends to cosmic consciousness via the fire channel. This awareness of the fire channel is the key pathway leading to cosmic consciousness. The level to which you ascend in the fire channel, the chakra at which you come to rest, depends upon your past-life karma.

The next task in advanced meditation is to ascend your consciousness through this middle channel in such a way that it does not break out of the fire channel and into either the solar or the lunar channels. As long as the energy remains in the fire channel, it is linear energy. If the energy breaks out into either of the other channels, it will become angular. Only with linear energy can we neutralize confining karma. Only with linear energy can we expand our state of consciousness into cosmic consciousness.

The primary force-fields of our being are conveyed through the solar and lunar channels. When we reach a state of meditation, the angular energies in the two outer channels collapse and become linear. Then they can enter into the fire channel and begin moving upward. When this happens, our consciousness begins to expand into cosmic consciousness. This is an essential point. When a person uses a technique that is *not* a meditation technique (for example, a concentration technique), the energies in the two channels do not collapse and do not become linear. Thus, they cannot enter into the fire channel.

In the physical world, angular energy is simply called energy. In the psychological realm, angular energy is called emotionality. Linear energy is emotionless Angular energy is emotional energy. Gaining emotional energy is not the function of meditation. The function of meditation is to quiet the body, to quiet the emotions, to still the mind and then to transcend to a state of pure consciousness.

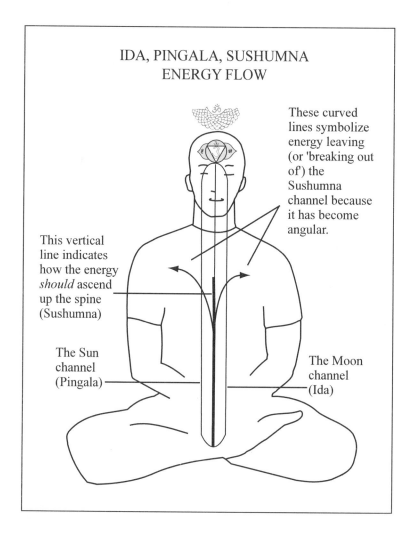

IDA, PINGALA, SUSHUMNA
ENERGY FLOW

These curved lines symbolize energy leaving (or 'breaking out of') the Sushumna channel because it has become angular.

This vertical line indicates how the energy *should* ascend up the spine (Sushumna)

The Sun channel (Pingala)

The Moon channel (Ida)

Angular energy is represented by a wavy motion; it angulates. It has the power to do and accomplish things in the physical realm as well as in the mental realm. When angular energies meet, there is a battle as they seek to change each other. On the other hand, when two or more linear energies meet, they do not interfere with each other and there is no battle. They can exist in the same space, at the same time, without affecting each other.

Angular energies exist everywhere in our being except in the very center of the fire channel. The energy in the lunar (left) channel is emotional energy. The energy in the solar (right) channel is intellectual energy. The energy in the fire (center) channel is a feeling state.

People frequently inquire about the difference between emotions and feelings. "Aren't they the same thing?" The answer is "No, they are very different from each other." Feelings are not emotions, and emotions are not feelings. Feeling, mystically speaking, is linear, whereas emotionality is non-linear energy. They are quite distinct, despite the fact that in common usage the words are interchangeable.

Webster's Collegiate dictionary defines the word "emotion" as:
   … An affective state of consciousness in which joy, sorrow, fear, etc., is experienced, as distinguished from cognitive and volitional states of consciousness.

The dictionary, however, gives many definitions of the word "feeling." As a point of reference, I have included 12 different meanings below:

   1. *The power of perceiving by touch, or by any physical sensation not connected with sight, hearing, taste, or smell.*

   2. *The general state of consciousness considered independently of particular sensations, thoughts, etc.*

   3. *A consciousness or vague awareness as in "a feeling of inferiority."*

   4. *The capacity for emotion, specifically compassion.*

   5. *A sentiment, attitude, or opinion.*

   6. *Sensibilities, susceptibilities.*

   7. *Fine emotional endowment.*

   8. *Emotion or sympathetic perception revealed by an artist.*

   9. *Sensitive, sentient.*

   10. *Readily affected by emotion.*

   11. *Indicating or characterized by emotion.*

   12. *Syn. Feeling, emotion. Emotion is applied to an intensified feeling. Feeling is a general term for a subjective point of view as well as for specific sensations.*

You can see from this that, in the English language, the words "emotion" and "feeling" are quite similar and are used interchangeably. This is not always true in the study of psychology and it is never true in yoga and mysticism, in which emotions and feelings do not have the same meaning. Emotions are angular energy and battle with all other angular energies. Feelings are non-angular energies and do not battle or interfere with things or emotions. Thus, they can control emotions rather than intensifying emotions by battling them. In life we want to move into a feeling state. Meditation is one of the best and fastest ways to attain a feeling state.

The word "emotion" is derived from two Greek words: *E* and *motion*, meaning "to put into motion." Introduced into the English language via the French when William conquered England in 1066, it first appeared in middle French circa 1575 from the word *esmotion*, which means "to set in motion" or "to move the feelings." It most likely came into French from Latin when Caesar conquered France (then known as Gaul). The Latin word *exmovere* means "to move" or "to put into motion."

In the psychology of yoga, the phrase that refers to the word "emotion" is *angular energy*. Emotion is a compulsive force of the mind. It is mind-energy that forces one to think or do something. However, the word "feeling" refers to *a state of awareness in which there is only awareness.* It has no compulsion. Feeling is pure awareness. It is awareness without any compulsive force within or behind it.

An example will clarify the distinction between emotion and feeling states. Let us say that two souls meditate and experience what they call "a deep, profound encounter." The first person is stimulated to go out and convert the world to think as he thinks. He does this because he believes that his way is the *only* true way. He is compelled to do this. The mystic, the yogi, would say that his experience was an emotional experience and not a meditation. The psychologist would say that he had a hallucination, which is comprised of emotional energy.

After having his experience, the second person remains silent and reflects on the experience. He comes to understand that all paths lead to Truth. He understands that some take a little longer, some go by different routes, but in time all reach Truth. Thus, he has no compulsion to try to change anyone's meditation technique or to change the world. If someone were to ask him for his method, he may or may not give it to that person, for he is not compelled to do so. Thus, the mystic would say that he had a "feeling," a vision, which is linear.

In mysticism, these two types of experiences, *emotional hallucinations* and *feeling visions,* are shortened to "hallucinations" and "visions."

Another simple example may be helpful. A person sits down and begins to meditate on a banana split. Suddenly he decides that he has meditated long enough and that he should take a stroll to get some fresh air. Next he thinks that he should stop at the drugstore and get a magazine. While he is there, he thinks that he should sit at the counter and read a magazine. Next he decides that he cannot just sit there; he should buy something. So he orders a banana split.

I hope it is clear that this was not meditating. His "meditation" was not a meditation at all. It was a state of emotional desire in which the ego mindset named his activity "meditation." Whether he was consciously aware of it or not, his mental vehicle was literally moved to go out and buy a banana split. He was compelled by his emotions. His mind, and thus his body, were put into motion to go out and buy a banana split.

If, in truth, he were meditating on a banana split, even if one of his friends suddenly tapped him on the shoulder and said, "We've all decided to go out and get a banana split. Do you want to come?," he would open his eyes and say, "No, I have a banana split right now ... and it's not fattening." In other words, meditation tends to hold one to the object upon which one is meditating. I hope that this clarifies more fully the difference between emotions and feelings, between non-meditative and meditative states.

As one reaches deeper states of consciousness through meditation, the flow of thoughts streaming through the mind moves to an elevated level of awareness. In the lower levels of consciousness, all thought is infected with emotions. The higher the level of awareness, the lower the emotional infection. At the highest level, there is no emotional infection whatsoever.

The life force of the average person is ruled by emotions rather than by reason and consideration. On the lower levels, we are all slaves and prisoners of our own emotional thought patterns. It is the only contact we have with Life. We see Life only according to the thoughts that are flowing through our minds. These thoughts are forced upon us because of the nature of our emotionality. Rarely, if ever, do we see what is truly happening outside ourselves or inside ourselves.

This happens on a personal level but also on a cultural level. History is ever changing according to the emotional values, and thus the thoughts, of the conqueror. In recorded history, the dates and activities of the countries involved are generally correct, but the place of battle and the reason for the war are always changed. Take the example of the Battle of San Juan Hill. They tell us that the Roughriders rode up that hill to victory. In truth, however, it is common knowledge that this battle took place some distance from the hill. And did you know that the famous picture of the American flag being placed on top of Mount Suabatchi was a posed picture? In this picture, they intentionally selected people to include the "correct" race, religion and color for the cultural patterning they wanted to present.

What happens in recorded history is a subjective, ever-changing series of events that is totally modified by the unconscious emotions and by the conscious emotional needs of the victors. History books are always a reflection of the conqueror and never an accurate reflection of history. Politicians, victors, generals and those in charge alter things and events for their self-serving purposes and needs.

Beware of everything you read. Be even more careful about what you think you know. Be even more careful about what you believe. This is the path of the mystic.

In the process of attaining a state of meditation, the meditator locks a thought pattern back into his mind while removing the emotions linked to that thought pattern. He takes a thought and turns it back upon his mind again and again. This is called concentration, the first step to attaining meditation. As emotions are removed or substantially dissipated, this process becomes easier and easier until the mind stabilizes itself and is fixed in deep concentration. Thus, a non-changing state of consciousness is established. At some point in this deep concentration, the meditator can let go of the effort that holds the mind to the thought; he can hold that thought effortlessly. In so doing, he attains a state of meditation.

As the meditator moves deeper into meditation, he reaches a galactic, unchanging state called *vritti nirodha*. This term means the process of the cessation of all thought—but without losing consciousness! The mind has become focused. It has attained one-pointedness. When the mind becomes extremely active and excited by the activities of emotion, cognition and volitional function, as well as incoming sensations, it has no power to focus. A mind that is not focused is an impotent mind, and a mind that cannot focus is a mind wasted.

It is helpful to understand the goals of yoga:

• The first goal in yoga is to soften the emotions so that the mind can become focused.

• The second stage is to quiet the flow of incoming sensations.

• The third stage is to slow down the incoming cognitive mind processes.

• The fourth stage is to reduce the volitional functions, those functions of the mind that are non-compulsory, that is, logical thought patterns.

• The fifth stage is to stop the cognitive mind processes.

• The sixth stage, which runs throughout all of the preceding stages, is to remove all of the volitional functions from one's mindset, leaving a free-flowing feeling state of consciousness.

• The seventh stage is to attain quiescence of the mind.

• The eighth and last stage is to attain an absolute stillness of the mind. This state of absolute stillness is known in yoga as *vritti nirodha.*

It is imperative to understand that all of these stages can be mastered only by first creating a sane lifestyle. Once a sane lifestyle has been established, breathing techniques can be practiced. This can be followed by using mantra techniques and then by using mental affirmations. All of these stages lead to a state of deeper concentration and then to meditation. After meditation has been mastered to some degree, one can slip into the outer fringes of samadhi. This stage of samadhi follows meditation as day follows night.

The state of samadhi has three levels. In each level, the sushumanic awareness varies.

The first level exists within the outer fringes of samadhi. Although this state is quite strong, it is the weakest of the three.

The second level exists within fractional samadhi, which is stronger.

The third level exists within total or absolute samadhi. Here the sushumanic awareness is the strongest.

Mystically and spiritually, emotions are considered negative because they compel us to think, say and do things, as it were, against our will. Emotions are always destructive to us and to those around us. They limit our horizon of awareness and narrow that which we are aware of and that which we can become aware of. They distort all that we see and all that we think.

According to the mystical viewpoint, and contrary to what most people believe, there are no positive emotions. All emotions are negative, whereas all feelings are positive. Mystically, emotions are negative because they move the mind away from sushumanic awareness; that is, they move the mind away from balanced awareness.

One of the emotions that most people consider positive is love. Yet look at all the destruction and pain that has been caused by this so-called positive emotion. Take the example of two people falling in love. In the initial stages, things appear to be wonderful. But look at all of the possessive things that occur because they are in love and at the vicious things done when one of them falls in love with another person. This type of love is an emotion. If it were a feeling state, and if indeed this person truly loved the other person, he would do everything possible to help his partner form a positive relationship with the other person. His attitude would be: "If you love someone else and would be happier with that person, you have my blessings." In my guru's language, this type of love is called *unselfish love*. The first type of love is called *selfish love* or just *love*. Some yogis would call the second type of love, that is, unselfish love, *compassion*. I call it *wisdom*. The rest of the world would call it crazy.

Yet, the truth is, if you love a person, you want to give that person that which will make him happy. Giving that person up should bring great joy if you know that you have helped to make him happy. If a person wants to possess someone or something, it is not truly love; it is an emotion that people call love. We need to clearly differentiate unselfish love, which is a feeling state, from selfish love, which is an emotion. Clearly, the type of love most people experience is selfish love. This possessive type of emotion brings a great deal of anguish and pain—not only into the person's life but also to all other people in that person's life.

One of the goals of the spiritual seeker is to attain liberation from the enemy within. The enemy within is a double-headed dragon: one head is *unawareness* and the other is *compulsiveness*. We are unaware of what is happening both within and outside. We are unaware of the "larger picture" in Life.

We are totally unaware of the greater things in Life, and thus we become compulsive regarding the lesser things of which we are aware. We are much like the man who, during the winter months, is cold but unaware of the heating unit existing in the house he has rented. He is only aware of the fire down the road. Thus, he is compelled to run out to that fire to warm himself.

The mystical approach is to neutralize emotions. When this happens, our lack of awareness markedly diminishes. We become more aware of both internal and external impulses, enabling us to guide our "ship of state" in a wiser direction. As we act more wisely, the imbalanced forces balance themselves and we become aware of the larger picture in Life.

We can now speed up our spiritual evolution. This is possible only because in removing or markedly softening our emotions, we begin to become mature. Maturity is the first and most essential step in gaining cosmic consciousness, because our emotions and thinking are then brought into a state of balanced awareness. This balanced awareness is a primal feeling.

When this transpires, everything becomes still. Rather than seeing what we desire, what we need to see or what we have been emotionally conditioned to see, we see what is truly happening—inside ourselves and others and universally. There is a transformation of our ego personality, a softening of the ego's needs and greed. This feeling state of awareness enables "seeing" without subjectivity.

An example might make clear the way in which we tend to react from a place of subjectivity. A man walks down the street. He is in an emotional state, because he feels the world has done him wrong. He has failed at something and is really upset. Though it is a beautiful, sunny day and everyone is smiling, the man is convinced that everyone is making fun of him. He thinks, "He's laughing at me. She's laughing at me. They're all laughing at me." This emotion takes the external objective reality of a smile and converts it into a subjective negative state in his mind.

The ancient texts often refer to this objective/subjective reality using the symbolism of a pond. Look into a quiet, still pond and see the reflection of a mountain. There is a double image: the actual mountain and its reflection. If someone were to drop a pebble into the lake, one of the mountains would begin to move. These ripples enable one to distinguish between the real mountain and the reflected one. In the same way, the ripples in the mind show us that which is not the Reality. The ripples in our minds are only a vague, mirrored image of Reality.

A state of meditation is not difficult to achieve if the instructions received are not faulty. One of the most common misconceptions is that we need to meditate for many hours in order to get a glimpse of Reality. However, a person cannot meditate for that length of time because meditation must be *effortless* in order to truly be meditation. During such a long period of time, the mind would become *effortful.* It is true that with a great deal of practice one can learn to concentrate for hours, but the average person like you and I cannot suspend the mind in meditation for hours, even after practicing meditation for many decades.

We overcome the difficulty of the mind seeking to do everything with effort by practicing and holding a state of meditation for only one or two seconds at each session. This is the secret. Because this is a very short period, it does not take much effort to hold the mind effortlessly. It is very difficult to produce a totally relaxed state of mind for ten or twenty minutes each and every day. Thus, just practice for three to five seconds and focus on something pleasant. This will assist your meditation. You are going for depth rather than length. Practice this three to six times a day.

I suggest you begin with the object of beauty meditation technique. If you are not familiar with it, it is explained in *Beginner's Guide to Meditation* and later in this text. If you are familiar with this technique, use it again, going for depth of meditation, not length of meditation.

Whatever technique you use, you need to familiarize yourself with it, whether you use it for a few seconds or a few minutes. You need to practice the technique often enough to become comfortable with it.

Each meditation school has symbols that it uses. Each meditation technique can have meaning to you if you understand these symbols. These symbols should not evoke any emotional reaction. A detached attitude needs to be established regarding the object of meditation and the symbols surrounding that object. This is best attained by first practicing detachment in your everyday life. Every day you need to learn to become more and more detached ... detached but not *indifferent*. Learn to slow down so that when you close your eyes, you will already be close to a meditative state. If you are running at eighty miles an hour, your lifestyle will be detrimental to meditation and to your spiritual life.

The technique and approach that you use must be comfortable and somewhat familiar to you. As your mastery of detachment progresses, you can meditate for longer periods of time throughout the day. This is usually done by dividing these long periods into short segments throughout the day. That is, meditating for a short time, then putting your mind to something for a longer period of time and then returning to your meditation for a short time again. Repeat this cycle a number of times throughout the day.

You are seeking depth, not length, of meditation. In so doing, your mind will not tire of the meditation. Remember that a tired mind will become effortful. In meditating thusly, you will be able to return to your meditation often. You will look forward to your next meditation session. This practice will help deepen your meditation, and the time span will increase automatically *without* effort.

In case you have not read the first two books in this meditation series, permit me to say that meditation is learned in three stages:

The first stage in learning to meditate effortlessly is simply to learn to sit still. Develop the habit of sitting still for three to five minutes at a time a few times each day at a consistent time each day. Your body must be absolutely motionless, without any tension whatsoever. Practice body stillness at the same time, in the same place and in the same posture each and every day. This will train your body to become motionless. It will also train your mind to become still in preparation for meditation.

In Kita Kamakura, Japan, where I spent some time, there was a Zen monastery in which the monks meditated daily. The first time I entered the hall and saw these monks, it was truly a marvel. They were so motionless and tensionless that they appeared to be made of wood or concrete. As they meditated, I heard a double clap and all but one monk stood up. As I observed this, I finally realized that the monk who remained sitting was made out of carved wood. This experience was a lesson for me and the new monks. It was intended to produce an insight, a *satori*, as to what meditation is truly all about. And it did!

The next stage for attaining a meditative state is to train the mind not to seek out "bells and whistles"—and most people do expect bells and whistles. Understand that striving for this type of experiences leads the mind away from meditation. One can hear bells and whistles if that is what one is seeking, but these will only produce states of concentration, not meditation.

After a while, a person will become bored with the technique. At this point, he usually looks for another method—a new method that will stimulate his mind. But in fact, to be effective, the technique must be repeated often so that it *does* become boring to the mind. It is at this point that one must continue practicing the method so that the habit becomes established and effortless. Then the mind will break open into a meditative state.

What usually happens is that as soon as a person becomes a little bored with a technique, he switches to another technique and starts all over again. He works very hard to master the new technique. The cycle is repeated. Once again, he spends all of his time in a state of concentration rather than a state of meditation.

When you are learning to meditate and boredom manifests, know that you are right on the brink of reaching meditation. It is at the edge of boredom that the mind looks for something new. Continue with the same method, and your mind will move to a "newness." Rather than switching to a different meditation technique, continuing with the same method will help you attain the newness of a *transcendental state of consciousness.* Your mind will move into a state of meditation or it will fall asleep.

Learning meditation is just like learning to type. If you have ever watched a person learn to type, you know that in the beginning stages he cannot be disturbed because he needs to concentrate on the keys. Once he has learned to type, however, he can type and talk at the same time; typing has become an automatic process. It is exactly the same with meditation. It has to become automatic. That is to say, *effortless* (for the conscious mind). In the same way that typing is automatic, the act of meditation must become automatic so that the mind can move away from conscious thinking about how to meditate to actually meditating at lower levels of the mind.

Yoga is a spiritual psychology dealing with states of consciousness. It is also a metaphysical science relating to the physical world. It relates and correlates various states of consciousness to mental and physical health. Yoga is also a mystical science in that it views these states of consciousness as precursors to physical events.

In yoga psychology, angular energy is called emotionality. The more angular the energies are, the more emotionality a person will experience or express. Meditation occurs when we take the internal angular energies and center them, making them more linear.

Most of us experience this centering of angular energy at one time or another when we become very emotional and then realize that we must remain calm. We usually use will power to calm these strong angular energies. As we do this, the energy moves toward the center channel, and we immediately calm down. For example, we may experience this when our boss is critical. We become angry, but we know that to retort could mean losing our job.

A number of schools teach that meditation occurs only when the mind focuses upon God. They add that focusing the mind upon anything else is just a state of concentration. This is not true; it is simply their religious definition of meditation. There are certain teachers who say that concentration is centering the mind upon a given thing, whereas meditation is centering the mind upon "no-thing." Yoga, however, relates the states of concentration and meditation to the concepts of *effortful* and *effortless* actions of the mind. This concept is more functional.

Meditation is a state of full attention *without* tension. Often you see people meditating or doing what they believe to be meditation, yet you can see that they have a great deal of tension. Their bodies may be still, but this stillness is filled with extreme tension. It may be a state of concentration, but it is not meditation.

As you move toward a state of meditation, you can perceive if your full attention is with or without tension just by being more aware. Become more self-aware and ask yourself, "How restless is my body? How restless is my mind? How tense is my body? How tense is my mind?" Finally, ask yourself, "How much effort am I putting into this meditation?"

When you finish your meditation, there are a number of things that reveal whether or not you have been meditating. Two factors are more apparent than others. First, if you are all geared up to accomplish something, you have not been in a state of meditation. If, however, you want to just remain sitting to enjoy the quietude, you have been in a state of meditation. This state of quietude, of contentment, is known as *santosha*. This state is vital because it is the stage just before the feeling state of cosmic consciousness. Contentment is not laziness. It is a state of active being that is not passive. The state of contentment contains the fullness of Life. Everything of value, everything of beauty, everything of meaning is present in contentment, in santosha. There is nothing more to do ... nothing more to seek. The contentment factor definitely shows. You and those around you will feel it.

On a subtler level, your personality will improve as you practice meditation. There will be a softening and a mellowing of your personality. The rough edges will automatically become smoother. At first, this will not be obvious to you. Other people will observe the improvement long before you do. They will say things like, "Did you lose some weight?" or "Did you change your hairstyle?" They will feel something radiating from you that is very positive but because it is so subtle at first, they will not be exactly sure what it is that has changed.

This does not mean that you will never get upset but it does mean that you will not get upset as often or as deeply. In time, you will never become upset. These are important differences because *intensity* and *duration* are the primary forces that bind us to our nightmares and "day-mares" of emotionality and, consequently, our own self-confinement. Thus, we need to be sure that we are meditating and meditating deeply.

The problem with most people, most of the time, is that they live in a constant state of restlessness and irritability, and thus mal-contentment. This leads to continual frustration. Their minds manifest negative emotions such as anger, jealousy and hatred, that are destructive to themselves, their families, and their civilization. These negative states of emotionality are destructive to the dreams and goals of everyone.

Psychologists talk about psychological blind spots. Meditation removes our blind spots. It softens the negative psychological attitudes, which are always destructive. Meditation enables us to expand our horizon of awareness, to change the subconscious, limiting patterns into positive, conscious, delimiting forces. Meditation enables us to break out of our tunnel vision and to develop our awareness on a broader horizon. Even more beneficial, it causes our awareness to expand vertically. This ascending vertical awareness is a movement into the higher, inner planes of consciousness.

As we move into higher planes of consciousness, we begin to:

• Clearly see the subtler physical laws along with the subtler patterns existing within the physical universe.

• Clearly see the subtler mental laws, which first manifest as subtle symbols in the brain stem.

• Clearly see the subtler laws manifesting in consciousness.

• Gain insight into the relationship between symbols in the brain and the laws manifesting in the mind and in the physical world.

• Gain insight into the awareness of other worlds.

• Feel and understand the inner relationship between the higher and lower realms, as well as the grosser and subtler worlds.

An example will be helpful in clarifying these concepts. Very high in the sky, there is water vapor. When the temperature cools, rain begins to fall. As it becomes quite colder, snow is formed. As the snow falls into warmer conditions, it begins to melt. As the temperature warms, the wet snow is converted into rain again. Eventually, this water hits the ground as rain and forms small pools of water. Because of the sun's warmth, these pools of water ascend into the sky as water vapor. The water circulates up and down, changing its form: vapor, water, snow, water, vapor, etc. In this example, we can see how the water goes through three basic states of physical matter: vapor, liquid and solid.

Mystics use water as the symbol of mankind's mental processes. The mind process is three-fold, referred to in Sanskrit as *gunas*. Most people's mental processes are frozen solid. The secret of a wise and happy life is to break free from whatever frozen mindset we have developed. These frozen mindsets, referred to as *tamasic* mindsets, are karmic patterns that are very difficult to break. Although they are hard to break, they can easily be melted by the warmth of the sun.

In Western culture, it is said that most people's hearts are as cold as ice. The secret of meditation is to melt the hardened heart by radiating spiritual warmth. We all need to break away, to a greater or lesser degree, from the confinement of our hardened heart. It produces a very cold attitude toward everything. As we begin to radiate spiritual warmth from within, we soften our own hearts, as well as the hardened hearts of mankind.

To generate spiritual warmth we need to reflect, understand and accomplish a number of things.

1. We need to develop the ability to adjust, adapt and acclimate to all life conditions. We need to move through various transformations at will and thus freely explore the dimensions of consciousness.

2. Mystically speaking, human beings live in a fairly set pattern mentally, physically, and karmically. We need to recognize that all changes occur slowly. We need to be very patient with other people and with ourselves.

3. We need to recognize that almost all personalities are fixed. For most of us, it is not possible to change our prejudices and loyalties. The mind, once it locks into an emotion, once it freezes into an emotion, tends to remain there, acting against our own better judgment and even against our own will.

This problem stems from our early childhood experiences and is based upon inherent past-life attitudes, moods and fears. As fullgrown adults, we are still battling with these earlier attitudes. The only difference is that as we grow older, we become more unconscious of these attitudes. We soon realize that trying to fight these emotions with logic is not very effective.

We tend to see successful people in terms of social value rather than in terms of spiritual value. Take General Patton as an example. In history, he will remain as one of the greatest generals of the Western world. However, few people ever question whether he had any real choice in becoming who he was. I doubt that he could have broken this pattern even if he had wanted to. The same is true of almost all people who become famous. It is their compulsion that drives them to fame. The mystical truth is that they came into this life with very little choice. Their past-life conditioning has forced them to fulfill a karmic desire for fame.

We must try to become independent of the compulsions of our past lives. When I was very young, the only place I could be found was in a library. However, I could never persuade my brother to go to the library or to become interested in books. He was always in the gymnasium lifting weights. He was building physical muscle while I was trying to build mental muscle. The problem is that we both had a compulsion: mine, to study and his, to build muscle.

Depending on the segment of our population to which you relate, one of us would have been considered more of a good guy. Mystically, however, we were both in error. We both needed to overcome the compulsiveness of our own mindset. I should have gone to the gymnasium more often, and he should have gone to the library more often. This would have been proof of self-mastery over our mindsets. It would have enabled each of us to create a more balanced life and thus a wiser lifestyle.

Each soul tends to build that which is already strong within him. We tend to stay away from that which is weak within us. This is where the danger lies. This is why we need to overcome our major compulsive drives. The mystics state that we need only to momentarily put our personality, our loyalties and our prejudices aside. If we can do this momentarily, we will be able to balance our lives. We need to see this only momentarily. We do not have to see life for a great length of time in order to know something. We need only see it for a brief period of time. Because we have memory, we can remember it afterward.

At this present moment, in this present incarnation, we have a great gift. It is called recollection. It is called memory. Unfortunately, it is quite limited for most of us because we are held to tunnel vision. Our emotions, which seem to give so much meaning to most people, are by their very nature self-limiting. These emotions keep us at the level we are at.

We are all aware that if an iceberg extends above the ocean by 100 feet, the depth of that iceberg extends below the water by some 900 feet. In the same way, the upper level of awareness is nothing compared to the lower levels of the subconscious. This does not even take into account the unconscious layers of consciousness or of the super-conscious.

In truth, the subconscious memory of an average person is about 900 times more voluminous than that of his conscious memory. The unconscious memory of an average person is about 9,000 times more voluminous than that of his subconscious memory.

And even though the super-conscious memory is above the surface, its memory is 90,000 times more voluminous than that of the unconscious memory. Remember, we are talking about memory, not about experiences. The conscious memory is only 1/432,000 of the experience of all memory combined.

I often relate these four levels of the mind to the symbolism of a lake on a cold winter morning. If you get up early enough, occasionally you can see a mist rising off the surface of the lake. The water is not a hard, flat surface. In a way, you can literally see a second lake right above this denser one. There is always a transformation of the liquid lake into a vapor lake, yet it cannot always be seen. In the same way, I refer to the transformation of consciousness.

Mystically, we exist in a lower or unaware state. We exist in a constricted state of consciousness from which most of us are unable to break free. Through meditation, we seek to move into a much more expansive state of consciousness. When we experience this transformation, we are able to make better and wiser judgments that bring us greater freedom.

Many of us are like an ant sitting on top of his anthill saying, "I am lord of the universe." If this ant were mystically inclined in any way, he might want to gain a better insight into himself. He would not be able to understand his true Self—his higher nature—by simply relating himself back to his anthill or back to some sort of sociological study of the ant culture. These constructions are too limited and too narrow. In order to attain this understanding, he must find means to expand his horizons of awareness. In so doing, he will recognize that the anthill is only one of many force-fields. As he moves away from his anthill, he will see that there are many similar anthills, but he will also see that there are many dissimilar ants. It is essential that he emotionally leave his anthill so that he can compare his own force-field to other force-fields. Next he must go even further in order to compare his ant force-field to other "non-ant" force-fields. When he has accomplished this, he will be able to understand what "anthood" is truly all about.

In the same way, mankind needs to continually become aware of his total cosmic consciousness. For it is here that the ultimate analysis of the entirety can be made. Then, for the first time, mankind can begin to talk about and understand what *mankind* is really all about. In so doing, he will realize, as do all mystics, that we are not very high on the totem pole of life. Man's ego is of such a nature that his emotionality refuses to allow him to break free from his ego-hood. Thus, he emotionally insists that he is at the top of the totem pole of life when in fact he is not! As a matter of fact, he is quite close to the bottom. Until he can let go of his cosmic superiority complex, he will never be able to see his place in the total scheme of things.

Om Shanti

CHAPTER TWO
The Crest Jewel Lies Hidden Within

I would like to relate a story that has great symbolic meaning and to recommend that you practice the technique suggested in the story.

Once upon a yogi time, there was a powerful king. He was exceedingly wealthy and successful. One day he thought, "Because my life has been so full, I should make a pilgrimage." Normally his servants carried him on a palanquin, but on this pilgrimage he was determined to walk. Also, he decided to fast and abstain from water.

On the day he began his pilgrimage, it was 100 degrees in the shade. Because he was not accustomed to walking and fasting, he became quite hot in a short time. He kept thinking, " I would really like some water. But if I ask for water, my servants will not admire me." So he continued walking. At high noon, he came to a bend in the road and saw a pond of water. This was too much! He could not contain himself! He was so thirsty he did not ask his servants for water but immediately ran to the pond and scooped up water with his palms. In his rush to do this, the crest jewel was ripped from his turban and fell into the pond.

Crest jewels are giant-size jewels, the most perfect of gems. They have immense value. Thus, the king immediately screamed to one of his servants, "I have lost my crest jewel! Come find it!" A servant jumped into the water and started looking for it. The king screamed again and another servant jumped into the pond. When these two servants could not find his precious crest jewel, other servants jumped into the pond to search for the king's treasure. The king sat down and lamented, "My crest jewel, my most valuable possession. I've lost it! I've lost it!"

Then, out of the corner of his eye, the king saw a little yogi walking down the road toward him. The king thought, "This yogi will help me." He called to the yogi, and the yogi came over and asked, "Your majesty, how might I serve you?"

The king replied, "I've lost my crest jewel!"

"Oh, that's nothing. I can find it for you."

"Will you?"

"Yes. It's no problem."

The king thought that the yogi had given him the power to find his jewel. Therefore, the king jumped up and started to run toward the water. But as the king stood up, the yogi requested, "Please sit down, your majesty." Thus, the king sat down.

The yogi continued, "The first thing you must do is order your servants to get out of the water."

"No," the king said, "Let them continue looking for the crest jewel while you help me find it."

"No, no, get them out of the water! That is a requirement," said the yogi.

"No, no!" responded the king.

"Goodbye, your majesty. I can't help you if you will not listen to me," said the yogi as he stood up and started walking away.

The king pleaded, "Please sit back down and help me!" In desperation, the king decided to remove all of his servants from the pond. At this point, the yogi pulled out a little book from his pouch. At first the king became very excited thinking that it was a book of charms for finding lost objects. But then the king saw it was the *Gita,* and he asked, "Are you going to read some magic chants?"

"No," said the yogi. Hearing this, the king ordered his servants back into the water.

Again, the yogi said, "If they go in the water, I leave!" Thus, the king ordered his servants to sit back down and he sat there in desperation.

As the yogi read the *Gita* aloud for awhile, the king become very interested, exclaiming, "That is really fascinating." After some time, the yogi put the *Gita* away and said, "Now the crest jewel can be found."

Surprised with the way the yogi abruptly stopped reading, the king asked, "Aren't you going to read more?"

"No. The crest jewel awaits," replied the yogi. They both stood up and walked toward the pond. Because the yogi had been reading for quite some time, the mud in the water, which had been stirred up by the servants looking for the crest jewel, had had time to settle. The water was now clear, and as the yogi looked into the calm pond he could see the fish swimming around. He could also see the footprints the servants had made. And in the clear still water he could see a little round hump of mud.

The yogi said to the king, "Look! You can see all that is in the water. You can even see the contour of the bottom of the pond. And from the mirrored surface of the pond, you can even see the sun above." He then reached into the water and pulled the hump of mud out of the water. It was the king's most precious treasure, his crest jewel.

This simple story, like all yoga stories, is didactic. It illustrates, symbolically, that the mind is a pond and that the crest jewel is our self-awareness that we lost. In the thrust to quell our thirst, our desires, we have lost our most precious treasure! Thus, we immediately throw our servants—our thoughts, our emotions, and our will power—into the pond to find it. These servants activate and disturb the mind. Then we throw in more thoughts and more emotions arise, which only muddy the water more.

I am not saying, "Don't think" or "Don't study." I am saying that if you wish to find your crest jewel, your self-awareness, you must be able to remove all the thoughts and emotions that muddy up the waters of your mind. Give the waters of emotion time to settle. In time, you will be able to see not only *into* the pond, but from its mirror-like surface, you will also be able to see what exists *above* the pond, even if you are looking down.

The Zen monks relate the wisdom of this story in their own fashion when they say, "Sitting quietly, doing nothing, spring comes!"

We need to slow down so that we can become attuned to nature, which moves at a much slower pace. We need to allow nature to quiet us. When we permit this to happen, our perceptions of everything become clearer on all levels. We have clarity instead of confusion.

Yogis and mystics have always said that education is a powerful tool and that you should avail yourself of as much education as possible. However, formal education is often a matter of memorizing data, and though data certainly is valuable, we must all learn to think. *Think!* It is one of the greatest abilities we possess. Think, but do not emote! Use your mind, but cultivate the ability to turn off your "emotional button" and to keep it off. You should be able to quiet your mind at will so that you can enter into the outer fringes of samadhi and thus expand your horizon of awareness and resolve any problems that arise in life.

Quieting the mind is a prerequisite technique to advanced meditation. Below are some guidelines for simple practice that will help you to attain a state of quietude.

1. Choose a time, an hour, that is most convenient for you, a time when you will not be interrupted. Most likely, this will be when the world is asleep. Each person's life, and consequently, his chosen time will be quite different. Just select a time that is convenient, a time that works for you.

Some people say they have difficulty sitting at the same time each day. Work to overcome this. If you choose a convenient hour, it will help. If you are unable to maintain a specific time, it indicates you do not yet have your life in the order necessary to pursue the awakening path. It could also indicate that you have selected an hour that is not convenient. If you select an hour very early in the morning or very late at night, it is more likely to be convenient. Sitting and meditating at the same time each and every day is a discipline requiring insight and endeavor in everyday life. This effort alone will help one to mature and unfold.

Many students start out in the correct way only to find their meditation time beginning to shift a little forward or backward. Do not let this happen. Do not let your meditation session drift. If you find that your session is "slipping" and that it is starting later and later or earlier and earlier, know that you are losing control of your earth life. If you see this happening, return to your original meditation time the next day and every day thereafter.

Just as everyone knows that suppertime is at a given time, when you meditate at the same time each and every day, your family will know and accept this as your personal time. It might even encourage them to meditate.

Let us say that you have chosen 6:30 a.m. as your meditation time. The best approach is to begin sitting in posture at about 6:25 a.m. Just begin by relaxing the body and establishing full attention without tension. Thus, when 6:30 a.m. arrives, you will be ready to begin your meditation. If need be, place a small clock with a very quiet alarm in front of you. When it goes off, begin your meditation. Some students set the alarm for the set period and meditate until it goes off. Thus, they do not have to worry about whether or not they have meditated for the proper length of time. This can be helpful in the early months.

Over and above this, allow me to say that meditating at different times is certainly better than not meditating at all. However, to get the most from advanced meditation, find the right time to meditate and meditate daily. Make the time to meditate. Meditate daily.

Because human psychology is what it is, you must come out of your meditation a "better" person. Otherwise your family will think that your meditation was a waste of time. And so might you. This can create problems.

2. Select a place that is quiet and comfortable for you. This is very important.

3. Find a posture that is comfortable and stable for you. If you have serious back problems or other disabilities, lie down comfortably. It is far better to lie down and meditate than to sit up and not meditate. It is far better to meditate lying down, totally relaxed, than to sit in full lotus, attempting to meditate when your body is experiencing total discomfort. If you sit on the floor, you will be about three feet tall, and this will lower your blood pressure. Lying down will lower it even more. This will assist in quieting your mind. Find the middle ground.

Simple physical problems that at first interfere with meditating in a vertical posture often tend to correct themselves with continued meditation practice until you are able to meditate comfortably in a vertical posture. Remember that we are all conditioned to fall asleep when we lie down. Therefore, if you use a horizontal pose, guard against becoming unconscious.

Again, the key point is that first we must make our physical body comfortable. Then we can work at making our minds comfortable. Later, we can make our astral bodies comfortable.

4. Next, proceed with a stretching session. This should consist of very gentle stretching, which will loosen the spinal column

and also have positive effects on your blood pressure. It will also open the astral channels, making it easier for the life force to flow through the center channel of the astral body.

5. Now simply sit for a few seconds until your mind quiets down, and then close your eyes and fix them at the root of the nose between the eyebrows. This is where the Ajna chakra exists. Your awareness should be focused at this chakra during your meditation.

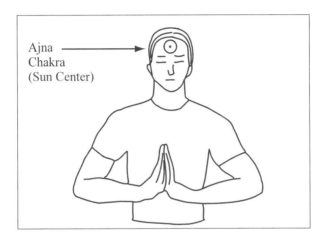

Ajna
Chakra
(Sun Center)

Our eyes continually move back and forth. The eyes and the eyelids move in sequence with the activity or nervousness of the mind. If we focus upon a given point when we meditate, it will help quiet the mind more quickly.

The mind can focus upon one of three places during meditation:

The first place to focus the mind is at the root of the nose between the eyebrows. This is where the ajna chakra, also called the single eye, exists. This is the best place to focus the mind during meditation.

The second place to focus the mind is at the solar plexus. This is also a good place, although from a mystical standpoint, it is better to be looking upward to the higher planes than downward to the lower planes.

The third place to focus the mind is at the tip of the nose. However, if focusing at this point is not done properly, eye problems can develop. Thus, I do not recommend using it.

When your mind is focused during meditation and the eyelids flutter a great deal, it means you are trying much too hard. Just focus and gaze at a fixed point. Do not stare. At this stage, you are actually seeking to quietly concentrate, not meditate. Just focus gently and do not let the eye movements become a distraction. In time, the mind will quiet down, and the eyes and the movement of the eyelids will be less agitated and less distracting.

If this becomes a problem, open your eyes and very gently close them again. Remember that when you go to sleep, your eyes automatically turn inward and upward toward the root of the nose between the eyebrows. This is normal and automatic. Mystically, when we do this in meditation, we are trying to go to sleep without losing consciousness. If we succeed, we will be able to explore the inner planes of consciousness.

Again, it has been shown that dreaming occurs only when the eyes are moving like windshield wipers. When the eyes are not moving, no dreaming is taking place. The idea is to stop dreaming.

Dreams are important. Dreams and the symbols existing within our dreams are extremely significant. However, in our meditation we are seeking to transcend even these dream states and to ascend to an even higher plane of existence.

For the average person, most dreams occur in the lower astral realm. Thus, they have many hallucinatory properties. In advanced meditation, we seek to experience vision states, which are not hallucinatory. Hallucinatory dreams have no external knowledge-bearing data, although not all dreams are hallucinatory. Visions, on the other hand, do reveal knowledge regarding the external world.

Here are a few techniques that will help to still the eyes and thus induce deeper meditative states. These methods will also assist in transforming your dreams into visional dreams.

• Take the edges of the two index fingers and extend them, turning them parallel to the eyes. Place the fingers below the eyes at the edge of the bone. Do not press on the eyeball; this could impair your vision over time. The fingers should rest on the bone below the eyes. Most people find that placing the fingers gently between the bottom of the eyeball and the ridge of the bone helps to hold the eyes steady. Remember that this method must be done gently.

• It is helpful to strengthen the eye muscles so that you do not need to use your fingers to steady them. This is done with a technique called *trataka*. Sit quietly while focusing the eyes upon an object or a mark on a wall. Open your eyes a little wider than usual and without blinking gaze for five or ten seconds. Then close your eyes and rest them for a while. Repeat the process two or three times. Be sure to rest and close the eyes between each session. While using this method, do not stare at the point. Just gently and continuously gaze at the mark, symbol or object.

Some texts say that you should gaze at a lit candle. In my opinion, gazing at a lit candle can harm the eyes because the intensity of the candle is much stronger than most people believe. Thus, I do not recommend this method.

• Another excellent method for strengthening the eye muscles is to look rapidly to the left and then to the right. Quickly repeat this movement. Now change the eye movement, and move the eyes rapidly up and down. Repeat these movements for a while. Next move the eyes rapidly in a diagonal direction. Think of a large clock in front of you and move your eyes from the number 5 to the number 11. Do this rapidly, again and again. This technique can be performed with the eyes either open or closed.

Now fix your eyes on the number 2. Rapidly move your eyes to the number 8. Repeat this back and forth movement a few times. Finally, rotate your eyes clockwise a few turns and then move them in a counterclockwise direction. Reverse the rotation a few times. Rest and repeat the total process two to five times. When you exercise the eyes for a few minutes, the muscles of the eyes and eyelids will become stronger. Many people say that practicing these exercises has helped them eliminate the need for glasses.

6. After your gaze has become steady, you are ready to begin meditating. As stated before, you start by meditating for only five or ten seconds. Then you might want to switch to a gentle breathing technique. After a minute or so, return to your meditation for a few seconds. If you prefer, you might chant mentally for a minute or so. Return again to your meditation session for a few seconds. After switching back and forth a few times, just sit in silence for a short time.

7. Your meditation at this stage is quite simple: Be motionless without any strain whatsoever. Just enjoy the quietude!

As you begin to meditate, your relaxed mind will suddenly think of five things you should be doing or that you have forgotten to do. This is good because it reveals that your mind is beginning to relax. This is the first stage in gaining a meditative state. Do not get upset. Do not get frustrated. If this repressed recall happens, just say to yourself, "That's right. These are things to be done. They are important. However, the most important thing at this moment is that I gain a deep meditative state. Right now, the most important thing is to just enjoy the quietude. Right now, the important thing is for me to become even more tranquil." Remember that the enemy is the scattered mind.

The mind will tend to run off in a hundred directions. When it does, you very gently bring it back to simply enjoying the stillness. If you get angry or upset, you will destroy your meditation because you will have fed the mind. You will have given the surface mind angular energy, causing it to become even more agitated. If this happens, just start all over again. Do not get upset. Just bring the mind back to enjoy the quiet. Each time you *quietly and gently* bring your mind back to the stillness, you have succeeded in your meditation. Understand this, and you will make great progress in your meditation.

In the first stages, your meditation may be very light, but it is meditation nonetheless. It is a very important precursor to deeper meditation, which is the basis of advanced meditation. As you practice it, look passively at the mind to gain insight into why it is emotionally wired to respond the way it does. Slow it down. Quiet the mind. Stop its running, ranting and raving.

A significant and fundamental stage in learning meditation is to get the mind to enjoy doing nothing, not even thinking, during your meditation time. This is not laziness; it is not lethargy. Rather, it is active enjoyment of the stillness of the mind. Again, be aware. Beware of moving into a state of unconsciousness or passivity. Meditation is an active state in which "thinking" stops—without losing consciousness—and your intuitive consciousness starts functioning.

When you come out of your meditation, you may want to jot down a few notes regarding things that disturbed your meditation, things that you realized you should or should not do, things that you should or should not change. Jot down any insights revealed about yourself, or Life, etc. This is important because shortly after you come out of meditation, that which you think is firmly planted in your mind will fade away. Often the most shocking revelations that you are absolutely certain will remain forever in your mind in this lifetime disappear. It is very easy to forget subtler inner insights when the mind is again faced with the forces of the conscious mind and the external world.

The problem is not so much the incoming sense data; it is the mind's reaction to that data. Many decades ago when I was in India, I meditated in a Jain Temple. It was so quiet that you could hear the proverbial pin drop on the stone floor. Some years later, I meditated in a Buddhist monastery where you could hear everything that was happening in the streets. You could hear dogs barking and people shouting as they were selling their wares. It was a noise-pit, I complained. I asked, "How do you expect anyone to meditate with all of this noise?"

The head monk said, "I understand. Come with me." He took me into another room at the back of the temple that was very quiet. He then played classical music and asked, "Will this help? How's this?"

"Oh, that's wonderful. That's beautiful," I said.

He then abruptly stopped the music and retorted, "How could you possibly meditate with all of that noisy music!"

It was a *satori* for me. The barking of the dogs was a sound. The shouting of the people was a sound. The music was a sound. However, I rejected some of these sounds as distracting and accepted the classical music as non-disturbing.

Life has little to do with the incoming sense data. It has much more to do with the reaction of the mind to that data. The key was to accept sound as sound. With that *satori* fixed in my mind, I returned to the meditation chamber and accepted life with all of its wonderful noise. As soon as I accepted all of the noises of life, they moved into the background of my mind, and I was able to meditate. What I thought of as music and what I thought of as noise were only interpretations of my mind.

So it is with all things and conditions in life. If the guy next door is blasting his radio with awful sounds, so what? If you accept this as part of the music of life, you will not be disturbed; you will be able to move from the surface of your mind into a meditative state. When we accept all of life (the music of life or the noise of life), it becomes clear that these exist merely in our heads, that everything important exists inside our own heads. By accepting the noise, we can meditate. And in the deep states of meditation, a *satori* will flow forth. Move!

Practice this method one to five times a day for just a few seconds and find the music of life within and then move to a quieter neighborhood! Remember: Practice every day—at the same time, in the same place, in the same direction and in the same posture.

After your meditation, quietly go about your external earth life duties.

Om Shanti

CHAPTER THREE
Meditation and the Psychology of Kriya Yoga

The mystics practice meditation to expand awareness and thus explore the inner worlds. In essence, yoga and mysticism are fundamental pathways for attaining knowledge of the macrocosm and the microcosm.

With the accumulation of knowledge comes wisdom. With wisdom comes the power to overcome internal self-limiting forces and an understanding of how to work with the external forces of nature. This brings liberation from ignorance, unawareness, superstition and incompetence. Competency is the ability to use skillful means to attain that which needs to be attained.

Yoga science is concerned with self-awareness and the exploration of consciousness. This enables us to more clearly see the options that we have in our lives at any given moment. Each of us is able to become more free. Each of us is able to overcome limitations. All limitations? Yes, because the ultimate principle of spirituality recognizes that all limitation is *self*-limitation. It is self-limitation owing to the fact that the self is ignorant, unaware or incompetent. All limitation is self-imposed, in one of these ways:

1. Going against the laws of nature, e.g., putting one's hand on a hot object. This is unawareness.

2. Not being able to say or do that which needs to be said or done, even though one knows the method. This is incompetence.

3. Not knowing how to harmonize oneself with the laws of nature. This is ignorance.

When asked the question, "Why did the person put his hand on that hot object?", mystics point out that there are three possible answers:

1. The person was not thinking. He was not aware of what his body was doing.

2. He did not know nor did he perceive that the object was hot.

3. He was subconsciously trying to punish himself.

All of this comes down to one factor: the lack of conscious awareness on the part of the individual. Historically, the Sanskrit word for this is *avidya*. The term means "without knowledge," but it is most often translated as "ignorance." Words are very hard to translate, for in their very translation the deeper meaning, the connotation, is often lost. Therefore, in trying to preserve the connotation of the word *avidya*, I translate it as "forgetfulness." We just cannot remember; we have forgotten the lessons of the past. They have slipped from conscious memory into unconscious forgetfulness. With this lack of awareness, we do not think, we do not perceive and we do nothing to correct our underlying subconscious attitudes that are self-destructive.

After this, the mystics learn how to examine, enlarge and deepen awareness. They learn to focus awareness, which leads to important discoveries regarding the nature of consciousness, especially the nature of balanced self-conscious awareness.

Mystics know there is a link between unawareness and the creation and continuation of pain and unhappiness. They know there is a link between self-conscious awareness and freedom. They know there is a link between unbalanced awareness and forgetfulness. Finally, the mystics know that there is a link between balanced self-conscious awareness and the ability to create. Mystically, this ability to create relates to artistic creation as well esoteric creation of new and higher states of consciousness. With the attainment of these new states of consciousness, people and events that are attuned to these states of consciousness materialize in our lives.

By focusing and becoming more deeply aware of his experiences, the mystic comprehends the meaning of existence itself and understands his place within that existence. The degree to which he is willing to invest time and energy into the exploration of awareness is the degree to which he will discover for himself the mysteries of Life.

In yoga and mysticism, there are methods for exploring awareness and consciousness. These methods are the spiritual tools for revelation. Our spiritual tools should always be used skillfully. In this area of self-improvement, two thoughts should be kept in mind:

• Self-improvement should always be done with a minimum amount of conflict.

• The self-improvement that comes from the skillful use of our spiritual tools reveals a deepening awareness of the nature of Life itself, enabling change to take place without strong desire and emotionality.

Yoga and mysticism involve the search for self-discovery and self-unfoldment. They provide methods by which we can become more self-aware. This leads to the doorway of discovery. Open this door, unfold and become more aware of Life itself—with all its meaning and mystery. This doorway reveals the celestial stars of inner light and Life.

When opening this door to Life, you will most likely become aware of things you might not approve of—not only in the world but also within yourself. At this point, one or two things will generally happen:

You will try to deny or escape from the things within your natural social conditioning and/or environment, or

You will find yourself immediately trying to change these experiences.

Trying to escape or change these experiences generally pulls us back into the lower planes of existence. This occurs because emotionality, which alters the thought process, causes disruptive changes in consciousness. These changes first occur internally. When we become emotional, our thinking changes according to the nature of the emotion. As our thinking changes, so our perception of the world changes. Thus, our external actions and reactions change. It is a fundamental principle of yoga that as we control our emotions, we are able to see the world more clearly. Consequently, we act and react in a more positive fashion.

Ultimately, we seek to move beyond our negative reactions to our experiences in order to transcend them. In so doing, we attain a more expansive and cosmic viewpoint of life. This allows us to put our earth life into proper perspective. We now see the earth life as a microcosm existing within the macrocosm—whole, complete and in total harmony with that macrocosm.

In gaining this insight, what often seems negative over a short period of time is seen as positive and beneficial over a long period of time; that is in the scheme of things. Thus, it is best to simply remain aware of the experience without judging it. Just accept it as a flow of consciousness. In this way, you rebalance your self-awareness and your attitude toward that experience. Then you can transmute it. You can do this only if the energy in the subconscious level of your mind is somewhat balanced. You cannot transmute a negative experience with either fear energy or disapproval energy.

You should seek to penetrate deeper into those things that are repulsive to you and find the wonders of consciousness that lie just beyond the form of that which is repulsive. If you enter deeply enough into the consciousness of your own universe, these so-called negative states will transform into positive states of consciousness. There will be no emotional need to force them to change because the change will take place effortlessly when your ego is no longer locked to these forms. The point is that first you must penetrate into your experiences and your reactions to those experiences—and then go beyond them.

Through mysticism, one learns to flow with the stream of consciousness and its contents without emotionality. When you refrain from demanding that this stream of consciousness go where you wish, you begin piercing into and beyond that stream of consciousness. Not demanding that it change as you wish is the beginning of seeing Reality as it is.

The first rule of mystical exploration is to learn to accept the stream of consciousness and its thoughts. If you seek to change this stream, you will be doing so because your ego does not approve of what it sees. This will stop your mind from flowing more deeply into your inner consciousness. Without entering more deeply into your inner consciousness, you will not be able to touch the Reality beyond your ego state.

Having reached Reality, you will change your stream of consciousness. Most importantly, you will have changed it with insight and wisdom. Thus, evolutionary forces are released. Trying to change the stream of consciousness before you see the Reality behind it will hinder you from seeing the forces that have caused it to be as it is. Unless you balance the causal forces, the stream cannot be *permanently* changed or altered.

You can lift your consciousness above and beyond any given stream to a subtler, less adulterated stream of consciousness. This is much like swimming in the ocean and entering into a cold spot. If you simply "will" this stream of cold water to change, you will be disappointed; it will not change. What you need to do is swim beyond that stream into a warmer one.

We all seem to be hypnotized or fascinated by the things flowing through our consciousness and thus through our lives. We need to de-hypnotize or de-fascinate ourselves from the negative forces flowing into our mind. In so doing, we can move to subtler and higher planes of existence and become freer in our minds, in our consciousness, in our lives and in consciousness itself. If we wish to move into the heart of Life, we must learn to stop disapproving of Life and learn to accept it. We need to accept *all* of Life.

When I was very young, I entered into a Japanese house with my shoes on. Rightly so, they disapproved. When I went to China, I took my shoes off before entering into a Chinese house. Rightly so, they disapproved. In each country, there are specific rules people follow. Each rule is correct in its own right.

In the same way, each experience on this earth plane has rules to follow. For example, if your head is above water, I might say, "Keep breathing." However, if your head is under water, I would say, "Do not breathe. Hold your breath." The two are contrary, but both are correct—each according to the nature of the realm in which you find yourself. Likewise, within each stream of consciousness, there are rules and principles that need to be followed. The study of mysticism and yoga is useful for learning these basic rules and principles and for becoming aware as to whether or not they should be applied.

As mystics, we need to learn not to judge these basic states of consciousness but rather to penetrate into them and go beyond them so that we can understand and balance them. When we transcend them, we enter into subtler states of consciousness, which are the matrix of creation. It is here that the force-fields of emotion, thought, action and reaction begin to manifest. When we have somewhat mastered being nonjudgmental of these inner states, we will become nonjudgmental of people and situations in the external environment. Even so, I wish to clarify myself in this discussion. I am saying, "Judge not a rattlesnake … but *do* protect yourself."

The average earthling exerts an enormous amount of energy because he is continually locked into fighting with the different parts of his mind and personality. By mastering our capacity to be nonjudgmental, we master the ability to adjust to change. By freely making changes, we free up a great deal of energy. This energy can then be used and directed toward deepening our search into self-awareness and consciousness. In so doing, we can understand how these energies function and/or malfunction. With this knowledge, we can balance our karma at a very fundamental level. This will help our lives to rapidly and easily improve. By following this mystical methodology, we can discover more spiritual tools by which to solve even more expansive problems, allowing exploration of yet deeper levels of consciousness and of Life itself.

We are reaching for the method of gaining awareness of awareness. Thus confusion, forgetfulness and ignorance are removed. Skillful means are gained. By discovering our own humanness, by discovering our own reality, by discovering our own true values, we discover what we really want to accomplish in this lifetime. This leads to more comfort with ourselves, our existence and other beings. It allows us to be more harmoniously creative.

THE TIME WORLDS

We have been discussing the importance of penetrating more deeply into consciousness and developing the ability to see with greater clarity the content therein. There are many realms of consciousness that are covered, like spheres around spheres or like the skins of an onion. These spheres are known as *worlds.* The true Self is at the very center of these spheres, and the nature of each sphere depends upon how distant it is from the true Self. Different schools give different names to these worlds. Here is a suggested list regarding these psychological realms:

• The present external world
• The present internal world
• The true past world
• The erroneous, fabricated past world
• The true future world
• The timeless world

World One: *The present external world.* The awareness of the present external world is the authentic and factual contact with external events and objects at the present moment. It is the awareness of the sense data: what one sees, hears, touches, smells or tastes in the eternal now. It is exact and accurate.

World Two: *The present internal world.* The awareness of the present internal world takes the sense data from the first world and alters it with its value judgments based on our fears, hopes, emotions, etc. Thus, the authentic and factual sense data is no longer factual.

The remaining worlds do not exist in the present time realm. They deal with images, events and subtle objects.

World Three: *The true past world.* The awareness of the true past world is the realm of undistorted total memory. Most people never find or enter into this realm.

World Four: *The erroneous, fabricated past world.* The awareness of the erroneous, fabricated past world is the realm of distorted and/or non-total memory. This is where most people live.

World Five: *The false future world.* The awareness of the future world is the realm of expectation, anticipation and fear regarding tomorrow.

World Six: *The true future world.* The awareness of the true future world is the realm of pure awareness or premonition, totally undistorted regarding tomorrow.

World Seven: *The timeless world.* The timeless world is the realm of self-awareness rather than the awareness of things and events (internal or external) of that Self.

Most earthlings live almost totally in the erroneous past or the false future worlds. Very little time is spent in the present. Thus, most lives are lived in a secondary world rather than in a primary world. However, if we can become more aware of our awareness, our consciousness will move from the secondary worlds to the primary world. The more we become aware of the eternal now, the more we can become aware of our reality and of the Reality.

In Indian thought, the Self is called the *atma* or the *jiva,* which lives within a more galactic universe called the Reality or Sri Brahman. The goal of the Self is to live in the present true world of the timeless realm.

Everything exists in the eternal now. The mind of man is locked into a past of regrets or a future of apprehension. Our concept and understanding of the future is as false as our concept of the past because they are both established on two of our emotions—fear and desire.

Examine your awareness right now. Begin to develop insight into the properties of your basic awareness of this moment, this eternal now. If you do this, you will have a clearer understanding of what I am discussing. If daily you take the time and energy to closely examine your awareness of this eternal present moment, you will perceive your past and the future very differently than before.

It is necessary to practice this daily in order to gain deeper insight. In order to develop deeper insight into the meaning and purpose of Life, you need to examine the awareness of this eternal moment again and again, in different mental states and in different circumstances. Only in this way can you discover the reality of your own life and its meaning.

Each time you enter into your own stream of consciousness, you become aware of different components of your existence because the time factor has changed. All encounters show different elements of your consciousness and of Life. The purpose of all yogic methods is to intensify and expand your awareness and your self-awareness, for sustaining contact with your own reality and with Reality itself.

A FIVE-FOLD METHOD FOR DEEPER AWARENESS

There is a technique for delving deeper into consciousness. It is most effective if performed just before your daily meditation and every night just before falling asleep. Practice this method for the rest of this incarnation. The five steps of this method are:

1. *Observing.* Close your eyes, relax and become a passive observer of the contents of your mind for a few moments. Watch your stream of consciousness with detachment. Do not allow the contents of your mind to cause you to become emotional. It might help to say something like: "Now I am aware of (such and such) and it belongs to the time world of ... (the past, the present, or the future)." In short, be aware that you are aware, and be aware of the contents of the stream of consciousness. Do not judge! Just be aware of what is happening in your stream of consciousness and the effect it is having on your mind. Realize that it might be affecting your mind but not the Self, not the "you as awareness." In the world of your consciousness, at any given moment, be aware of the degree you are lost in the world of the erroneous, fabricated past or the world of the false future.

2. *Focusing.* Remain in a relaxed state and re-examine your stream of consciousness. Be aware that your awareness is a beacon and that whatever it focuses on will become clearer. Notice that at the same moment all other things will tend to disappear into the shadows of the background of your mind. This occurs because the modern mind has been trained to look for one truth, to look for one thing to the exclusion of all else.

Our minds must be retrained to become more focused without losing the awareness of that which is not in the center of our focus. In the process of watching your stream of consciousness, notice how abruptly one thought or emotion replaces another thought or emotion. Learn to focus your awareness, and at the same time expand the focus of that awareness. As you focus your awareness, become aware of what flows in and what immediately flows out. Notice what stays for shorter or longer periods of time. Most of all, see if you can understand why these changes occur.

3. *Generalizing.* In your relaxed state, allow your mind to generalize. Generalizing means bringing concepts and events together into a general pattern. It is an activity in which the mind records events and then categorizes them into a common base. The conscious mind separates everything into little compartments. The mind must learn to collect separate events, whether they are internal or external, and unify them. It must learn to take data and organize it into larger and larger categories that contain a common basis. For example, you may have the following symbols in a dream: a red balloon, a red car and a piece of red cloth. These can and should be reduced to a common category: red things. Or you may have a collection of tanks, guns, bullets, bayonets and hand grenades. With generalization, these objects can be placed into the common category of "Mars things." Some personalities do this better and faster than other types of personalities.

When we learn to generalize, our awareness of objects and events will become much clearer. In using the process of generalization, we can more easily see the relationship between thoughts and events, between thoughts and things.

When the mind is tired, it will stop generalizing. At this point, rest and remember to re-focus. Unify concepts, thoughts, emotions and objects, placing them into their proper categories. At the same time, do not get lost in the stream of thoughts and emotions. Stay awake. Stay aware. Learn to keep the true Self, the atma, apart from that stream. Do not get lost in the "dream" of the stream. Do not get lost in the "dream" of your everyday earth life. Be aware. Become more aware. Stay aware. Clearly see the distinction between consciousness and the content of that consciousness.

4. *The selective process.* Remaining in your relaxed state, observe the selective process of the mind. Of the thousands of experiences, intellectual and emotional, that are possible to experience at any given moment, we normally select only a few to reach the surface of our conscious mind. Why these? The gatekeeper of the mind selects only a few experiences that it permits to enter the conscious realm. The gatekeeper directs our attention to certain objects and events to which we have a deeper, subconscious attachment.

Seek to remember the types of events, people and objects that generally flow in the stream of your consciousness. Seek to understand what types of things you "hold" in this selective process. Why does it function as it does? Gain control over this process so that your awareness can fully open the gateway. Be aware that you can move beyond the everyday gate of experiences. This is the aim of yoga and one of the key goals of mysticism.

5. *The avoidance process.* The opposite of the selective process is the avoidance process. In a relaxed state, observe the avoidance process of your mind. This is the process of *not selecting* certain thoughts and/or emotions. The mind of each type of personality normally will not focus in certain areas. It must be trained to enter into these "forbidden" zones. Once again, you see the need for the daily practice of detachment. By remaining detached, we can enter into those zones that are closed off to the conscious mind and gain the vital missing experiences. In so doing, we can become more whole, and we can correct, improve and free ourselves from our own self-confinement.

Om Shanti

CHAPTER FOUR
Methods for Your Spiritual Unfoldment

In this chapter, a number of different meditation techniques will be discussed. Practice each one for a short time to determine which method is most suitable for you.

1. INSIGHT MEDITATION—A Buddhist Technique

This technique is for developing mindfulness. It is a very powerful technique. It is difficult for most Westerners to practice because social conditioning teaches them to be mindful of what is happening outside their minds. Their ego state is more externalized. Thus, this method is well worth the struggle.

Take a small portion of your consciousness and place it at the back and top of your skull. Then take this portion of your consciousness and (mentally) constantly look down into your mind/body complex with mindfulness.

This technique has three levels:

Level One: The first level is an extensive mindfulness of your physical body. It can be done with your eyes open or closed. Watch your body with mental awareness. Watch what is happening to it. For example, as this small portion of your consciousness is aware of your body, you may think, "I am sitting on one leg … My eyes are twitching … My arm is about to move … My hand is scratching my head … My arm is moving downward … My nose itches ... My left arm is moving upward … My fingers are rubbing my nose ... My arm is moving downward again," etc.

As you practice this technique, your mind repeats everything that your body is doing as it is doing it. For example, "My arm is lifting." To some personalities, this may seem silly. However, remember that this is only the first stage. Let us continue to the next level.

Level Two: After you have mastered the first level, you can move to the second stage. Here the mind anticipates what the body is going to do. In watching and being aware of the body, you may say, for example, "My body is sitting and it is about to get up ... My body is getting up and is about to walk ... My body is walking and is about to go into the kitchen ... My body is in the kitchen and is about to turn around ... My body has turned around and is about to sit down ... My body is sitting down and is about to reach for the newspaper."

In the first stage, your mind is mentally repeating what your body is doing. In the second stage, you seek to anticipate what your body is about to do but has not yet begun to do. The process is to observe how far in advance your awareness can foresee what your body's next action will be. Certain personalities have the potential to become obsessive with this method. If it bothers you in any way, just stop using it.

Level Three: The final stage of this technique is to continually focus that small portion of your awareness on your mind. This third stage has three sub-stages:

Sub-stage One: Observe the mind's actions. Think to yourself, "My mind is thinking about paying the phone bill ... My mind is thinking about my father ... My mind is irritated with my spouse ... My mind is emotional ...

Sub-stage Two: Observe the mind and anticipate what its next thought will be: "My mind is thinking about yoga and it is about to think of food ... My mind is thinking about food and it is about to think about studying Sanskrit ... My mind is about to think of food ... It is about to become irritated about last week's trip."

Sub-stage Three: Seek to gain greater leeway time in being aware of what the next thought pattern will be. For example, in the above examples, the first thought pattern surrounds a set of thoughts regarding yoga, the second set of thoughts surrounds food, the third set surrounds studying and the fourth set surrounds irritation. Now you want to extend your awareness so that you have greater and greater lead-time before a change in the pattern actually occurs. The greater the lead time, the more time you will have to change or improve the set of thoughts that have not yet occurred but are going to occur unless your awareness intervenes.

Soon you will become very aware of everything that is happening in your mind. You will begin to understand why the thought patterns emerge as they do, the true cause of irritation and why the emotionality flares up. This leads to the mindfulness that you are neither your body nor your mind. Finally, there arises an awareness that the small portion of consciousness, which seemed at first to be only a small part of your mind, turns out to be a doorway to the over-soul.

As this method is practiced, great insights arise as to how and why the mind functions. Thus, this method is referred to as *insight meditation*. It is said that as you practice this technique, ultimately there is an insight that is totally inexpressible. Some people refer to it as *Nirvana*. Being inexpressible does not mean that it cannot be experienced. It means that one is unable to communicate it to another person unless that person has already experienced that state himself.

It is just like trying to explain love or like trying to explain the color blue to a person who has been blind since birth. In the same way, it is said that you cannot communicate enlightenment to unenlightened souls. Personally, I believe this and other concepts can be communicated to others. We simply cannot communicate them in everyday language. By the use of symbols and other non-verbal communications, super-subtle concepts can be communicated. Furthermore, these states can be transferred to others. This is the main reason for studying symbolism and internal ritual.

Returning to the insight method, when practicing this technique no effort should be put forth to become detached. It is practiced simply to gain insight, to see what is happening in the mind and how it works. A potentially greater power to control the mind states arises when it comes about through effortless actions. This method emphasizes the importance of awareness. Be aware. Be aware. Gain insight.

Some people state that this method has a dualistic pattern. Some say it has a schizophrenic patterning. Yes, it does emphasize the seer and that which is seen, the knower and that which is known. But this does not bother me because mystics are by nature schizophrenic. That is to say, they are walking in this and also in other worlds—often at the same time. However, this schism is not dissociative in any way, shape or form.

In the mystic, one part of the consciousness is looking back at another part—perchance as a third part watches both parts. However, this schism is not schizophrenic. One part of the mind is simply a passive observer, but there is no conflict with the other part. There should be no conflict whatsoever. In schizophrenia, the

mind is divided into more than one part and these parts are disso-
ciated. The individual is unaware of, and/or does not have any control over, the other parts.

Continuing with the technique, one keeps going further and
further into the inner recesses of the mind until the level of the "no-
mind" is reached. It is poetically expressed from a *satori* I had in
Japan:

> *The mirror, the mind,*
> *Rub, rub, rub.*
> *No mirror, no mind,*
> *Then, what is this?*

The *Upanishads* state it this way: the knower, the known, and
the act of knowing. The knower is seeking to know the object that
is to be known through the act of meditation. Other texts talk
about the seer, the seen, and the act of seeing.

2. OM MANI PADME HUM—A Tibetan Method

The next meditation technique is a Tibetan method of meditation. It is easier and less demanding than insight meditation. It is
the chanting of the mantra, "OM MANI PADME HUM."

When it is chanted, it sounds like: OM MAD-MAY PAD-
MAY HUM. The vibration of the first word is OM and sounds like
the word 'home' without the 'h'.

The vibration of the second word is MAD-MAY, pronounced
like MOD as in the word "mo-dern," and MAY as in the month of
May.

The vibration of the third word is PAD-MAY, pronounced
POD as in the word "pea-pod," and MAY as in the month of May.

The vibration of the fourth word is HUM, pronounced
"whoooom," much like the English word "whom."

People tend to think this mantra is a sentence that has meaning, but it is not. It is a series of fundamental mantric vibrations or
sounds hooked together, which literally affect the subconscious
mind and positively affect the conscious mind. Mystics say these
vibrations affect all matter, not just your mind and body.

We know that sounds affect life very dramatically. The next
time you watch a movie, notice what makes it a movie. It is the

soundtrack. Without these sounds, the effect of the movie is flat. Turn off the sound and watch the movie. You will immediately see that the movie is not much of a movie without the sound. What makes a love story so powerful? It is the music. What makes a heroic story so forceful? It is the music. Certain people, including musicians, have learned how to use the power of mantra but often for the wrong purpose. They have learned some of the secrets of the power of vibration: the power of sound.

Because this mantra looks like a sentence, we are conditioned to ask, "What does this mantra mean?" The mystic would say that it means two things. First, it means OM MANI PADME HUM. Second, it means whatever state of consciousness is manifested as one chants it at the proper time, for the proper length of time and in the proper way.

Exoterically, the mystic would say the meaning of OM MANI PADME HUM is: *The jewel is in the lotus.* Esoterically, it means what is revealed when it is chanted.

The Buddhists have many mantras. They use the OM (AUM) mantra sound from the Hindu system. The Buddhists place the OM at the end of their mantras whereas the Hindus place it at the beginning of their mantras, with two exceptions. The OM MANI PADME HUM mantra is one of these exceptions. This means that it is a very special mantra. It also demonstrates that the placement of the sound is vital in mantra.

Sit in a meditation posture and relax. Keep your spine straight. Gently close your eyes and focus at the ajna chakra. Begin chanting the mantra: OM MANI PADME HUM. Chant with a few seconds of silence in between each mantra. With each chant, the silence in between chants should become longer and longer by a few seconds. There should be a definite feeling of absolute quietness.

This technique will lift you above your body and mind. It will lift you above body consciousness and mind consciousness and bring you to a state of pure consciousness. As you move to this state of pure consciousness, many wonderful secrets regarding Life, contentment, and creation will be revealed.

The breathing pattern is also significant in this technique. Just before chanting, inhale fully and quickly through the open mouth. Exhale as you chant. Inhale again only after emptying the breath through chanting.

Please note the pitch of each sound, as seen in the diagram below:

THE UP AND DOWN PITCH
OF THE OM MANI PADME HUM MANTRA

This method works not so much by letting go of the world and world consciousness as by attracting and attaching your awareness to the mantric sounds that mystically "strike" the four lower chakras. This process elevates one to the Mercury chakra.

As you chant the mantra, you will feel peacefulness and joy begin to flow into your being. This awareness will begin to churn a little more actively once you inwardly focus on the mantra. It will move you gently away from surface consciousness and to the awareness of the supreme Self, the atma. It will produce permanent, positive effects.

This mantra is a six-fold mantra, that is, it is made up of six mantric sound vibrations. Thus, it should be chanted six times in each round. There is a short silence at the end of each mantra and a much longer period of silence at the end of each round. As you advance in the mastery of this technique, increase the number of rounds to six. Once you are deep within the mantra, the number of rounds should be increased to twelve with the mantra chanted twelve times in each round.

Also, the period of silence in between rounds should be extended. While chanting, shift your awareness from the thinking pattern and become more aware of the feeling state within your tranquil mind. I said the feeling state, not the emotional state.

At first, as with any meditation method, this mantra should be practiced three to five times a day. Begin by chanting for only twenty to forty seconds at each sitting. The peace and joy that manifest will draw you into deeper layers of consciousness. The bliss that you feel will rapidly, of its own nature, absorb you into longer sessions. This will occur automatically and without effort; the meditation will be extended effortlessly.

This mantra meditation can be practiced three to five times a day whereas the insight meditation should be practiced for a few minutes, three to five times a day to begin with and then extended to twenty-four hours a day, even while in the sleep state.

3. A CHRISTIAN MANTRA TECHNIQUE

The third technique is a mantra used by the Coptic Christians. This mantra is: *Eloi, Eloi, Lama Sabach-Thani*. It is a biblical statement attributed to Jesus and historically has been translated as: "My God, my God, why hast Thou forsaken me?" or "My Lord, my Lord, why hast Thou forsaken me?" Contrary to popular belief, its correct translation is "My Lord, my Lord, everything that has been done, has been done for *this* moment."

This mantra is from Matthew 27:46. Interestingly, it is the only part of the New Testament that was left in the Armenian language. Armenian, the language spoken by Jesus, is the Western Semitic language of the Armenians. From the time of Achaemenid, it was the Linqua Franca in Southwest Asia as well as the everyday language in Palestine, Syria and Mesopotamia. It was later replaced by Arabic. Armenians are members of a group of Western Semitic people prominent in the history of ancient Syria and Mesopotamia circa 1100 to 700 B.C.E. Aramaic is also the original tongue of a Christian sect known as the Coptic Christian Church. It is the original Christian Church of Egypt governed by a patriarch and characterized by the adherence to *monophyletism*, a doctrine that maintains Christ's nature to be partly divine and partly human. Coptic is an Afro-Asiatic language that descended from the ancient Egyptians. It is extinct except in the liturgy and literature of the Coptic Christian Church.

When you chant this mantra, in time it will reveal why you incarnated here. Thus, it will reveal your destiny. It will also remind you that everything you do to keep your body alive and well leads to the moment of daily meditative prayer.

Decades ago, I frequently used this mantra just before giving the Temple's Sunday noon meditation. The previous week had always been hectic and difficult. Much work had to be done to keep the Temple alive and functioning. It was filled with numerous administrative duties and planning. Thus, just before I started the noon meditation, I chanted this mantra to remind my students and myself that it was the work done during the previous week that made "this moment" possible.

As in all mantra recitation (*japa*), this mantra should be chanted many times in a meditative pose while holding a reflective attitude. It is an interesting mantra. I suggest that you chant it for a few minutes, for a few days, and experience its effect upon your mind.

4. AN ISLAMIC SUFI MANTRA METHOD

You do not hear too much about mantra in the Islamic faith. However, in Islam, a mystical tradition known as Sufi or Sufism, does use a number of ancient mantras. One such mantra is well known in the West because stage magicians have always used it. This mantra is ABRA-CA-DABRA. It is always incorrectly pronounced. The correct pronunciation for this mantra is ACRA-KA-DABRA, with the emphasis on the KA. It must be chanted over and over again until you become lost in the sound of the mantra. When you chant this mantra for three to five minutes, you will experience an unusual state of consciousness. Some people express it as disagreeable or unpleasant. Nonetheless, I suggest you chant it because it will enable you to see the powerful effect mantra has on the mind.

Later tonight, chant ACRA-KA-DABRA for a few minutes, and follow it by chanting the Tibetan mantra OM MANI PADME HUM for a few minutes. Then compare the two different states of consciousness that are produced. Be aware. Beware. Do not judge that one is better than the other. Just become aware of how different mantras affect the mind in different ways.

By switching back and forth between these two mantras, with your everyday state of consciousness in-between, you will have three mind states together. The differences might produce an insight. Your mind will begin to think, "Wow! I didn't realize that mind states could change so quickly and so distinctly."

I will leave you with these two mantra techniques. Think about them. Practice them. Compare them.

5. THE HINDU AUM TECHNIQUE

The mantra meditation technique called OM-tracking uses the mantra OM (AUM), which is the sound vibration of the Reality.

In Hinduism, the name of Reality is *Sri Brahman,* not *Sri Brahma.* These two concepts are different. The translation of the word *Brahman* is "Reality" whereas the word *Brahma* means "the god of creation." Sri Brahman projected Sri Brahma so that he could project all entirety. I prefer the word *Reality* because if we call it "god," then we must ask, "Which god? The Hindu god? The Islamic god? The Christian god? The Buddhist god? Or the Jain god? To which god are we referring?" The word "Reality" transcends all of this. Reality is Reality. It has no form, no shape, no size and no personality. Reality is what exists.

Whatever I know of reality is only a very small part of that Reality. I know what I know. I can also reach further into the unknown Reality and make it known to my consciousness. Yet this I also know: It is as it is, and as it is, it should be. If this were not so, it would be otherwise.

We are seeking to go beyond manmade concepts. Thus, we move into the use of symbols, then to mantric sounds, then to cosmic consciousness. OM is a vibration. It is real. It is a part of, not apart from, Reality.

Here is how the OM-tracking technique is performed:

First, inhale through the open mouth as fully and as quickly as you can. Do not inhale so rapidly that you start to cough or choke. The OM mantra is now slowly chanted out loud. Be sure to extend the mantra as long as possible, allowing it to flow out as an unbroken stream of sound. Do not extend it to the degree that the sound begins to break.

As you chant OM, visualize it exiting your mouth in front of you and then circling around in a mental track and returning back into your right ear. This is how the method received its name. As the sound moves along the track, listen for it in the right ear as if you were going to hear it mystically.

Mantra is a very powerful method in itself, but when used with a yantra, it becomes even more effective. Mantra and yantra go together. A yantra is a diagram which one visualizes. It is generally a circle (like a circular track) or a complex set of circles sometimes enclosed in a square.

In this OM-tracking method, the yantra consists of a horizontal circle that runs from the mouth around and into the right ear, and from the right ear back out the mouth. This horizontal track is visualized as the mantra is chanted.

You may ask if there is any significance in listening for the astral sound in the right ear. There are a number of mystical reasons for doing this. The main reason is that if heard in the right ear, it very positively energizes the right channel of your being (the pingala), the energy of the awakened state. The left ear corresponds to the left channel of your being (ida) and relates more to dream states.

DIAGRAM OF THE AUM-TRACKING

With each tracking, the circle becomes larger and larger, and the inner AUM-sound returns to the ear.

The darker line symbolizes the chanting of AUM and the smooth line indicates the silent listening for the AUM-sound as it returns into the right ear.

As you begin to chant the OM, do not extend it too long. When the mantra is complete, you will have mentally moved halfway around the circle. Now sit in silence and mentally bring the sound along the remaining track, back into your right ear, while listening for the astral sound. In performing this tracking, you will have to mentally enlarge the circle or track to the degree that you can comfortably link it to your breathing pattern. When you find the correctly sized track, you will be practicing the technique properly. This may be a block long or longer. The longer the duration of the chant, the larger the track must be.

Once you have mentally brought the sound back to your right ear, rest a few seconds. Then mentally bring the sound along the track to your tongue and then to your mouth. Chant the mantra again. Without stress or strain, allow the mantra to be extended a bit longer. Keep making the duration of the chant longer and longer and the size of the track larger and larger—all without strain. Thus, with each new mantra, the duration of silence also becomes longer and longer. When you reach your right ear, listen in silence for the astral sound.

As you mentally make the circle larger, you might find it helpful to visualize a ball of light just ahead of the OM sound. Speed the movement of the ball of light so that the mantra circulates through the entire circle in the same period of time as before. If you started with a three-foot circle and extended it to a mile, the OM sound must now be chanted more slowly so that it can circulate through this distance and back in the same one-breath cycle in the same amount of time.

Although the speed of the mantra becomes faster, it should always be chanted at approximately the same vibration. It is the mind that is moving more rapidly, returning to the ear more rapidly. As the mind speeds up more and more, you will find yourself caught up in this circle and will momentarily forget everything else. You will be brought into the inner circle of awareness.

I suggest you do this OM-Tracking Technique for one to three minutes. In time, you will have somewhat mastered it and should increase it from five to seven minutes. Track for three to seven rounds at first. Later you can increase the rounds to 11. Be aware of any feeling state that arises.

This method produces tranquility, serenity and equanimity. It also burns off negative karma, which you will remember is one of the forces holding us to this plane of consciousness. If a person continues to practice this technique, in a relatively short period of time he will begin to neutralize his negative habits and extreme emotions. For example, if he is angry all the time, this method will soften the anger. He will not be angry as often, and the anger will not be as intense.

People often ask if they can use a recording of the OM mantra while practicing this method. The answer is no. The reasons are many. The two most important are, first, only *you* can match the visualization to the mantra you are chanting. If you use a tape, there will be a tendency to set the visualization of the mantra to the sound on the tape. This is not advisable. Second, using a tape makes the process much too passive. Your own mind should build the track. When your own mind builds the track, a positive groove is made in the mind. In short, for the mantra to be effective, the power must come from inside you, not from externals.

Whatever you do, whatever technique you practice, the most vital thing to remember is that there must be awareness of awareness. If a technique is uncomfortable, you should be aware of this, as well as of the degree of discomfort. Then correct it or use another method. If a technique makes you feel shaky, you should be aware of this and change methods. As you practice a technique, be aware of what is happening in and to your body and mind and also in your consciousness. Be aware of what this mindfulness reveals. It is important to record these revelations in your meditation journal so you can make any needed changes. It also will provide you with a record of your progress.

Om Shanti

CHAPTER FIVE
Advanced Meditation

In this chapter, I would like to clearly define advanced meditation. What constitutes advanced meditation? What is *not* advanced meditation?

Advanced meditation is not defined by its duration. It does not necessarily mean meditating for longer periods.

Advanced meditation is far more dependent on intensity. First and foremost, it is meditation at a deeper level.

As the meditator goes more deeply into his mind via advanced meditation, he truly loses the awareness of the external world, but *without* losing consciousness! This is vital.

The time factor in this inner world overrides the so-called external time factor. This is essential. When one transcends the earth's time factor, one's horizon of awareness expands beyond earth life and beyond ethnocentricity.

In advanced meditation, the meditator's one-pointedness seeks out the "goal-less goal"—samadhi. When the intent of the meditator is to go beyond stilling the mind, he has almost reached advanced meditation.

When the meditator uses his meditation to help other beings, advanced meditation is attained. This state of consciousness starts within the outer fringes of samadhi. When one seeks to help others, he rapidly moves into full samadhi.

Although every seeker may not reach full samadhi, every seeker can attain the outer fringes of samadhi, the doorway to absolute samadhi.

Advanced meditation is not some sort of personality self-development. It is not self-improvement for the purpose of becoming the best sports player, the best dancer, the best salesman or the best at anything. There is a significant distinction between self-development and self-unfoldment. The function of advanced meditation is to move one toward self-unfoldment—consciousness as it existed in spirit before it became enmeshed, entangled, confined and constricted with the body/mind complex.

The structure of the human personality permits five fundamental pathways to reunite micro-consciousness with macro-consciousness.

The first is the social pathway. This pathway relates to training students in fellowship, brotherly love and service. This is called Karma Yoga, the yoga of unselfish work. It is an extremely important yoga, which, unfortunately, many people dislike. Thus, it is often played down. It is the most ancient pathway and requires a great deal of self-discipline.

The second is the physical pathway, having to do with disciplining the physical body, as opposed to disciplining one's social being. It is referred to as Hatha Yoga and has to do with making the body very supple. This pathway is misunderstood and often downplayed. It is a complete system in and of itself, and it is also one of the greatest systems. Unfortunately many people are lazy in this area.

The third is the mental pathway. It is called Raja Yoga or Jnana (Gnana) Yoga. It is the path of the philosopher, but its essence is not merely memorizing data. This path enables one to gain wisdom and thus to mature.

The fourth is referred to as the pathway of meditation, or Dhyana Yoga. It is the path of self-awareness, and it is different from the mental path.

The last path is the mystical or esoteric pathway. It is the path of the occult scientist who studies the relationship and the effects of objects on consciousness as well as the effects of consciousness on objects and events. This is the path of Kriya Yoga and Laya Yoga.

All these yogas have a great deal in common and use many of the same techniques. But each path has a greater emphasis on one method and one goal than the others. Any person who has a guru rapidly comes to understand that the guru uses all four pathways. They are all tied together; they all emphasize meditation. However, because each student's personality and karma differ, the guru often recommends one path for a particular student.

A great deal of havoc and harm has been done to yoga and meditation over the last few decades. One reason is the result of the desire to "repackage" and sell New Age products and services. This "repackaging" and its promotions have released a great deal of misinformation.

Many people have incorrectly come to the conclusion that meditation is nothing more than relaxation. But meditation is not relaxation, and relaxation is not meditation.

Many people erroneously think that meditation is some sort of autosuggestion bordering on autohypnosis.

Many people erroneously think that meditation is a means to increase one's capacity to "do" things better (to be a better salesman, a better basketball player, etc.).

Many people think that meditation is a way to acquire more money, more fame or more of something else. This is not the case.

Many people think that meditation is a kind of quiet prayer. This is not accurate.

These are not the functions of meditation. Quite the contrary, meditation is a way of getting rid of things, thoughts and ambition.

What exactly *is* advanced meditation? Here are three definitions:

1. Advanced meditation is a technique that enables the earthling to move from body/mind consciousness to transcendental consciousness.

2. Advanced meditation is a method that enables the earthling to shift his awareness from body consciousness to cosmic consciousness.

3. Advanced meditation is a procedure for moving from awareness to self-awareness and then to balanced self-conscious awareness.

One might ask, "What is the purpose of meditation?" The ultimate answer to this question is that there is no purpose! It is much like asking, "What is the purpose of happiness?" or "What is the purpose of love?" There are benefits to being happy and to being in love, but they should not be confused with the purpose of being happy or being in love.

I could say that, in truth, most people are not really in love nor do they love. They use love to "get something." True love is not aimed at getting anything. It is simply an expression of the realization of who and what we are. As with love, so with meditation. Those who meditate, meditate because of an awareness of who and what they are. With meditation, the realization is, "I am not the body. I am not the brain. I am not the mind." With this awareness, one moves toward transcendental consciousness.

MEDITATION AND THE HOLY BREATH

There are two types of breathing. The first is *exoteric* or *gross breathing*, which keeps one conscious in one's physical body. However, because this type of breathing is weak, everyday consciousness is weak. Then there is *esoteric* or *astral breathing*, which keeps one conscious of and in one's astral body.

From a physiological standpoint, the process of meditation is very complex. It reaches into the mind-body complex, which directly relates to our breathing and really cannot be separated from it. If our breathing stops for a period of time, there is only an interruption between the mind/body complex and consciousness, which is reconnected with the next breath. If our breathing stops completely, there will be a break between the mind/body complex and consciousness. As long as we are breathing, we will remain conscious of and in our body.

Mystical tradition explains that when you inhale, either automatically or with control, *prana*, the life force, flows from the cosmos into your own subjective individual universe. It moves into your mind/body complex through the moon center, the *chandra* chakra. The scientific term for this area of the body is the medulla oblongata. In mystical schools, it is called "the mouth of God."

As this energy flows into your mind/body complex, it flows down your spinal column. When you exhale, the energy ascends to the top of your spinal column, radiating out through the single eye, the ajna chakra. This flow of energy forms a large wedge or a "V" with wings. See the diagram below.

This prana flows into your being as pure energy, meaning that this energy has not yet been given form, design, color or shape. Thus it is nameless. It is called pure energy when it enters your astral body via the chakra system. As it is flowing downward and upward through the chakras, it takes on the coloration of those chakras (of that time/space moment). This pure energy is given a definite shape, color and form. It is now called impure, meaning that it has attributes. You have given this energy color and form, and thus, name. You have unconsciously become part of the creative process and have therefore reshaped the energy. You have become like the potter working with clay. With your mind/body complex, you have remolded the clay (at least momentarily) into a

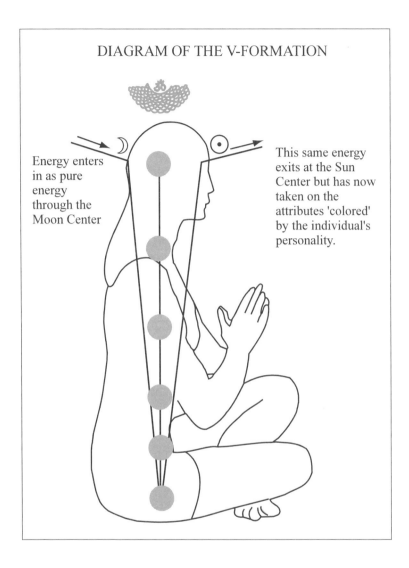

DIAGRAM OF THE V-FORMATION

Energy enters
in as pure
energy
through the
Moon Center

This same energy
exits at the Sun
Center but has now
taken on the
attributes 'colored'
by the individual's
personality.

design, shape, form, pattern and color. Your subconscious mind immediately assigns a function to it. In mysticism, these two types of energies are known as linear energy and angular energy. They are also known as untainted energy and tainted energy.

As you quietly watch your breathing for a long period of time, you can feel the energy descend and ascend. With more self-awareness, you will discover that when you become more emotional, the

"V-shaped" wedge becomes wider; when you become less emotional, the "V-shaped" wedge becomes narrower. When there is no emotionality in our lives, there is no V-shaped patterning. There is only a straight line like an "i." The dot on the top of the i symbolizes the head of the person who has detached him/herself from the five lower chakras.

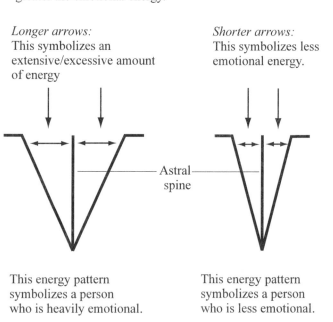

THE WEDGING PATTERNS

The amount of energy released is indicated by the distance from the center line (astral spine) and the angle as it moves away from that line. The greater the length of the line, the greater the emotional energy.

Longer arrows:
This symbolizes an extensive/excessive amount of energy

Shorter arrows:
This symbolizes less emotional energy.

Astral spine

This energy pattern symbolizes a person who is heavily emotional.

This energy pattern symbolizes a person who is less emotional.

The mystics say that we should strive to lessen our emotionality and, at least once a day, reach a state of total non-emotionality—even if it is only for a second.

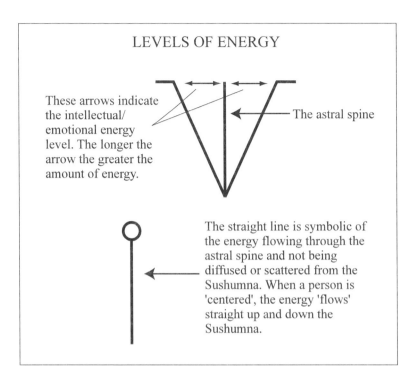

LEVELS OF ENERGY

These arrows indicate the intellectual/ emotional energy level. The longer the arrow the greater the amount of energy.

The astral spine

The straight line is symbolic of the energy flowing through the astral spine and not being diffused or scattered from the Sushumna. When a person is 'centered', the energy 'flows' straight up and down the Sushumna.

The wedge in the V-shaped pattern is a gauge indicating how close or how far away the energies are from the center of the spine. When the energy descends straight up and down the spine, there is no V form at all. Consequently, when this occurs, the vast majority of energy comes in at the moon center and goes directly out the sun center. This is centered energy. In ancient days, a person who manifested this type of energy was known as a channeler. This term should not be confused with today's psychics or channelers.

In everyday life, the energies that flow to the right (pingala) and left (ida) of the center channel (sushumna) cause the V-shaped energy pattern to "crucify" us. Because these energies are so scattered, we have no control over them. They totally control us. The purpose of advanced meditation is to move us away from this "crucifixion." The goal is to attain and sustain blissful cosmic consciousness, which expresses the reality of our own microcosm as well as the reality of the macrocosm—and not the quality or talents of our mind, body or personality.

Most of the time, we are just concentrating and creating. We are creating things, situations, art, desires and needs. These are not wrong. The mystics are simply saying that the emphasis should be on the *creator,* not on the *creations.* Normally, we are so absorbed in doing, attempting, getting and conquering that we lose sight of the creator within us. Once we find the creator within, we can find the veritable creator—what is referred to in the kriya traditions as our elder brother.

What does this mystical concept mean? We are of the family of God. We are all on the same level. A childish way of saying this is, "Man without ego is God, and God with ego is man."

Mystically speaking, God was not created, for God is spirit and "lives" in timelessness. In the same way, some earthlings were not created, for their true nature is also spirit and "lives" in that same timelessness.

Mystically, there is danger in thinking that life is about the expression of our being. When we do this, we become so connected with trying to express ourselves that we become bottlenecked and fettered. Ultimately we need to step beyond or transcend our striving for self-expression and self-development, which we hear so much about today. We need to become more concerned with self-unfoldment, which has nothing to do with our self-expression.

Let me return to the concept of the big wedge in which the life energy is flowing at a distance from the axis of our being. In modern-day language, we would refer to this as being "boxed in" by our own angular energy. Thus, we arrive at a fourth definition of meditation: Meditation is the process by which linear energy, rather than angular energy, is produced.

There are numerous sets of symbols associated with the three channels in your astral body: the ida, pingala and sushumna. Some of these are the three mother letters, the trinity, or the trimurti. This concept relates to the sun and moon coming together to produce a planet, and the three together produce the divinity. If we take any three factors and put them together, their togetherness produces a fourth factor.

If we put these four factors together, two of which are alike, we obtain what the Greeks call the *tetragrammaton* (*tetra* meaning "four," and *grammaton* meaning "letters"). Religionists use this mystical concept to compress the word "good" into the word "God."

Did you know that the fundamental word for "god" in every language is a four-letter word, of which two of the letters are the same?

One of the reasons that the breath is considered sacred is that it has an inhalation, a hold, an exhalation, and another hold (IHEH). In English, these four-letter words symbolically comprise a primary biopsychological tetragrammaton.

What is significant is that this IHEH (like all tetragrammatons) can be arranged in 12 and only 12 patterns, and thus the importance of the mystical number 12. Did you know that there are exactly 12 cranial nerves leading from the brain to the spine? The earthling has 12 fundamental states of consciousness, and as we breathe a full breath, we symbolically move through these 12 basic states of consciousness.

By mastering the control of prana through pranayama, we can make contact or communion with these states of consciousness. Then we can become aware of the states of consciousness that are angular or out of balance, and we can bring them back into balance through the use of a mystical method.

One method for accomplishing this is to chant the twelve-lettered kriya mantra:

OM + NA-MO + BHA-GA-VA-TE + VA-SU + DE-VA-YA

As I said before, the goal is to convert the angular energy into linear energy. The next step is to allow only linear energy to enter into our astral body.

In the psychological science of kriya, angular energy is emotional energy, not just emotional thoughts. The more angular energy there is in the astral body, the more the mind becomes fixed on thoughts, things and events and the more difficult it is to become aware of the creator of these forces. The goal of meditation is to move away from awareness of objects and events and to develop greater awareness of the creator of those objects and events. When we become aware that we are the creators of those things and events, we gain more control over our lives. This is so vital that I will say it yet again: The more your awareness is focused on things and events, the less your awareness can be focused upon your true Self, spirit—the creator of those things and events.

For most people, life is just like the old story of the goose and the golden eggs that you hear about in European mythology. Most people pay so much attention to the golden eggs that they ignore the goose that lays them. Your inner consciousness, in a state of balanced self-conscious awareness, is the goose, the hamsa that lays the golden eggs of life. The golden eggs are the people, the events, and the things that are drawn into your life. As the life energy flows through your personality, you automatically modify it with your state of consciousness.

This is such an important factor that I will repeat it: As the energy flows into your subconscious being, your subconscious personality modifies it. For example, as an Aries-type individual inhales, this energy flows into his or her being and is modified by the Aries personality. Because of this, the energy flows out in the form of forcefulness in personal, business or other relationships. This energy is primarily directed toward self-aggrandizement. (When I refer to the Aries personality, I am referring to someone who has key astrological planets in Aries, such as the sun or moon, a predominance of planets in that sign or an Aries ascendant.)

In the same way, as the Taurus individual inhales, the life energy flows in but is modified by his or her Taurus personality. Because of this, the energy flows out in the form of determination in personal, business or other relationships. This energy is primarily directed toward collecting things.

As the Gemini person inhales, the life energy flows in and is modified by the Gemini personality. As this energy flows out, it does so in the form of inconsistency in personal, business or other relationships. This energy is primarily directed toward verbal expressions.

In the same manner, each of the 12 personality types modifies the basic life energy and converts it "like unto itself." However, we are moving into a different area of research that will be dealt with in another book.

Classically, there are 12 primary personality types: Aries, Taurus, Gemini, Cancer, Leo, Virgo, Libra, Scorpio, Sagittarius, Capricorn, Aquarius and Pisces. These symbolically relate to the 12 Disciples of Christ, the 12 Knights of the Round Table and other symbols relative to a given social structure—for example, the 12 Labors of Atlas or Hercules. This symbolic psychology, called mythology in modern times, is spoken of in different cultural patterns. Thus, many people think that these 12 symbols refer to different things, but they do not. They are related directly back to the 12 basic states of consciousness of mankind.

With each in-breath, each entity that has a cerebral/spinal axis pulls in formless energy that is automatically given a specific form according to the nature of its personality. As we meditate deeper, perfecting our technique, we begin to spiritually unfold. This is why one of the first indicators of spiritual unfoldment is a definite softening of one's ego personality and the release of compulsiveness. My guru says the clearest clue that we are spiritually unfolding is the disappearance of the rough edges from our personality. Our personality becomes more linear.

When linear energy is consciously experienced, for the first time in our lives we begin to experience life as it is rather than as we desire to see it or hope it to be. We have removed the colored filters from our eyes and mind as seen through our ascending sign, by which each soul sees the same world from a totally different perspective.

With this, mystical events called noetic experiences manifest and have great significance in bringing about our unfoldment into cosmic consciousness. Most of us see the world through our own special colored glasses, but because of the nature of our personality, we tend to "color" the life that we see. Very few people ever see truth or anything else as it is. When we no longer color the energy flowing in, we see the world as it really is. Once we get into the flow of linear energy, there is no coloration. We see the worlds beyond that which we have created. By turning our consciousness toward that reality, we find the ultimate state of awareness. This is what the path of mysticism is about.

We need a system by which to minimize the coloration of our mind filters and, consequently, the misinterpretation of life and experiences. One of the most ancient and valuable systems for doing this is dream interpretation, which, like many occult subjects, is mired in the mud of superstition. Nonetheless, it is a deep, esoteric science that is well worth your personal study. With the proper study of dreams, we remove many of these colored filters. Although it is true that dreams do contain some colorations, they contain fewer colorations than exist in our awakened state of consciousness.

A deep, clear, basic psychological study of dreams will reveal the nature of our subconscious and unconscious mind patterns. It will assist in removing the filters and help us to see more clearly and more profoundly. For most humans, dream awareness is one of the easiest ways to become aware of the forces that are flowing out of the subconscious mind. In dreams they flow out as symbols.

Meditation is a process of falling asleep consciously so that we can clearly and abundantly collect these symbols. In meditation, however, we do this while being more conscious and more aware. These symbols are colorations of our subconscious personality. Seeing and understanding them gives us the ability to remove them.

From a mystical standpoint, the value of dream interpretation differs from the value that psychiatrists and psychologists assign to it. Spiritually, dream interpretation is something much more profound, telling us how far away we are from the core of the creative being and how far away we are from the center of awareness within ourselves—the doorway to Reality.

To be sure that there is no miscommunication, allow me to say that by the words "creative being", I am not referring to a person who creates art. I am referring to the personal source by which people, objects and events come into each person's life. In very simple symbolic terms, this personal source magnetizes itself by the thoughts and emotions that it holds in its sheaths. It is drawn to those objects and events symbolized by the thoughts and emotions we hold consciously or subconsciously in our minds. The objects and events are not drawn to the personal source.

Stop reading now. Put this book down and think about what I just said. Think deeply about it. Reflect on it. Understand the difference between drawing things to yourself and you being propelled toward those things and events.

Yesterday morning I was reflecting on this chapter and a question arose in my mind, "Can a person breathe in negative vibrations?" (I am still talking about breathing, although in an indirect way). The answer is no. A person cannot breathe in bad vibrations. Neither can a person breathe in good vibrations. A person can only breathe in that which he already is. This is a mystical statement that is well worth reflecting on for 30 years or more. The only thing that you or I can breathe in is what we are already. Thus, the pathway is truly about seeking how to become what we are not. We do this by changing our thinking and emoting patterns.

We can breathe in pure prana. Prana is neither good nor bad. It is only prana. Prana is the only thing out there. All else lies within us. As prana enters our being through the moon chakra, it activates our personality. It becomes whatever our personality unconsciously tells the mind to become. The law of personality states that we always strive to become more of that which we are, to gain more of that which we already have. Reflecting on this should bring a very important realization. It is through this realization that we see the importance of understanding and studying the ancient science of the horoshastras, known as the Mother Science, the Science of Time and the Science of Symbols—esoteric astrology.

Some religions deal very curtly with the concept of time, and they generally deal with it only in terms of the end of the world or "end-time" as they call it. However, all religions deal with symbols in some way. As diligently as Western religion has attempted to reject and abandon symbolism, it has not been able to do so. Even though Christianity sought and continues to seek a completely literal interpretation of the Bible, it has been unable to do so. The Book of Revelations is nothing but symbol after symbol, and most Christians do not have the slightest understanding of what the Vision of John truly means. Thus, they call it "the mystery." Or they say that it is not for man to know. But then, I ask, "Why write about it?"

Returning to the question of the value of unformed energy, allow me to answer this question by using the symbolism of amorphous clay and a teacup. A teacup can only take the shape of a teacup (or a broken teacup). However, by its very nature, amorphous clay (that from which the teacup is made) can take any shape. Once the clay is baked into the shape of the teacup, it remains a teacup (or a broken teacup). Only if the baked clay is returned to its original form can it be reshaped and formed into a plate, a saucer or a tureen. Using this symbolism, the clay is everything. It is all-important because it can take on the shape of anything (via your consciousness). It is limited only by the horizon of your personality, that is, the horizon of your awareness.

Therefore, the next question that needs to be answered is, "How do we widen the horizon of our awareness?" The answer is that we do so by using the appropriate meditation technique. Although there are innumerable meditation techniques, there are only five fundamental categories of meditation. Each meditation method can be placed into one of these categories, and each of these categories leads to a different result.

THE FIVE CATEGORIES OF MEDITATION

The first category of meditation includes those methods in which the key purpose is to lead one to mindfulness. Mindfulness is extremely important. It is a state of consciousness in which we are aware of what is happening in our inner being as well as in the so-called outer world. The key function of mindfulness is to help you to be aware without evaluating or wanting to change anything. Mindfulness also leads to the awareness of what is about to happen but has not yet happened. Later, at a deeper level of meditation, one becomes aware of why these things occur and why changes take place. A mindfulness of what is happening and why it is happening is present in one's own physiology or psychology and, as the method is perfected, in the universe itself.

The second category of meditation includes those methods in which the key purpose is to produce fuller collectiveness. This means that the mind is now not only mindful, but it is also calm and imperturbable. Some teachers would say that in this state of fuller collectiveness the mind is self-composed. It is collected into a state of fuller realization of the nature of the Self and the world. In this second level, the mind brings together without conflict the energies of the Self and the world. In short, they are brought into linear lines of energy, and thus neither one affects the other.

The third category of meditation includes those methods in which the key function is to lead one to one-pointedness of inward consciousness. Although the energy streams are flowing up and down and in and out, at this level one can bring these energy streams to a point in which they have enormous intensity for expanding self-awareness.

Some gurus feel that the first three categories are not different but are simply different levels of meditation.

To gain a better understanding of what is happening within these three levels of meditation, both symbolically and literally, take a sheet of paper. If you roll it up, it becomes linear. If you roll up that symbolic line, you get a point, symbolic of collectiveness. In one-pointedness, you gather all the energy into one point, giving it great power to create or reveal greater awareness. The yogis call this point a *bindu*, which is the place where creative energy is released. There is one key bindu. It is at the moon center. There are other secondary bindus in the lower chakras.

I will say it again. Take a point, a dot and unroll it. What do you get? You get a line. Now unroll the line. What do you get? You get a plane. Now unroll the plane. What do you get? You get a cube. Take a cube and roll it up and you get a plane. Roll up a plane and you get a line. Roll up a line and you get a point. Hopefully, this example will help you understand the secret of how energy is released down through the various planes of existence.

The fourth category of meditation includes those methods in which the key function is to lead one to bliss or ecstasy. In the West, at least up until the late '20s, the word "ecstasy" was usually used to refer to these mystical states of consciousness. It referred to ecstatic states of communion with God or to states of consciousness transcendent of the earth plane. However, at that time, a movie director decided to produce a film called *Ecstasy* that portrayed a naked woman swimming in a pond. From that time on, in the Western mind, the term "ecstasy" was usually associated with sexuality rather than with God consciousness.

This category of meditation produces an ecstasy in which there is a fullness of mind. This fullness causes the mind to be forever filled with bliss. It is so full that the bliss never leaves. It may fluctuate from high to higher or from higher to high, but it never leaves. One does not have a longing to re-experience this bliss because once experienced, it remains forever. It leaves one with a deep and abiding contentment.

This level of meditation is quite different from the religious state of ecstasy in which the mind becomes depressed and dejected when the state leaves. This painful and insatiable longing for that which is missed is the so-called "dark night of the soul."

All four of the above levels of meditation have a strong sense of bliss and quietude in which there is a feeling that, at that moment, everything is as it should be. Within these four states there is bliss, contentment and noetic data. However, each of these levels of meditation varies in the intensity; each varies in the level of the meaningfulness of the noetic data.

In the fifth category of meditation, something happens that is not experienced in any of the first four categories. This fifth category includes those methods that lead to samadhi or cosmic consciousness. The methods of the fifth category are called primary techniques. In these methods, the life energy, the pranic currents that rotate through and around the spinal axis, literally become linear in their course. The energy is changed from angular energy to linear energy, which then moves into the bindu.

Thus, we have yet another vital factor for defining advanced meditation: Advanced meditation is meditation, if and only if, the angular energy is changed to linear energy and lifts, balances and centers itself in the bindu. This centering of the life energy lets us know that our meditation is working. Upon entering into the outer fringes of samadhi, the rough edges of our personality soften. Hostility goes away. Suspicion goes away. Fear goes away. Contentment enters and the personality becomes more caring and loving.

When one's meditation is in any of the first four categories, karma can be softened. When one's meditation is in any method of the fifth category, karma is dissolved. Thus, another definition of advanced meditation is that it is the process of demagnetizing the influence of angular energy. It is the demagnetizing influence on the angular energy in this fifth category that allows this energy to pull away from things. As it pulls away from things, the only place it can go is back to the Self. Thus, it goes from ideas, thoughts and emotions back to pure consciousness.

I should mention that:
• The fifth stage techniques are called primary techniques.
• The fourth stage techniques are called secondary techniques.
• The third stage techniques are called tertiary techniques.

This does not mean that the first four categories are unimportant. They are important and meaningful. Ultimately, however, advanced meditation depends on using techniques associated with the fifth category.

My guru said that if a person uses any one of the first four categories and stays with it, it will automatically lead to the outer fringes of samadhi. However, it will take much longer.

Of course, everyone wants to begin with the methods of the fifth category. This is why we do not make much progress upon the path. Walking the path must be an organized step-by-step ascension from emotional imprisonment to freedom from embodied consciousness.

When discussing meditative techniques, it should be clear that there are many different ways to meditate within each category. For example, Buddhism tends to emphasize the use of yantras and mandalas, whereas yogis tend to emphasize breathing techniques and mantras. We should not minimize or criticize any system of meditation. Rather, each soul needs to examine the various methods and determine how each can benefit him. Above all, each soul needs to ask the necessary question, "Does this technique have the ability to control the energy in my being?"

For most people, it takes many years of work to attain perfect conscious concentration before they can attain the fifth level of effortless meditation, which releases samadhi. When samadhi is attained, it lasts for only milliseconds at first. For the vast majority of people, however, samadhi manifests in very weak units and lasts for only nanoseconds. At first these "specks" are very weak, but over a long period of time they become stronger. They may be so weak at first that we do not even recognize them as states of consciousness existing on the outer fringes of samadhi. They may feel like periods of light cheerfulness in which negative events and people do not seem to bother us as much as before or they may bring insights into things, events and people. They may be periods in which everything we do seems quite effortless.

Over and above this, these subtle events do have a cumulative effect. In time, samadhi breaks forth in its full glory. Here we realize the experience for what it is. For most of our lives before entering the pathway, we were trained to energize our minds in order to get something or to accomplish something. Now it can be done effortlessly.

It is difficult for Westerners to meditate because of a very basic personality attitude that their culture fosters. They have been conditioned to believe that he who runs the fastest gets there first. He wins who energizes and does the most intense work for the longest period of time. In meditation, however, we must let go of this attitude. The art of meditation and the art of living are about reaching an effortless state.

Modern society has made an appalling mistake. It does not understand the true concept of winning. The error is that we think fame equates with greatness. Yet nothing is further from the truth; these two concepts are about as far apart as any two concepts can be. The great ones are usually hidden.

We should not remain poor in body or spirit. In other words, we can and should move from wealth to greater wealth, from happiness to greater happiness, from wisdom to greater wisdom. I am not implying that "things" are inferior. I am saying that we need a technique whereby we can pull ourselves away from things in order to find the creator of those things. Finding the creator of our experiences enables us to instantaneously re-experience anything that we have experienced, at any time, and at any place. How? By the magic of our memory. Memory is the greatest of gifts. This is the power of Venus, Taurus, and the "winged bull"—the memory tract that relates to the second house within the esoteric horoscope.

Mystically, life is about being aware. It is about being conscious. Life is consciousness; death is unconsciousness. Advanced meditation is the means to attain and thus sustain consciousness. Therefore, the mystic never dies.

One of the vital goals of advanced meditation is to attain and sustain a state of consciousness called un-embodied consciousness. We seek to move from embodied consciousness to unembodied consciousness. We seek to literally move out of our body consciously.

When we experience this advanced meditation stage, we are liberated from constrictive body consciousness. We are liberated because we have learned how to remain conscious while outside the physical body and how to personally experience living in and through our astral body. We touched upon this earlier when we talked about learning to dive into the dream state consciously. When we are in our astral body, we can find our own memory tract and thus read our personal history from the beginning of time and before.

When we move into the meditation states existing in categories one through four, we can reach the memory tract of life. However, in category five we can tap into the memory of our past lives. We can recall these experiences and thus be well on our way.

The psychology at work here is the same as when a person has a toothache and keeps repeating to himself, "I don't have a toothache." He believes this suggestion will get rid of his toothache. However, in truth, the more he focuses on his toothache, the more he will experience the pain. He rids himself of the toothache by not thinking about it. But how does he stop thinking about the toothache when it is so painful? He does this by thinking of something far more beautiful or far more fascinating. In the same manner, we let go of the noise in our minds by letting go of the world and the rat race in the world that exists in our head. We let go of the noise in our head by letting go of the emotional factors of the world, which also exist in our head. We let go of the noise by letting go of all of our compulsions, and by becoming truly detached from the world in our head.

Yet we must be sure to fulfill our obligations, our responsibilities and our commitments to life and in life. We must be detached but not indifferent. We need to be detached from things and remember that, ultimately, all learning is but a remembering. For most of us, samadhi is a remembrance of something already experienced, whether that was five years or five lifetimes ago. Still we have to work to bring it back to the surface of our minds. We need to learn to let go and remember.

There is another vital question: What is the distinction between experiencing samadhi and having the memory of experiencing samadhi? I am suggesting that perchance they might be the same thing. In Western psychology and philosophy, however, we do not think that the experience and the memory of that experience are the same thing. What do you think?

We are taught to forget dreams. When we were young, most of us were told to forget our dreams because they were not important. We were taught that things in the world are real but that thoughts and dreams are not. As we grow older, we come to understand that inner states are far more important than external states.

What is the difference between an experience and the memory of that experience? Is the only difference in the time factor? Being more philosophical, one might ask, "If I have already experienced something, why would I want to re-experience it?" One mystical answer might be that it is far more meaningful to re-experience something than to simply remember it. Is this too subtle a mystical statement? If we have had cosmic consciousness in our past lives, why are we striving so hard re-experience it? The answer is simple: Our memory of that state of consciousness is striving to gain (or regain) a greater awareness of it and of its meaning.

Some mystics say that if we did not have the memory of cosmic consciousness, we would not have the impetus to seek it. Others say that if we did not have the memory of cosmic consciousness, we would not have the aspiration to seek it out again.

Om Shanti

CHAPTER SIX
The Principles of Mantra in Meditation

Because mantra meditation is one of the most widely used forms of meditation, we will devote more time to a discussion of its many facets.

What is mantra? In simple terms, mantra is a patterning of sound vibrations. There is no conscious primary meaning to a vibration. It just exists. For example, the sound "Mmmmm" is universal. It is the sound "Mmmmm" in all languages. The same seems to be true of the sound "ma" or "mama." It may be written differently, but the sound is the same.

Mantra is a primary vibration that affects the subconscious and unconscious minds, as does the sound "mama." On a higher level, it also affects the super-conscious mind. Eastern schools of thought refer to mantra as thought-patterns produced by sound vibration. The old Jewish system refers to mantra as "words of power." The Christians and the Muslims refer to mantra as the repetition of the name of God. Mantra is a universal process that takes place in nature, automatically, manifesting at subconscious levels of the mind, affecting both the biology and the psychology of the brain and mind.

The pathmakers of old listened to nature and observed the effects that a given sound vibration produced. They repeated the sound with their voices. Then turning inward with a quiet mind, they mentally reproduced the sound vibration, observing the effects that it had on their mind and thus on their body. Finally, they modified these fundamental sound vibrations. That is to say, they added to or subtracted from them, thus creating the mantra. They then chanted these mantras and observed the effects they produced.

The mystics of all ages and cultures state that anything and everything can be accomplished if a person uses the right mantra. Because of this, mantra has been held as one of the most deeply guarded secrets of the oral tradition. Anything can be accomplished if a person has the right mantra and chants it in the correct way. For a mantra to be effective it must be used in the proper manner, intoned with the proper rhythm, used at the correct time and, most importantly, the chanter must have the appropriate mindset. Mantric vibrations affect the mind in a positive, constructive and healing manner.

When the pathmakers of old passed on their sacred wisdom to their students, they revealed what each mantra could accomplish. In the oral transference of the meaning of these subconscious sounds, mantra evolved. These subconscious primary vibrations were given conscious meaning, which were considered to be secondary. These secondary meanings, however, are somewhat insignificant compared to the subconscious mantric vibration. Nonetheless, mankind seeks to understand everything via his conscious mind.

In the Hindu philosophy, the fundamental sound vibrations from which mantras are created are called *bijas*, meaning "seed-sounds." These bija seeds are primary sounds. We put these primary vibrations together to form a mantra. These bijas are fundamental sound vibrations that unfold into specific experiences "when seeded." There are 12 of these bijas, a seed-sound for each of the 12 fundamental states of consciousness.

When a bija is seeded, it means that the fundamental forces existing within the bija mantra are not only released but also directed toward a predetermined goal. This is usually done by the maker of the mantra, the person who created the initial mantra. In one symbolic sense, the seeds are like vowels, and the consonants are like the rest of the mantra. They shape and determine the length of the vowels, as in the following: KA, TA, BA or AK, AT, AB, etc.

Remember that mantra has vibrations within itself. For example, there are bjia seeds or fundamental vibrations in the mantra AUM. They are:

- "Aaa,"
- "Uuu," and
- "Mmm."

Students often make the mistake of thinking that mantras are words, and they try to give them conscious meaning. However there are no words in mantra. There is only sound. In addition, when we use some type of writing system to symbolize these sounds, we create yet another level of symbolism. We create tertiary symbols of the mantra. Depending on the writing system used, these sounds are symbolized in various ways.

If we look at the Sanskrit language, in which the word *mantra* means "vowel," we see that these seed-sounds are symbolic of the 12 primary Sanskrit vowels: A, AA, I, II, U, UU, RI, LRI, E, AI, O, and AU. These 12 primary vowel sounds are often nasalized, symbolized in English with an "m" or an "n" with a little dot over them.

Some wise people may say that "A" is a bija sound, but "AA" is not. It is only a prolonged "A." If this is true, then it is true that all other long vowels should be deleted. Thus, we have a new system. In this new system, there would be only nine vowels: A, I, U, RI, LRI, E, AI, O and AU. In order to bring the total number of sounds back to 12, three more symbols would have to be added. Some say these three symbols would be the three nasals NA, NA and NA. The first NA has a long mark over the N; the second NA has a wavy line over the N; and the last NA has a dot under the N.

Please note that I am using Roman letters to symbolize these Sanskrit sounds, which causes the creation of yet another level of symbolism. Remember that the farther away a symbol is from its primary source, the weaker will be the effect of that symbol upon the mind. In other words, the fifth level of symbolism is much weaker than the second level of symbolism.

Because the English language has only five vowels, one might have to use semi-vowels, diphthongs and nasals to symbolize these 12 bijas. It should be clear that the more vowels a language has, the more suitable it is for mantra use. Ancient languages, as a whole, have far more vowels than do modern languages.

As you chant a mantra, you will become aware that you are suddenly inhaling a great deal of air but exhaling very slowing. This process of short duration to long duration mathematically gives a mystical factor relating to the power of the prana transferred to the mantra. As you repeat the mantra and thus the breathing pattern, you build up pranic energy to empower your mantra. For example, if you inhale for five seconds and exhale for 30 seconds, the power factor would be six. If you inhale for two seconds and exhale for 30 seconds, the power factor would be 15. If you inhale for one second and exhale for 30 seconds, the power factor would be 30. And if you inhale for one second and exhale for 60 seconds, the power factor would be 60.

This prana is distributed into three sections:
- that which relates to your physical body,
- that which relates to your mind and
- that which relates to the release of energy from your mind/body complex.

First, when chanting mantra, there is an enormous absorption of oxygen and prana, life energy, into your physical body. This added oxygen and life energy has a strong and positive purifying effect on the blood and thus on your total body. It improves your health and promotes longevity.

Second, as you draw in and absorb more oxygen and prana, the brain is fed more fully. Areas of the brain that have been dormant since physical birth begin to awaken, bringing greater clarity of thinking and greater dimensions of psychological functioning. In this way, the brain and mind are improved. They become sharper, more creative, more aware and more self-aware. All of this brings awareness of the laws of consciousness.

Third, as you continue to chant a mantra, you feed energy from the mind/body complex into the creative process of the mantra. This definitely can transform negative moods and attitudes into positive and constructive states of consciousness. Thus, the mantra is very powerful.

When you chant a mantra, the brain begins to unfold. The lotus opens. In Western psychology, it is said that the brain is nothing but gray matter. We know that the amount of gray matter that is activated in the ordinary person is somewhere around three-tenths of one percent of our total capacity. Some say that it is one percent; others say that it is three percent. Personally, I think that the conscious power of the conscious mind is around one millionth of one billionth of a percent. The vast majority of the mind is simply sleeping or dormant. Because of the lack of prana, it is inactive. As we put more and more oxygen and prana into the blood stream and as it goes to the brain, the gray matter begins to awaken. As this gray matter awakens, our IQ increases. Everything in our mental state improves. Ultimately this unfolds into cosmic consciousness and the jewel that is in the lotus is revealed.

The word *mantra* literally translated means "thought form" or "thought pattern" produced by vibrations. The concept behind mantra is the generation of new, positive and specific thought forms. The mantra is then repeated over and over until it overrides any negative thought form existing in our conscious or subconscious personality.

At some point in the repetition of the mantra, this fundamental thought pattern momentarily flashes through the mind, giving us insight into something specific we had not thought before. This specific new thought is the result of the mantra. It also gives us added insight into the nature of old thought patterns.

The mystical and psychological effects of mantra extend far beyond its external effects. Mantra has two levels of manifestation. First, it has an external manifestation. This is what the average person thinks the mantra is about. Second, it always has a mystical/psychological effect: greater insight into life, consciousness and the laws of consciousness, that is, how karma is created, stored, and manifested.

I want to emphasize again that when using a mantra technique, the power of the mantra does not generally manifest until the mind first becomes bored. It is only when the mind becomes bored with the technique that the mind begins to break away from the mantra and move to lower levels of awareness. It is in these lower levels that the mantra is energized.

It is good to experience the joy produced by using a method and to find joy in chanting. Your mind may get so caught up in the joy, however, that you may not realize the effect of the mantra. The goal of meditation goes beyond the joy and also beyond the method. The effect still takes place. But you can increase the power of the mantra by shifting your awareness away from the joy and away from the method and refocusing it on the desired result you are seeking. This will enable you to give clearer and better direction to its force.

Here I need to refer to a very deep, esoteric concept in mysticism: The bliss of God hides the true nature of God. Most people seek the joy of God and go no further. In the same manner, the joy of the mantra conceals the true meaning and effect of the mantra. Most students seek the joy of the mantra and do not seek the wisdom contained deeper within it, beyond the joy. In other words, we settle for the "gifts of God." My guru, Sri Shelliji, said that the bliss of God is God's last defense mechanism.

At or near the point of boredom, the mantric patterning will flash through the mind, probably more as a remembrance than as a new realization. At first, it will be difficult to tell them apart. But one must continue chanting, taking the mind past its restlessness and boredom until it becomes focused. One needs to stay with the mantra, and in time one's consciousness will break free from everyday thinking and emoting patterns. At that moment, one will see the world, one's Self, one's place in the world, and the place of all earthlings in the design of things. One will suddenly see all of this as a totality. There is a moment when the soul comes back to itself. There is a moment of total remembrance and acceptance of all that one remembers with clear mindfulness. As a matter of fact, if one does not accept all of Life, one will not be able to recall the full memory of Life itself.

Mantra is not only a spiritual term but a religious term as well. It relates to the Hebrew word *logos*, to the Jewish phrase, "Words of Power," to the Christian concept of "the Word" and to the Hindu word *Vak*. It is interesting to note that the Hindus wrote about *Vak* thousands of years before John wrote about "the Word."

In the ancient Vedas, it says:

"In the beginning was the Word. And the Word was God (Brahman). The Word created all that was created. And the Word is AUM." How about that? John, the mystic, used the very same words thousands of years later, but he did not say that the Word was AUM. He referred to the Word as "God." The closest Christians have come to the word AUM is AMEN.

Let me continue the discussion of mantra meditation. Mantra meditation removes three levels of thought:

• Those thoughts that are transitory, thoughts that exist for only a short time;

• Those thoughts that are progressed, repetitive thoughts that usually stay with us for two to eight months,

• Those thoughts that are natal, repetitive thoughts that tend to stay with us for most of our incarnation.

Once these three levels of thought are stripped away, we are free to transcend thought. The deeper we move into the method, the more we are able to eliminate these thought levels, though only momentarily. It is in this moment that cosmic consciousness can manifest. It does take preparation. It does take persistence. Symbolically, at this moment, the ice cube has melted. The water still exists, but it is much more fluid.

Mantra does not have to be chanted out loud. Actually, from a classical standpoint, mantra meditation is a threefold process; that is to say, mantra is performed on three levels: mantra, pajan, kirtan.

Mantra is the first level and is best referred to as muttering. At this level, we can hear ourselves but not too clearly or too distinctly. At this stage of chanting mantra, the more superficial thoughts, the transient thoughts, tend to quiet themselves and/or go away.

Pajan is the second level. After chanting for some time, we can center ourselves at this level. We now pick up the mantra and perform the pajan level of chanting. It is louder and stronger; it is more intense. Some people refer to this stage as singing. It softens the force of the thoughts and/or drives away the second layer of thinking, the progressed thoughts.

At this point, we have rid ourselves of transient and progressed thinking, the superficial thoughts, as well as those that are more emotionally attached to our thinking process.

Kirtan is the third level of the mantra process. Here we can rid ourselves of natal thinking, those thoughts that tend to stay with us most of our incarnation. Kirtan has been called loud singing. Others call it screaming harmoniously. Once we reach the point of kirtan, we stay in this mode for a short time or until all of these heavily glued thoughts are softened or removed from the surface mind. At this point, we reverse the process. We now return to pajan for a short time and then to the mantra stage for a short time.

Next we chant the mantra silently.

Then we chant silently without moving the tongue.

The final stage is complete and absolute stillness in which the mantra chants itself. It is within this stillness that true meditation takes place and the power of the mantra manifests.

We see that there are nine stages to the mantra process:

Three stages upward in which the voice is intensified. In order, these are mantra-pajan-kirtan.

Three stages downward in which the voice is lowered and the intensity decreases. In order, these are kirtan-pajan-mantra.

The final three stages are: silent mantra, silent mantra without moving the tongue, and lastly, total stillness of the mind, in which the mantra chants itself.

There are basic guidelines pointing out the patterns of mantra, such as timing, intonation, etc. There are also basic guidelines for pajan and kirtan. The guidelines for kirtan are much freer than the guidelines for pajan. The guidelines for pajan are much freer than the guidelines for mantra. In kirtan, the spirit moves one more freely, if one chooses to use such an expression. Within the guidelines of mantra, there is not much room for free expression of the spirit, for the purpose of the mantra proper is to direct the mind to a given place. It sets one's feet upon the right road. If one does not start upon the right road, all the effort and walking are meaningless.

Historically speaking, there are three types of mantra. To make life easier, I will use English terminology to explain them:

1. The first type of mantra is a singular mantra, a monosyllabic sound. With this type of mantra, one repeats a singular sound over and over again. There are different ways of chanting this monosyllabic sound in order to obtain different effects. An example of this type of mantra is RAM.

2. The second type of mantra is a dual-sound mantra. This type of mantra is very powerful. It is dual in nature and is generally linked to the breathing pattern. An example of this type of mantra is HAM-SAU (pronounced hahm-saw.)

3. The third type of mantra includes those that contain more than two mantric sounds. They might contain 5, 8, 12, 24, or 32 mantric sounds.

In general, mantras range from 1 to 32 mantric sounds. The most important of these include:
- The one-lettered mantra
- The five-lettered mantra (e.g., OM NAMA SHIVAYA). The term "five-lettered-mantra" refers to a mantra containing five sound vibrations.
- The six-lettered mantra (e.g. Tibetan mantra OM MANI PADME HUM).
- The 12-lettered mantra
- The 32-lettered mantra

I would like to mention that when in China, I was given some mantras. We do not hear much about Chinese mantras. The strange and wonderful thing is that within these mantras there are basic sounds that are not natural to the Chinese language. In Japan, I was given some Zen mantras that also had sounds that were not natural to the Japanese language. Carrying this research a little further, back in the '40s, I studied Egyptian religion in the archaeological library of the Field Museum. This religion often dealt with mantra. Again, these mantras contained sounds that were not natural to the Egyptian hieroglyphic language. In some of the more esoteric Sanskrit mantras, there were sounds that were not natural to Sanskrit. These not-natural Chinese, Japanese, Egyptian and Sanskrit mantric sounds were common among these different languages.

Yoganandaji told my guru that this indicated that mantra evolved from a common super-language. There is a theory that at one time on earth there was one language spoken by nearly everyone, and from which these mantras most likely originated. They were passed down to different cultures that later added to the mantras by using sounds from their own language. It is said that these diverse languages and cultures drew upon a prototype mantric language that predates the languages mentioned. Some say that this was the language of the ancient Atlantean civilization. Others say that it was the language of "space people" who originally landed on earth and gave us these words of power. I do not know whether this is true or not, but I do know that there was a far older language that had contact with these four cultures and beyond—for example, the Mayans. I was taught that these sounds are sounds of an astral language, and thus they are common to all languages.

Mantra is meaningful in many ways. It is a pattern that exists in total opposition to artificiality. Mantras are not what the words mean, though we often give meaning to the vibrations. The meaning is that which you experience after you recite the mantra for an extended period of time. The true meaning, the esoteric meaning of the mantra, is revealed only when you chant the mantra for a long time with an undistracted and concentrated mind. This esoteric meaning has three levels: the universal level, the cultural level and the individual level. It is only when all three of these levels are experienced through chanting that the esoteric level is fully revealed and understood. There are also three effects produced by each true mantra:

In the first level, every mantra has a positive physiological effect on one's health or at least on one organ of the body. It brings health and vitality to the physical body. For example, the Tibetan mantra OM MANI PADME HUM has a very powerful effect on the liver. On a physiological level, this mantra is vibrating at, and to, the liver. It is saying to the liver, "Be healthy. Gain greater and more positive vitality."

In the second level, every mantra produces a positive mental reaction that has three sub-levels. It produces tranquility, detachment and insight.

In the third level, every mantra produces a spiritual reverberation that transcends the body and mind. It produces a transcendental awareness for which there are no words. The best way I can express this reverberation is to say that it vibrates and resonates a state of consciousness that reveals the nature of Life, which at the same moment reveals the Self as the self-revealing Self.

Over and above what I have said, there are three other types of mantras:

The first type of mantra is composed of standard words from a native language. For example, in Sanskrit, we have the mantra OM NAMA SHIVA YA. In Tibetan, there is the mantra OM MANI PADME HUM.

The second type of mantra includes those mantras that are composed of sounds such as RIM, HUM, KIM, HRU and HRIM. These mantric sounds are not often found in most languages. Unfortunately, they are sometimes referred to as nonsensical sounds by sociologists because they are looking at them from the standpoint of the exoteric meaning of the words. These mantras are not nonsensical; they have deep meaning but their meaning is heavily disguised.

The third type of mantra includes those mantras that are composed of both standard words and these basic vibration sounds. An example of this type of mantra would be OM SHIVA HRIM, RIM PHAT.

Let us now return to the second type of mantra, which sociologists consider nonsensical. I want to explain how this type of mantra is constructed in order to clarify that it has definite meaning. This is one of the more closely guarded mysteries of mantra. Although I may be getting too deeply into the concept of mantra, this information may help you better understand the meaning of mantra. It is vital to know as much as you can about mantra meditation because it is one of the most powerful forms of meditation.

As an example, let us look at the mantric sound HRIM. At first, it looks like a nonsensical Sanskrit word. However, it has a definite meaning. This is how this mantric sound was constructed: H stands for HARI, which, according to the Vishnu Purana, is the most accessible mystical force of all the spiritual energies of the Reality. HARI is composed entirely of this essence. Thus, from Him and in Him is the Universe. Here we have two sub-levels of meaning:

1. This means that HARI is within us and we are in Him. Thus, His creative powers can be and are released within us. This does not mean that these creative powers are at our disposal at all times. It is only when we have the ability to properly chant the mantra, when our body and mind are in a peaceful, serene, and focused state of consciousness, that this creative energy is at our disposal. HARI is the supreme indwelling lord dwelling within our inner consciousness.

2. HARI is also one of the names of Lord Vishnu, who has the power to remove our limitations and deficiencies. The word HARI comes from the verbal root meaning "to take away," to remove our limitations and inadequacies. And of course, the negative forces are taken away through knowledge and wisdom.

RI symbolizes the word RITA, meaning *ritual,* or more clearly, the order of the universe that reveals the proper ritual of Life. It is a term used to symbolize the universal harmony of Life. In short, it means that Life is abundant and we should not experience lack in our lives.

RIM also symbolizes the word RINAM or *debt.* (Please note that the N and the M are nasalized sounds in these words.) The word-symbol debt refers to the debt that each of us has to the powers that be, to the sages and to our ancestors (including our parents).

Finally, M symbolizes the word *mantra,* which in this case is a form of speech that produces a material effect on the mind and body.

Thus, we have the sound HRIM, which comes from the following words:

HARI + RITA + RINAM + MANTRA.

These are reduced to:

H + RI + RI + M, producing HRIRIM.

The RI and RI overlap each other making the RI a long sounding RI. Thus, it is reduced to HRIM.

I have condensed 25 pages of information about mantra to explain the basis of the formation of sounds. I would also like to point out that in this section I have not mentioned a number of factors because of my spiritual code of silence.

What does the mantra HRIM mean exoterically? Exoterically, it means that the divine force exists within us. However, we need to find the ritual of harmony in order to be able to experience that divine source within ourselves.

If we use mantra correctly, we are able to pay back the debts that we owe or at least to help balance out these debts. How can this be? Debts cause karmic particles that accumulate in our astral bodies, and the force of this angular energy holds this karma to us. Mantra transforms some of this angular energy into linear energy. When this happens, the force-fields holding the karmic particles are weakened and/or removed. In either event, much of the karma is released. Consequently, when these debts are somewhat paid, our karma in this area is brought back into some degree of balance. Our deficiencies or lacks dissolve and abundance manifests. When this karma is released from our astral body, there is regeneration and a transformation of our consciousness. With this transformation comes awareness of our unwise actions of the past; there is an understanding of the foolishness of these past actions. Thus, we immediately seek to rectify them with positive, wise and helpful actions that will assist other people to improve their lives. In so doing, we repay this symbolic debt.

The regeneration or neutralization of the negative karma that we have incurred from unwise past-life actions occurs at the moment our attitude is transformed. We begin to manifest more positive helpful actions toward living creatures. The karma is neutralized at this moment. However, the total debt is really paid over an extended period of time by wise and helpful actions toward others. All of this awakens the realization, "How foolish I have been."

We chant mantra to change ourselves, to change the world. When we change, our attitudes and actions change. They become much more positive and are directed toward selflessly helping others. We begin to live a new and more skillful life.

It takes an enormous amount of self-discipline and internal striving to move away from the desire to seek revenge from those we feel have hurt us in reality or in our imagination. It takes an even greater amount of self-awareness and wisdom to understand that those souls have hurt us because they are enmeshed in their own negative karma. It is of vital necessity that we bless them. We who bless them are indeed blessed. We become free.

Returning to the basic concepts of mantra, it should be pointed out that each letter or sound of the mantra is associated with an appropriate visualization. In the inner mind, one can see the mantric sound via a short astral "film strip." Thus, one can see the mantra that one is chanting.

With each mantric sound that is chanted, there is a series of imagery symbols that the student is taught when he is learning the total mantra. It may take months to master each sound or set of sounds along with the corresponding imagery symbols. It sometimes takes up to two and a half years to learn the mantra taught by the guru or the master of the mantra. There are mantras, I am told, that take 12 years to master. By this time, the student may have been chanting each sub-mantric sound of that mantra for an hour or so each day. In so doing, when he chants the entire mantra, all the imagery and power of his past practice will flash through his mind, empowering the mantra. By the time the student masters a single mantra, it becomes unbelievably rich in visualization and also in *swahs,* various arm movements made while holding precise *mudras* as each sound is pronounced.

The time spent in chanting a mantra usually varies from 18 minutes on the low side to 108 minutes on the high side. Under certain circumstances, special mantras can be chanted four to six hours each day for three to four months in order to produce the desired effect of that mantra. Most often, however, one uses a "householder pattern," which means that the imagery and swahs are dropped.

In summary, the whole idea behind the technique of mantra meditation is to find an appropriate mantra. As you hold this mantra in the forefront of your mind, repeat it to yourself. At the same time, let all other thoughts fall away. Do not try to understand either the meaning of the mantra or its implications. Simply try to grasp the feeling of the mantra and allow the symbols to manifest from that mantra. Then consciously re-enforce those symbols.

Om Shanti

CHAPTER SEVEN
The Essence of Mantra Meditation

There are 108,000 dominant mantras, although the sacred texts talk about hundreds of thousands of secondary mantras. Mantra is most often associated with Hinduism, although it is not unique to Hinduism; almost every culture uses mantra. It is just that the Hindus have uniquely nurtured, developed, polished, perfected and preserved mantra.

Two vital factors always exist in all advanced meditation. Inhalation must be as short as possible and exhalation must be as long as possible. In breathing and mantra meditations, these two factors are key. This ratio in the meditative process is also known as the extension ratio, which we talked about earlier. The inhalation must be as short yet as full as possible, whereas the exhalation must be as long as possible. This must be performed without any stress or strain whatsoever. The ratio of inhalation to exhalation indicates the power factor of the mantra. That is, the power of the mantra depends on how short the inhalation time is, compared with the length of the exhalation time. The higher the ratio, the more effective the mantra will be in producing the desired results.

Let us say that the inhalation is 0.5 seconds and the exhalation is 17 seconds. The extension ratio would be 17/0.5 and thus the power factor would be 34. If, however, we increase the inhalation to two seconds and keep the exhalation at 17 seconds, the extension ratio would be 17/2, which is a power factor of only 8.5. There is a substantial difference in these two power factors; one is approximately four times more powerful. In other words, if we chant HAI RAM, JAI RAM, JAI JAI RAM for seven seconds after an inhalation of 0.5 seconds, the power factor will be 3.5.

Another important factor regarding mantra is the number of times the mantra is repeated. This repetition process is referred to as *japa*. If we take the example given above and chant the HAI RAM mantra three times in a row, the power factor is the square root of 3.5 x 3. Now, 3.5 x 3 = 10.5, and the square root of this number is only 3.2. However, if we chant this mantra five times while the other factors remain the same, we have the figure of 17/2 x 5, which is 42.5. The square root of this number is approximately 6.5. Here it would take at least four mantric repetitions to break even regarding the power factor. You can see that the more mantric repetitions one performs, the greater will be the power factor.

If we repeat the mantra seven times, the power factor will be the square root of 3.5 X 7. 3.5 x 7 = 24.5, and the square root of this number is approximately 5. If we chant the mantra 100 times maintaining the same breath ratio, the power factor will be the square root of 3.5 x 100 or approximately 19. If we chant it 500 times, the power factor would be approximately 42. It is clear that when using mantra, it is essential to chant it more than a few times because with the first few chants, we actually lower the power factor. This simply means that in order for a mantra to be effective, it should be used for an extended period of time.

Using the previous HAI RAM, JAI RAM mantra example, if the inhalation is 0.5 but we extend the exhalation from 7 to 34 seconds, the power factor will be markedly changed. In the earlier example, repeating the mantra 100 times gave us a power factor of 19. However, in this new example, we have a ratio of 34/0.5 or 68. Now 68 x 100 = 6800, and thus the power factor is the square root of 6800 or approximately 82.5. This is a much greater power factor than 19.

It should be noted, however, that some mantras can be more easily extended than other mantras. If one is using the hong-sau technique, for example, the timing factor is not specific because this mantra cannot and should not be extended by will power or by any other factor. Although the total hong-sau breathing pattern (inhalation and exhalation) most likely will be shorter at the beginning of each session, as one continues practicing the technique, the inhalation and exhalation will slow down and become extended.

According to Indian thought, there is a correct length of time to practice meditation. We call this a *muhurta*. A muhurta is 48 minutes of time. There are 24 hours in a day and 60 minutes in an hour, so we have 24 x 60 or 1,440 minutes in a day. Thus, a muhurta is 1440/48, or 1/30th of a day.

In Indian mysticism, there is a process by which a larger number is made into a smaller number or a smaller number is made into a larger number. In other words, we can take 48 minutes (a muhurta) and, in our mystical minds, turn it into 48 seconds. Here we arrive at the concept of the *upa-muhurta* (*upa* meaning "lesser" or "little"). Thus, an upa-muhurta is 48 seconds. With the use of this mystical method of the upa-muhurta, the benefits normally attained from 48 minutes of chanting are gained in just 48 seconds but only if one meditates for this length of time with a collective mind and without stress or strain.

After sustained repetition of the mantra, the mind is brought to rest; that is, one stops chanting and moves into the after-effect phase. If the chanting has been effective, the mantra meditation will change the breathing pattern and the range of the inhalation and exhalation will become quite short, generally from one-tenth of a second to one-half of a second. If the chanting has been truly effective, the after-effect phase will cause the breathing to slow down even more until the inhalation and exhalation both become zero seconds. In other words, when this ideal inhalation time is reached, when the breath has been suspended, the person has entered into a state of samadhi.

This is the goal that we all are working toward—entering samadhi without losing consciousness. When the yogi says, "without losing consciousness," he means without losing awareness of your inner states. At first one does lose awareness of the external world. However, in time and with practice, awareness of both worlds manifests. Back in the 1950s when my body slept at night, I was still aware of the external world. (It is amazing what people say around sleeping people. I often wonder what subliminal effect this has on the sleeping person.)

In order to make the mantra technique emphatic and effective, the total time of both the inhalation and exhalation should be at least 48 seconds, an upa-muhurta. This total time must be totally effortless.

If a person were to inhale for 2.0 seconds and chant (exhale) for 48 seconds, the influence factor or power factor would be 24. If the person were to inhale for 0.5 of a second and chant (exhale) for 48 seconds, the influence factor would be 96. However, if this person were to inhale for only 0.25 of a second and chant for 48 seconds, the influence factor would be an astounding 192.

Next, there are two types of mantra meditation. The first type is like the OM mantra in which there is only one mantra per breath. The longer it is projected in a single breath, the more powerful its effect will be. The second type of mantra is like the five-lettered mantra in which the more times it is repeated in a given breath, the more influence it has. No matter what mantra one uses, it is imperative to maintain your focus while practicing it. Mantras can be chanted either silently or aloud, depending on what the chanter is seeking to accomplish.

Some mantras should be chanted very rapidly whereas other mantras should only be chanted slowly. Yet it is possible to chant a mantra in various ways. For example, the OM mantra can be chanted many times with a single breath. However, it is best to chant one OM mantra as long as possible with one breath. Other mantras can be chanted either very rapidly or very slowly. It depends on the type of mantra that is being chanted and what the person is attempting to accomplish with that mantra.

One of the special mantras that can be chanted either way is the *panchakara mantra* or the five-lettered mantra OM NAMA SHIVA YA. At first this mantra appears to be a six-lettered mantra. However it becomes a five-lettered mantra by merging the MA with the SHI. Thus, it becomes OM NA *MASH*-VA YA. When it is chanted like this, it is reduced to a five-lettered mantra. Other schools drop the "A" in NAMA, and the mantra sounds like this: OM *NAM SHI*-VA YA. This reduction process is a very powerful method for intensifying the effect of the mantra.

This mantra can be chanted in two ways. The first is to chant it very rapidly and the second is to chant it very slowly. Most teachers generally suggest that the student first chant it aloud and quickly until the mind settles down. Then it should be chanted more slowly. Later it can be chanted even more slowly and very quietly. Once the seeker advances in the mastery of quieting his surface mind, this mantra should be chanted very slowly and silently.

If disrupting thoughts occur while chanting a mantra, the speed and/or the loudness of the mantra can be increased until the mind rebalances itself. When the mind is rebalanced, the level of the sound and speed should be reduced. As always, while the mantra is being quietly chanted, all emotionality must be set aside. The mind should be totally focused on the feeling state produced by the mantra. After coming out of your meditation, reflect on the thoughts that entered your mind during the meditation. Why did they occur then? Be sure to deal with these thoughts in order to balance them.

Modern people love to ask, "What does a given mantra mean?" As I have said before, the meaning of a mantra is the state of consciousness that is manifested when it is chanted. It is at this time that the secret of the mantra is revealed. The treasure of one's consciousness reveals the meaning of the mantra.

In exoteric terms, if pressed for the meaning of the five-lettered mantra, we would say it means: *Hail, oh thou auspicious indwelling light, the dissolver of all negativity.* This mantra removes all negativity.

The next critical factor in understanding the mantra meditative process is the pattern of the mantra. Again I will use the example of the five-lettered mantra. Being a five-lettered mantra, the pattern of chanting would be to chant it five times with each breath. This is called a round. This round should be repeated five times for a total of 25 mantras. Then it can be repeated five times for a total of 125 mantras. Next this round can be repeated five times for a total of 625 mantras. Then it can be repeated for a total of 3,125 mantras.

If the student has difficulty in chanting this mantra five times in one breath, he should practice pranayama and body cleansing. The number of rounds chanted will vary according to the capacity of the student. Each person should perform only the number of rounds that feels comfortable and stress free. This can range from 5 to 125 rounds. The length of time can range from approximately three minutes to many hours.

Usually a teacher will instruct the student to practice a given number of rounds. Sometimes by following this pattern, the mantra is repeated tens of thousands of times, even hundreds of thousands of times. The number of rounds for a cave yogi, for example, would be much greater than for that for a householder. The yogi might chant the mantra between 125 to 625 rounds in the manner just described.

The next vital factor in the mantra meditation process is the duration of silence following the repetition of the mantra. The duration is the length of time one remains in a meditative silence effortlessly. This aftereffect stage is only effective when the process is effortless. It is not dependent on duration.

The purpose of mantra meditation is to produce stillness of the mind. When the stillness is lost, the mantra should be chanted again to produce a deeper stillness. With each state of stillness, the meditation becomes deeper and longer until the effect of the mantra is reached or cosmic consciousness unfolds.

The value of mantra is that it can reveal to you something that your mind has not yet consciously perceived. The sounds used are actual sounds that exist in the astral world. One of the most important mantras in the Vedas is AUM. As previously stated, this mantra has come down into Western civilization in the words "Amen," "Amin," etc.

Our specific everyday state of consciousness, called "human consciousness," is produced by a series of vibrations. As long as these vibrations are maintained, we will sustain our everyday state of consciousness. These vibrations are produced by our unconscious mind; that is, they are unconsciously produced. However, they are sustained and reinforced by the activity of the conscious mind. The mind is fascinated by and held to these vibrations. If, however, mantra is practiced long enough, the mind lets go of this fascination and becomes free. Thus, these unconscious patterns can be changed and we can encounter experiences other than our everyday ones. These are often called astral experiences. In time, the mantra process will lead to the experience of cosmic consciousness.

According to tradition, a state of consciousness produced by a mantra can momentarily override an existing everyday state of consciousness, revealing new experiences. This new state of consciousness will be momentarily established. However, when the power of the habit of everyday living and emoting resurrects itself, this momentary state is overridden. Thus the need for *japa,* continual repetition of the mantra until the momentary state becomes an established daily state.

Japa is the process of stilling the mind by chanting, remaining quiet and then rechanting the mantra to still the mind at an even deeper level. It is by the repetition of the mantra that a given state of consciousness becomes a more permanent state.

MANTRA AND THE BREATHING PATTERN

The repetition of the mantra forces our breathing mechanism to establish a new and very particular pattern. This produces many psychological changes in consciousness. One of the major changes relates to the awake/asleep cycle. It is the breathing pattern that determines when we stay awake or fall asleep. By changing our breathing pattern and sustaining that pattern, we can move directly into the sleep state. However, upon entering the sleep state, most people become unconscious. Thus the practice of yoga is twofold:

Learning to remain aware while sleeping. In time, meditation helps one accomplish this, and meditation upon subtle matter helps even more.

Learning to remove the lower, negative emotions, or at least soften them, so that we can move to higher planes of consciousness after entering the sleep state.

The key reason that we are awake is because our breathing pattern is locked into the awakened state breathing pattern. There are certain people who are locked into this awakened breathing pattern and thus have difficulty falling asleep. If they changed their breathing pattern, they would be able to overcome insomnia.

When we fall asleep, we do so because of one key mystical thing: our breathing pattern re-establishes the sleep rhythm of breathing. Understanding this, mystics work to control their breathing pattern so that they can change it at will, enabling them to enter the sleep state at will. This is the first step in exploring the great cosmic universe.

In between the awake and asleep breathing patterns, we have the *dream* breathing pattern. By the repetition of certain mantras, mystics are able to go to sleep at will. With the repetition of other mantras, they are able to dream at will. By using still other mantras, they are able to control what they dream. This is the next mystical step. The goal is to climb higher and higher into the cosmos, that is, into subtler and subtler realms.

I repeat, the secret of mantra meditation is that when the sound vibration is repeated, it sets up a pattern that consequently changes the rhythm of our physiological breathing. This in turn changes our state of consciousness. It is only when we move away from our earthbound consciousness that we are able to truly see our universe and thus ourselves.

Do you remember the symbolism of the ant and his anthood? Unless this ant is able to somehow transcend his anthood, how can he understand his relationship to all other ants, to other anthills and to the universe? Now conceive that the ant is a symbol of the earthling. In the same way, we as earthlings must move beyond humanhood before we can move to devahood. Until we attain a state of devahood, we are not able to truly understand the nature of the earthling.

Unfortunately, the word *devahood* has often been translated as "Godhood," but this is not what it means. In the Hindu tradition, the word *deva* does not mean God. It means a being who has a lofty state of consciousness that far transcends that of human consciousness. Thus, when we attain a state of devahood, we can look back at our human life and say, "Now I understand the meaning of *man*. In my devahood on the astral plane, I understand the earthling in relationship to all things because I now have a larger perspective."

There are certain physical positions that should be maintained while chanting mantra and practicing other meditation techniques. These are:

- The spine is erect.
- The stomach muscles are taut.
- The chest is up and the shoulders back.
- The chin is level and the eyes closed.

When you are at full attention without tension, you can begin to chant your mantra.

The next important factor in the meditative process is that the influence or power of one's meditation, as well as the caliber of one's meditation, is directly proportional to the effortlessness of that meditation. We could also say that the influence and force of one's meditation is inversely proportional to the effort used in meditation.

Another essential factor regarding mantra is the emphasis of a specific sound pattern. This pattern can be changed according to what one is attempting to accomplish. In other words, we can change the effect of the mantra by simply emphasizing different sounds in the mantra. For example, when chanting the mantra OM NAMA SHIVA YA:

- We could emphasize the OM in "*OM* Nama Shiva Ya," or
- We could emphasize the NA in "Om *NA* Mashi Va Ya," or
- We could emphasize the SHIV in "Om Nama *SHIVa* Ya," and so on.

Classical Hindus, not yogis, take mantra as a total pattern and chant it in an acceptable classical manner. It is the yogi who is interested in the subdivisions of the mantra.

Mantric vibrations stimulate gray matter. In a quasi-scientific way, most neurologists refer to gray matter as that which enables an entity to think (in our sector of time and space). Gray matter is primarily in the brain, but it also descends into the lower spine as two ganglia "threads," the ida and pingala nadis. These threads join at the throat and then separate and continue downward. They join again at the heart area and then separate again. They descend further into the solar plexus, where they again join together and form the largest ganglion of gray matter. From here the ganglia separate and then join again at the level of the small of the back. They then separate and join again at the base of the spine. They no longer separate.

The gathering together of these two ganglia at the five vital areas on the spine form the five lower chakras, called the Mercury chakra, the Venus chakra, the Mars chakra, the Jupiter chakra, and the Saturn chakra.

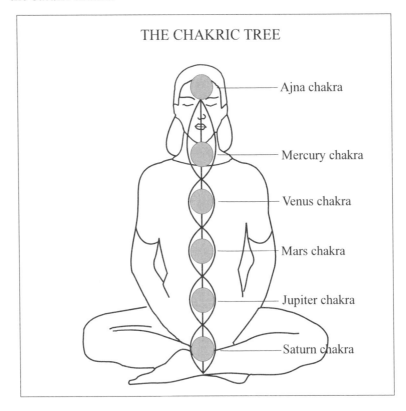

THE CHAKRIC TREE

- Ajna chakra
- Mercury chakra
- Venus chakra
- Mars chakra
- Jupiter chakra
- Saturn chakra

The ganglia along the spine have actual and also symbolic correspondents to the astral areas of the subtler worlds. These chakras are miniature brains that some people believe to be the location of the subconscious mind. However, the area of the unconscious mind is located in the *talas,* which symbolically exist in the areas of the upper legs.

Mantra meditation not only stimulates gray matter into conscious activity, it also causes one to become more select and focused. Mantra brings selectivity to the mind so that it is able to become aware of certain very subtle forces and objects. It does this by producing stimulation to the appropriate area of the gray matter.

For mantra to be truly effective, it must become automatic. Do you remember the example of the person learning to type? When he is first learning to type, he may say, "Don't disturb me. I'm trying to type." If you disturb him, he will make mistakes. However, once the subconscious mind controls his fingers, he can type and carry on a conversation without having to consciously focus on the keys. This is so because he is typing with the Mercury chakra, the cervical area of the spine. The typing is now automatic, freeing the conscious mind to do other things. In exactly the same way, we have to practice the meditative technique until it becomes automatic in the lower levels of the mind. When this happens, the meaningful effects of meditation will begin to manifest.

We talked about these levels of awareness when we referred to the five categories of meditation that lead to mindfulness, fuller collectiveness, one-pointedness, bliss or ecstasy and finally to the fifth stage, samadhi. Some mantra meditation techniques will walk you through all five of these stages. They are called twelve-lettered mantras. The uniqueness of the twelve-lettered mantra is that it ultimately reproduces the five stages. The constant repetition of the twelve-lettered mantra moves one through the five stages without having to keep returning to get the second, third and fourth initiations. Continuously chanting the twelve-lettered mantra through the self-evolving stages moves one into the higher stages of meditation, where one finds oneself on the outer fringes of samadhi.

One of these twelve-lettered mantras is: OM NAMO BHA-GAVATE VASU DEVAYA.

Although there are a number of ways to chant this mantra, the most classical way is to chant it in a monotone like this: OM NA MO BHA GA *BAA,* TE BAY SU DE *BA* YA.

Two other factors should be mentioned. First, the BAA sound is like "baa" in "baa baa black sheep," and it is held three times longer then the other sounds. Second, the BA sound is like "ba" in the word "badminton."

The meaning of the mantra is the state of consciousness produced when the mantra has been properly chanted for a correct period of time. However, if we exoterically analyze this twelve-lettered mantra, we come up with the following meaning:

First, *Bhagavate* means *lord* as in the English expression, "lord of the manor." In England, the function of the lord of the manor is to take charge of the entire manor. He must keep it in good repair and take care of the people who live on it. He cannot sell the manor. In short, he is responsible for the property and its people. This meaning is quite different from the Western concept of lord referred to in religious terms.

Second, the word *deva* means *a celestial entity*. It is difficult for most modern people to distinguish between an astral, a heavenly and a celestial being. The average person considers anything higher than a human being to be a god or an angel. Devas, however, are groups of celestial entities. They are much higher than astral or heavenly beings, and as such, have much more power than the angels referred to in Western tradition. Yet, like angels, they have a very specific area of command.

Third, in simple terms, *Vasu Deva* is a celestial being. *Vasu* means *the breathing principle*. Along with other factors, he is lord of the prana. In English, we would say that he is lord of the breath. When the breath leaves, our physical body dies. When Vasu Deva leaves, our physical body dies. For almost everyone, when the physical body dies, unconsciousness results. More accurately, when Vasu Deva leaves, the average person becomes unconscious. Prana is the energy that keeps our bodies and also our minds conscious. In yoga, Vasu Deva is not God; he is one of many forces that hold our body and mind together. However, for mankind, he is a vital force and a pathway in human evolution.

Fourth, it is true that some Hindus refer to Vasu Deva as the indwelling reality, or the indwelling divinity. Here we arrive at a wonderful symbol. In a very complex and true psychological way, Vasu Deva is a symbol of the son of God. Yes, Vasu is the son of God, and his father's name is also Vasu. They have the same name; they are one. You probably know his father by the name of Lord Krishna.

Thus, yogically, OM NAMO BHAGAVATE VASU DEVAYA means:

I hail and prostrate to the holy indwelling reality within, which sustains my body, mind, and the total microcosm.

This simply means that we do not have to climb a physical ladder to get to heaven. We simply have to climb our astral spinal column. The symbol of Jacob's ladder is not an external symbol.

You might remember that the Buddha sat under the base of the bodhi tree. The Jewish mystics talk about the tree of Life. And the Hindus talk about the wish-fulfilling tree. All of these tree symbols relate to our astral spinal column with all of its chakras. They are like the rungs of Jacob's ladder. In the West, this is symbolized by the Christmas tree. The lights on the Christmas tree are symbolic of the chakras. Usually there is also a star or key light at the top of the tree, symbolic of the single eye or the ajna chakra.

Om Shanti

CHAPTER EIGHT
Comparative Meditation Techniques

In the discussion of comparative meditative techniques, we have talked a great deal about mantra meditation. I would like to move on and discuss some Buddhist methods. Although Buddhism also uses mantra, it is better known for its use of mandalas and yantras. A mantra is a sound vibration or a given thought form whereas a yantra is a diagram of a vibration. A yantra is the visual equivalent of a mantra.

A MAHAYANA BUDDHIST MANDALA TECHNIQUE

Mandalas and yantras originally were devised by the Hindus and have been used by them since ancient times. With the birth of Buddhism, the use of mandalas was carried over into this new school of thought. Mahayana Buddhism, the largest Buddhist sect, also uses the mandala technique.

A mandala is a circular and symbolic representation of the macrocosm and also of the personal microcosmic forces. A mandala is used in a particular type of meditation. It is a symbolic map of a given part of the universe or cosmos, as well as an area inside the body. Mandalas are visual representations used in meditation to focus the mind. With the mandala, one sees a map of the microcosmos and the doorways to other realms. Tibetan Buddhists often paint their mandalas using colored sand, much like the Southwestern American Indians.

SRI YANTRA

A yantra is another type of visual representation used in meditation to focus the mind. However, it uses geometric shapes (not circles) to symbolize the macrocosmic and microcosmic forces. One of the most famous yantras used by both Hindus and Buddhists is called Sri Yantra and is composed of nine interpenetrating triangles, which symbolize the interpenetrating male and female energies of the cosmos.

With the yantra, one also sees the energy fields in the cosmos and can use these to evoke different states of consciousness that automatically move the meditator into different realms. Although yantras are two dimensional, they are conceived of and visualized as having three dimensions.

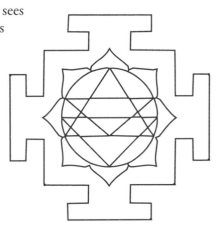

This is a Hindu and also a Buddhist yantra one can meditate upon.

Usually yantras refer to patterns that are visualized whereas mandalas refer to patterns that are created externally and gazed upon. In this chapter, these terms are used interchangably as they both refer to diagrams that are used to focus, concentrate and move consciousness to specific areas of the universe. They are visual methods for revealing where our consciousness exists. They are maps and methods for getting from "here" to "there." Both are mystical tools for practicing concentration and meditation.

Like mantras, mandalas do not always make conscious sense at first. As one spends time mentally constructing and meditating upon these diagrams, there will be a moment, a flash, in which the mind suddenly gains insight into their meaning and use.

Allow me give to you an example of how to meditate with or construct a yantra. In meditation posture, mentally draw a circle and color it yellow. Put a white dot in the center of the circle. Now put four arms on it, and then put a square around the four arms, and a triangle around all of this. You now have a special yantra called *Yantra of the Universe* that can be used for meditating.

Many people have poor visualization powers, and thus yantras or mandalas are a great help in assisting them. These visualization methods of meditation are performed by continuing to look at a diagram and then closing the eyes and visualizing it. This process is repeated over and over again until the mind can hold the mental picture of the diagram. In so doing, the mind suddenly grasps that there is a way out of this maze of embodied consciousness. It sees that there is a way out of the universe of name and form. You suddenly realize that you can be free from body-consciousness. The yantra or mantra has shown the way. The diagram has produced a new state of consciousness in which you remain conscious in your unembodied state, if you have done your other mental practices.

My guru refers to this state of being as on the outer fringes of samadhi. In this state, you are no longer stuck in your mind/body complex with all of its limitations. This "seeing" helps you to remain in a state of balanced awareness, detached from extreme states of emotionality. Also, and very important, the outer fringes of samadhi is a state of consciousness that dissolves negative karma.

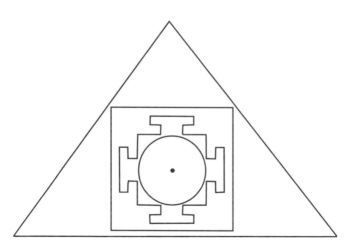

YANTRA OF THE UNIVERSE

A TIBETAN METHOD

In the Tibetan school of Buddhism, the visualization process often takes place at eye-level or a half-inch above it and at a distance of one yoke in front of you. A yoke is 18 inches away. However, some people say it is 24 inches. Whichever it is, simply use the distance that is best suited to your mind.

Imagine a pinpoint of light in front of you, about half an inch above eye level. The eyes can either be open or closed. Now visualize the point of light a yoke away, and from this point of light begin to build and visualize the yantra. Use a standard yantra or mandala or diagram thirteen.

The process begins by mentally drawing a circle around your pinpoint of light. This circle should be four inches in diameter. Mentally paint the inside of the circle with a proper color. As you mentally paint the circle, leave the center dot unpainted. Allow it to continue to radiate white light.

Select the color based on what you are trying to accomplish. If you were living in a monastery, the abbot might suggest a specific color to paint your circle. For instance, if you were very lethargic, he might suggest that you paint the circle red. If your color is red (a color you may be using to gain more energy), the first step is to paint the circle red a number of times each day until you can see the red disc with its dot of white light very clearly in your mind's eye. Red is a symbol of life's vitality. It is the energy of Mars, the god of vitality. After visualizing the circle for a number of days, weeks or months, you will suddenly find that your body/mind complex is less lethargic and much more energetic.

Various colors have different effects upon the subconscious mind. For example, if you are restless and/or insecure, you might paint the circle green. In modern terms, this ancient system of yantra is referred to as color therapy. In short, it is color therapy, internalized. However, it is more than just color therapy. It is visualization with color and symbols.

Next you move to the second rung of this three-rung process by placing another configuration on the yantra. You now place a square around the circle.

In the third rung, you add a small doorway that leads to a tunnel at the top of the square. This tunnel leads to another time/space dimension.

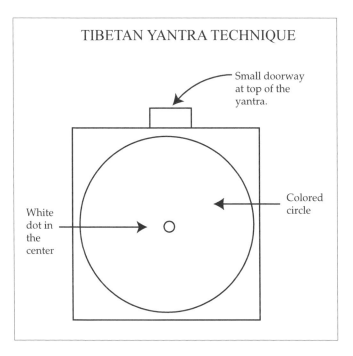

After a little practice, this extraordinary and crucial technique will enable you to see what is happening deep within your mind. This is how the yantra looks:

This visualization technique should be practiced for only a short period of time each day, ranging from 10 seconds to 3 minutes. The key point to keep in mind is that you should not strain the eyes or exhaust the brain.

Today these visualization techniques have become quite popular in certain schools of holistic healing. There are a number of very prominent doctors and psychiatrists who believe these visualization techniques can give one the ability to overcome disease.

THE GURU'S METHOD

When I was staying with my guru in the late forties, we often talked about healing. He once said to me, "There is one system that exceeds them all in terms of visualization for healing. Sit with your eyes closed and keep the spine erect. Visualize that you are standing under a waterfall. Water is a very powerful symbol of purification.

Visualize the water flowing over your head and shoulders and also washing through your body. This visualization of water will wash negativity out of your system, even negative karma." Then he added, "This may even help you become illumined sooner." He chuckled and that was the last of his discourse.

You can begin your practice for a few minutes each day. After a week, you can increase the period of practice to five minutes. After two more weeks, you can increase the period to ten minutes. After a few more weeks, you can practice the technique as long as you can remain quiet and keep the mind unstressed.

A THERAVEDA TECHNIQUE

Theravada is the original Buddhist school. It is more fundamental and more internal and requires far more self-discipline than the other Buddhist schools. It holds to the belief that almost everyone is so busy and occupied with taking care of other people that they have forgotten to put the proper focus on their own spiritual unfoldment. A person who adopts this concept is one who leads the life of an *arhat*.

This school of Buddhism has an excellent meditative technique. It begins by sitting still in yogic posture. The eyes are kept open or closed. The attention is focused on the stomach area and then on becoming more aware of the breathing pattern in the stomach area.

As the diaphragm rises and the stomach distends, think "rising." When the stomach drops and the diaphragm lowers, think "falling." With the awareness of this up and down movement of the diaphragm, one continues thinking, "rising ... falling ... rising ... falling," and simply becomes totally aware of this motion of the diaphragm. Practice this daily until your awareness of this process becomes almost automatic. Do this until you are aware of this physiological movement even in your sleep.

As you gain a deep, continuous awareness of the rising and falling of the diaphragm, you will automatically and effortlessly focus upon it. Then the mind will mentally follow the rising and falling of the breathing pattern. You will begin to realize that the only thing that has been rising and falling is thoughts in your mind. At that point, this type of meditation brings forth a deep awareness of one-pointedness. There will be a movement away from a heavy collectiveness to a single-pointedness, leading to the awareness of the unembodied consciousness.

When you first begin to use this process, the mind can focus only with great effort upon the rhythm of the semi-automatic breathing pattern. After practicing it for some time, however, the mind's action will become more effortless and relaxed.

One of the problems with this technique is that in the initial stage the mind tends to interfere with the semi-automatic breathing pattern. Thus, some people may feel a slight "suffocating" sensation as they practice it. This is a fairly common difficulty for some people who practice various breathing techniques. If you feel this difficulty, stop and rest, and then return to the practice.

Practice this technique for a few days, watching your breathing motion. Do it for two or three minutes each day. Some people may find it somewhat stressful at first, but the vast majority of people will not experience any problems. For everyone, it will be most meaningful.

The Theravedas, like some yogis, use techniques that bypass the state of ecstasy. They drive around it to reach a point of awareness that produces quietude. One of the ideals of this Buddhist school is to totally escape the mindfulness of the reality of individual consciousness and move to the Reality—Buddhahood or Bodhi-chit, the enlightened mind. These methods move toward *Nirvana* or a void of no-desire, not a void of non-existence. These techniques enable the meditator to rapidly let go of the personality complex.

The term *Nirvana* does not mean *no flame of consciousness* as many Western writers and some Buddhist scholars claim. It means *no flame of desire*. In this state of meditation, one goes beyond the ego-personality and thus the desires of that ego-personality.

From these practices arise what is called *the state of the unborn*. This enables the individual to reach his primordial state of existence, his pre-earth body form—not just his pre-human body form, but his pre-earth body form, the formless one.

A ZEN BUDDHIST TECHNIQUE

There is a third major school of Buddhism, the Buddhism of Japan, which came to Japan in the ninth century through a great Chinese sage named Bodhi-Dharma. He belonged to the Chinese mystical school called Chan. Chan is a romanized word that is pronounced *J'an* in the Chinese language. The Japanese had difficulty in pronouncing the 'J', and thus it became Zan or Zen.

One of the Zen methods of meditation is a technique called the *koan*. A koan is a mental puzzle that cannot be logically solved. The best-known of all Zen koans is, "What is the sound of the clapping of one hand?"

Three words need to be distinguished in relation to the concept of the koan:

We are all familiar with the first two—logical and illogical.

The third word is *alogical,* meaning that which is neither logical nor illogical. It has a pattern beyond the other two concepts, and it is a giant step beyond the Greek thinking of either/or, which has caused so many problems in the world. In the either/or patterning, for example, "You are either for or against it. You are either loyal to me or not." However, with this third framework, you have a choice: "You are neither for nor against it. You are neither loyal nor disloyal to me."

The student's mind, seeking to answer the unanswerable puzzle of the koan, is transitioned into a new state that is best called an *alogical* state of consciousness. Within this new state of consciousness, a satori arises that answers the question and reveals a deeper meaning within Life.

While practicing a koan technique, the student goes over and over and over the concept, turning his mind towards an answer. In a monastery, the monk in charge would press him for an answer. Thus, the student is pressured both internally and externally. This psychological pressure is the vital link in the process of solving the koan. It is all-important because within a short period of time something happens. Because the mind has no logical framework or structure with which to answer the question, and because the mind is structured to answer questions, it does answer it—but in an alogical manner. I repeat, the mind answers alogically, not illogically. The mind has broken the bonds of its limited consciousness and has reached a state of satori.

It has been very difficult for modern man to break away from Aristotelian logic, which is a binary logic: It is either true or not true. One of the great advancements of the computer age is that it has moved man's mind beyond this either/or binary logic. This is sometimes referred to as either/or/neither logic. It is not binary.

A satori is an insight into the nature of things that the logical mind simply cannot grasp. The satori is a direct experience into the problem for which one is seeking an answer. This satori reveals further insight into the cosmic nature of things and into the way of life of the earthling.

Let us say that I have a pen and a piece of paper. On this paper, with this pen, I am writing the word "candy," and I am also drawing a picture of a piece of candy. Try to take this word and/or picture and eat it. Do you get any nourishment from it? Did you get a satori? In Asia, it is said that "Painted cakes fill not the stomach."

Words are only concepts in our heads and have little or nothing to do with life. Words only have to do with some sort of mental activity and identification that has nothing to do with life either. We have been sold a bill of goods: words, words, words and more words. We live in a world of words, not within the real world. The conundrum is that I am using words in an attempt to explain this.

Can you imagine Mahatma Gandhi standing up and saying, "My beloved, when you propagate your esoteric cogitations or articulate your superficial sentimentalities and psychological observations, beware of platitudinous ponderosities?" How effective do you think this statement would be in communicating with people?

Lao Tsu, the great Chinese mystic, said many things, two of which were most important:

"Fine words are seldom ever true ... and true words are seldom ever fine."

"He who speaks, knows not, and he who knows, speaks not."

A JAPANESE SHINGON METHOD

Shingon is the Japanese mystical school of Buddhism. One of its methods is to simply become aware by becoming aware of the silence. What is silence? It *is* a sound. In a temple, the head priest assists the seeker in becoming aware of this silence by asking him to make a sound. He will say, "Pronounce the sound 'aaaaaah.' Now, in the middle of this sound, stop!" In this way, this sound is repeated over and over again, faster and faster. The repetition of this method produces a spontaneous awareness: a satori! The attainment of this satori occurs at different time spans for different people. Nonetheless, it does produce smaller satoris within days. It is a method that will produce great insights.

THE AGAMA TECHNIQUE

There are Hindu texts called the *Agamas,* which means "that which has come down" (from ancient times). The *Agamas* are traditional teachings contained in non-Vedic literature. The earliest of these texts belongs to the Shaivite sects. In northern India, they were written in Sanskrit. However, in southern India they were recorded in Tamil. The word *agama* is also used to describe the Jaina sacred texts, another non-Vedic religion of India. Unlike the *Vedas,* the *Agamas* were available to non-Brahmins and women. A number of mantra techniques are given in these texts.

One Agama technique is to chant ahh, and unlike the Shingon method, in the repetition, one moves the stop closer and closer to the beginning of the "ahh" sound.

The same text mentions another mantra sound. It is a shorter sound or "ehh." Pronounce the sound "ehh," and in the middle of this sound, stop the vocalization. Repeat the sound over and over again: "ehh ... ehh ... ehh" ... and in the middle of that sound, stop suddenly. Then begin to stop the sound earlier and earlier as you did with the "ahh" mantra. These two mantras produce a state of enlightenment, but each produces different insights into Life.

Combine these sounds and repeat over and over, trying to stop in the middle of each sound, while at the same time moving the two closer and closer together, thus producing an Ah-Eh mantric vibration.

These profound methods will have a definite positive psychological effect upon your mind. If practiced consistently over time, they will reveal deep mystical insights into the nature of thoughts, language, and thus creation. This technique may seem illogical to some students, but in truth it is alogical.

As you practice this technique and are drawn further and further into the sound, you will be drawn further and further into yourself and away from language. Thus, you will be able to break free from the ego personality. Somewhere in the middle of this practice, you will suddenly realize, "Ahhha!"—and there will be an insight. This type of meditation dissolves your conscious and unconscious expectations and limitations.

A CHRISTIAN VISUALIZATION TECHNIQUE

Christian methods of meditation are often linked to visualization. The first part of this technique is performed by thinking of a cross and then visualizing it. Next think of Christ and visualize him on the cross. Then reflect on any negative emotions that arise and balance them. One of the ways this can be done is by meditating upon opposite states of consciousness such as love, beauty and harmony. If you overcome these internal emotions, you will be able to gain greater insight into your own internal nature as well as your motives.

The second step is to visualize the victory cross on which Christ is resurrected and no longer karmically held to the cross of crucifixion. See what emotions arise in your mind and balance them out. The length of time for practicing this technique can be adjusted according to your individual needs and abilities. However, because of the emotions that this technique tends to evoke in most people, it should be practiced only for a very short period.

This technique can be considered a pre-meditation technique because it is a process by which you can purify or balance the emotions of your soul. With this process, you begin to prepare yourself for deeper states of meditation.

The third step in this method is to reflect on the cosmic meaning of the symbols—that is, Christ, the cross, and all the other symbols—as they relate to your and your life. In other words, how much are you really self-sacrificing? Is this self-sacrificing really a sacrifice or is it a negative desire for self-punishment?

As you begin to practice this Christian visualization technique, reflecting on the emotions that are evoked and working to balance them, various stages of awareness will evolve and manifest in your soul. You most likely will move through three internal stages, producing insights into your life. These three emotional stages are:

1. The Self as sinner
2. God as the good
3. The world as creation

As these emotions become more balanced, and as you evolve further with the assistance of this deeper reflection, you will become more aware of levels of consciousness that are more positive and evolved. These levels of awareness are:

1. The Self as part of Life
2. The Self as part of the good
3. The Self as one with God
4. From goodness only goodness can flow.

In the last stage of this meditation method, you will move away from the negative states of everyday living as conceived by your mind/personality. You will move away from pain, suffering and sorrow as conceived by church doctrine. Instead, you will move to the mystical experience of love, joy and attainment.

Some people criticize this method for being too negative. This may be true for some people. However, many people are stuck in a pit of pain based on early childhood teachings that foster the belief that Life is negative and that in order to be holy, one must suffer. This method can help these people to move out of their pain and into a more constructive way of thinking and thus of living. It does this in a number of ways:

First it awakens one to the realization that there are others who are suffering.

Next it awakens one to the realization that other people's pain is often greater than their own.

Most importantly, it gives one insight into one's own actions that have caused the pain.

If you do not feel that you are trapped in your pain, it is probably wise to bypass this method. However, I find that many people are not aware of the "pain-pits" in which they are living.

This meditation method can bring an awareness of several critical factors to the meditator's surface mind, the most prevalent being the idea of suffering. First, people often have the idea that God's suffering and their suffering are one and the same. Though we tend to think God suffers, it is merely that we project our suffering onto Him. I believe this to be true, for God is God, and therefore does not and cannot suffer. Second, there are people who think they *should* be suffering because they feel they are bad people. This is engendered by their belief that they were born in sin. If we follow this train of thought, we have to conclude that if God is suffering or has suffered, God too must be bad. Yet we know this is not true, for the fundamental concept of God is goodness. Third, there are those who think, "If God is good and has suffered, if I want to be good, I too must suffer."

Whatever type of thinking underlies these negative attitudes, there is an exaggerated focus on suffering. There are those who think, "Perchance I should accept my suffering as a part of Life. If Christ suffered in silence, maybe I should suffer in silence, too." Thus, they live a life of suffering in silence. However, when one reaches the final stage of this meditation, there is a realization that Life is *not* about suffering. This is just not the case! Life is about joy and happiness. The idea of suffering, which is not an Eastern concept, pervades Christian thinking. It is an attitude that is often heavily distorted by the church and misunderstood by the masses.

The next concept revolves around the question, "Why does God allow so much suffering?" At this level, there is often a subliminal link between the idea of suffering and the concepts of love, duty and service—the key concept being love. Love and suffer. In other words, people often believe that in order to love, they must suffer.

When we speak of love or giving, we come to an interesting thought. If we give of our excesses, we are not really giving. Isn't that a fantastic concept? When we give, we must do so because of compassion and unselfish love and for no other reason. I do understand that this concept can easily be misunderstood. However, if you meditate on it, you will come up with the right answer. What is the right answer? I would best answer this by telling you a true story:

Many decades ago, Mahaji came to the United States and asked for money. There was a student who had been coming to the Temple of Kriya Yoga for a number of years. He became fascinated with Mahaji's concept of love and gave him all of his wealth, which was quite extensive. Shortly afterward, Mahaji returned to India and stayed there. A few months later, the young man returned to study at the Temple. One day, shortly after his return, I heard a discussion he was having with a number of other students. They asked him, "How does it feel to have been duped out of all of your wealth?"

To this, he replied: "Mahaji taught love, and I felt attuned to it. He asked me for my wealth, and I gave it to him. I gave it freely and without any reservation. Thus, I was not duped!"

They retorted, "Do you mean you have no regrets?"

The young man hesitated for a few moments and said, "Yes. Yes, I do. I wish I had some money so that I could go to India to be with him."

I think that the lesson to be learned here is very clear: He (you and I) should not give *everything* that we have. We must keep some for ourselves, so we can feed our own body, mind, and soul. I do hope you understand this story.

I think that the person using this Christian method must use it with an understanding that suffering is separate from love. Human love is a very complex emotion. The post-meditation state of this method is to separate love into its three stages so that one can more fully understand and balance this most destructive emotion.

The first stage is *eros,* sexual love.

From this stage one moves to *philia,* friendship love.

From this stage, one hopefully moves to the last stage called *agape,* selfless love. My guru called it unselfish love.

As a person uses this technique and evolves his state of consciousness from suffering to love, he will gain an awareness of how mankind should think and act wisely. This is definitely a level of God-consciousness, called Christ-consciousness by some.

Everyone and everything is in an unconscious movement toward attaining a realization of Reality. However, it is only by the use of conscious effort that the path is made shorter, safer, and permanent. Each approach and method is the best approach for someone.

A JEWISH MYSTICISM METHOD

The next method of comparative meditation I would like to discuss is a Jewish mystical method. Jewish mysticism, more accurately called Kabala, uses the Tree of Life method with its triple pillars: the middle pillar, the pillar of justice and the pillar of suffering. With this method, one goes beyond the outer pillars and reaches the middle pillar (which I was taught is beyond justice and injustice; beyond suffering and non-suffering). The state of consciousness in the middle pillar is that of balanced being.

Like many philosophies coming out of the Middle East, this system also emphasizes suffering. For some people, the Tree of Life method is an excellent approach for reducing, resolving and eliminating the negativity within their soul. The soul is the memory bank of the spirit.

At some point, every meditation technique is simply a movement away from whatever direction the senses take us. More specifically, when we exist more in one of the outer pillars, the energy is focused more on emotionality. When we exist more in the other outer pillar, the energy is focused more on sterile logic. Some people are more to the left pillar than others, and some people are more to the right pillar than others. Very few people are in the middle pillar. As you practice this centering technique, you escape from the two extremes of emotionality and sterile logic.

Jewish mysticism heavily relates to the alphabet; for some Jewish mystics, the alphabet is paramount. The Hebrew alphabet is called the "alef-bet" because of its first two letters, alef and bet. The alphabet is the mechanism that is the missing link between the sending and the receiving of our desire, whatever that desire might be. The alphabet is the mechanism for moving a thought from the physical plane to the higher metaphysical planes and for returning that which exists in the higher metaphysical planes back to this physical plane. This is done via the sounds of the alphabet, that is, via mantra. Speech attunes us to the earth plane whereas mantra attunes us to the higher planes.

It is the alphabet and its thoughts that are circulating and linking the higher and lower planes. Within each human being there exists a censor that is a psychological mechanism. The link between the higher and the lower worlds is not working because this censor of ego and greed is saying, "I am not going to share anything with my enemies." This really means that the person feels his enemy is not worthy of receiving. This censor, this gate, stops the flow of thought between the two worlds. This breaks the link. The gifts of God cannot flow down into the physical plane and therefore we cannot receive them for ourselves. Some call this blockage ignorance. Some call it greed. Some call it selfishness. If we ourselves wish to receive, we must open this censor by giving to our enemies.

The brilliance of the middle pillar method is that it enables us to take the most precious gift we have or can conceive of and give it to one whom we detest or deplore. In giving to our enemy, we open this censor wider, allowing subconscious as well as super-conscious material and information to flow into our ordinary states of consciousness. When it is open, we ourselves can receive that which we value.

In practicing the middle pillar method, we are able to understand that energy is released from numerous levels:

The first level of energy release is the alphabet. A string of thoughts is passed along by angels (angles). It is passed along from one angel (angle) to another until it reaches its destination. The effect is returned in the same manner.

The second level of energy release is the realization that any resistance to the fulfillment of the energy's purpose is never external to us. It is always internal.

The third level of energy release is the realization that the divine force fulfilling the meditation is never separated from us. It is not separated from us by finite distance or by infinite distance.

The fourth level of energy release is the realization that distance, time and motion are not separated from us since all three of these factors are in our own physical/mental being.

The fifth level of energy release is the creation of a circuit existing between the divine and ourselves.

We must learn to open the censor gate. We need to create a circuit that will enable us to impart and to share equal to our capacity to receive. The link between the microcosm and the macrocosm is the procedure and practice of receiving and giving. In this method, it is the giving and receiving that opens the censor gate. Some mystics call this the creation of the circuit.

The first step in this middle pillar method is to want cosmic consciousness more than anything else, to want it at any price.

The second step is to prove this to yourself by giving gracefully to your worst enemy in thought or in deed.

The third step is to become completely relaxed and then to ask, "What is the most precious thing that I own?" You need to think and reflect on this to be sure that you choose your most valuable possession. Some teachers state that you should reflect on what you consider to be the most wonderful gift you, yourself, could receive.

The fourth step is to go through your mind and think of the person in your life whom you dislike the most. Visualize your worst enemy and mentally give him or her this most precious gift. You may find that your mind cannot or will not do this. This realization, along with all the thoughts that flash through your mind, should bring many realizations, if not enlightenment. If your mind will not or cannot give this precious gift, try again and again. If you stay with it, you will be able to give the gift to this hated enemy. If you are able to give the gift, the last step is to give the gift with love, kindness and the feeling that you are truly happy that he or she is receiving it. By giving your greatest treasure to your worst enemy, you build a circuit to the divine. The divine is now able to disperse divine gifts to you via the circuit that you have created by truly giving.

With this practice, we open the gate that restricts the flow of super-conscious states of consciousness into our everyday functions. After all, if we can give our most precious gift to the soul we perceive to be most unworthy, we are opening the gate in our subconscious mind that allows us to feel worthy to receive. Most people do not feel worthy and thus (according to this system), they do not receive. One of the benefits of this method is that it gives us the ability to examine the inner depths of our mind. Whether we give the gift or not, by practicing this technique, we gain great insights into our mind and into Life.

To repeat, this technique consists of taking that which is most precious to you and giving it to your worst enemy. If you cannot do this, you will not be able to receive. If you can do this, you will be able to receive. Why? Because your willingness to give your greatest gift to your worst enemy opens the door so that you can receive the gifts of Life. The blessings of Life are there. It is we who have closed the gate, and we insist on keeping it closed by not sharing. If we can learn to give that which we value the most to the person whom we dislike the most, we gain the power to open the gate. The degree to which we can give is the degree to which we can receive. This is the secret of the Kabalistic method.

Om Shanti

CHAPTER NINE
The Inner Workings of the Mind

I would like to address some frequently asked questions about meditation. The first is, "Can I change the personality of another person by chanting a mantra for them?" I do not think that a person can change anyone else's personality by chanting for that person. Moreover, the purpose of mantra is not to change another person. Its purpose is not even to change God's mind. The purpose of mantra is to transform ourselves so we are more able to help others via example or wisdom. The only thing we can breathe in is that which we already have within our being. We can pass on data and knowledge. We can momentarily help people. We can momentarily inspire people. If they take these gifts and use them, they will unfold. However, no human being can change the destiny of another. We can only be the bringers of their own karma.

The second question is, "Must we attain a meditative state in order to grow spiritually?" The answer is, "Yes, absolutely!" We cannot attain any stage of enlightenment without first attaining a meditative state of consciousness. We must not only attain a state of meditation; we must sustain that state. All books, scriptures and teachers concur on this point. It is much easier to attain a meditative state, as difficult as it might be, than to maintain such a state.

Consider the story of the young student who thought he had studied long enough at an ashram. He thought it was time to leave and get married, so he asked his guru for advice. The guru answered, "Yes, it is very easy to find a woman. It is very easy to get married. However, it is much more difficult to *stay* married, and it is impossible to stay *happily* married unless you are alert, wise and unselfish. These qualities are the result of meditation. Furthermore, you should remember that there are pathways to meditation, including reading, reflection and lecturing compassionately." If you use this example and replace the word *marriage* with any other word to which you can relate, you will have the secret of all mysticism.

As difficult as it might be, it is easy to move through life. As difficult as it may be, it is easy to create. However, it is much more difficult to sustain that which you have created, and it is almost impossible to sustain that creation harmoniously.

In truth, the only thing that is easy to do is to destroy that which another person has created because we all have within our astral body many seeds of negative karma. The concept behind meditation, and the reason we meditate, is to gain deeper insight into Life so that we have greater ability to create and sustain that creation harmoniously. In so doing, we can truly help people, rather than just interfering in their lives.

The next question is, "Can a person attain a state of meditation instantaneously?" Again, the answer is, no. (Although, psychologically, it is wise to leave this possibility open.) For everyone, it takes years of hard, self-directed effort to produce a state of meditation in which the blessings of bliss, wisdom, happiness and insight manifest. This meditative state is called samadhi. When this state of consciousness is attained, it is attained in a millisecond of time. Once attained, it will never be forgotten. That is one of the marks of a samadhi state.

It is just like finding real love, something that very few people have ever experienced. Once it is experienced, no matter how long one lives, he will never forget it. The experience of love is what makes gentlemen or gentlewomen out of barbarians, saints out of sinners and sages out of fools.

The key point here lies in our memory tract. I ask you to meditate on the question, "What is the difference between an experience and the memory of that experience?" Have you ever traveled to a large city? If you have, right at this moment think of that city. Were you thinking of that city before I mentioned it? I am sure you were not. The truth is that when you think of one of these places, you are actually there; for it, and you, exist in your memory bank.

In the same way, once you have experienced a millisecond of samadhi, that which the samadhi reveals is yours forever. Actually it was already in your consciousness (super-consciously) at that time. However, now that you have experienced it, it will remain in your consciousness consciously.

Have you ever been in a room when the lights went off? Do you remember how difficult it was to keep your eyes open in that room?

When our physical eyes are closed, we cannot see anything. When we are in darkness, we cannot see anything. However, the "single eye" remains open at all times. When we are single-eyed, we can "see" in the "dark." The dark is a symbol of non-memory or forgetfulness. The memory of an experience and the experience itself are not mutually exclusive. They might not even be different states of consciousness.

The experience of samadhi stays with us, no matter what other experiences or states we may be experiencing on the surface of our mind and sometimes at a deeper level.

MEDITATION AND STRESS

A number of psychologists did research on mantra and found that meditation produces a state in which the body becomes more relaxed and the consciousness becomes more mindful. Although meditation is not the same as relaxation, relaxation is one of the benefits of meditation. It is reported that over 80 percent of the sicknesses prompting people to see doctors are psychosomatic. This means that it is not microorganisms that cause disease in the body. The causes are induced by mental attitudes such as fear and anger, which result from stress and strain. The remaining diseases are the result of chemical poisoning, resulting in autoimmune diseases. More and more doctors are concluding that even these diseases are triggered by stress. Thus, it is clear that any method that helps us to relax is of great value.

On a mental level, the more stressed and emotional we become, the less effectively the mind functions. Relaxation and free association go together. Though we should not deny the benefits arising from relaxation, we must not confuse relaxation with meditation. They are different states.

There are four types of people. The first group includes people who are absolutely bored. Because of the intensity of their boredom, they are constantly looking for a "high." They want to be amused. They want to escape the dull reality of their lives. They mistakenly believe that the titillation of their senses is the one thing that will keep them sane.

The second group of souls, which includes religionists, goes to the opposite extreme. They deprive themselves to the point of suffering. They have a fanatic need to prove that they are holy. How do they prove this holiness? Because they tend to equate holiness with suffering, they think that the more they suffer, the holier they will become. I do not have a problem when they live this out in their own lives, but I do have a problem when they actively work to make others "holy."

Many years ago when my mother was dying in the hospital, I visited her quite frequently. During this time, there was a Christian patient in the bed next to hers. One day this woman was screaming with pain. Her pastor came to visit her that day. As he saw her lying there in terrible agony, he grabbed her hand and said, "God must really love you because he has given you so much pain." This stopped her …for a few seconds.

Many people equate holiness with pain, and thus they consciously and unconsciously work very hard to bring pain into their lives. Sadly, they can become highly successful at this.

Meditation is a way of getting rid of something. One of the key things it gets rid of is pain. In all of your "getting rid of," get rid of your garbage called suffering. Mystically, pain is not the name of the game. It truly is not. The purpose of Life, the purpose of mysticism, is to reveal to you that Life is an ecstasy, a joy and a wonderment.

Someone once said that if we do not learn through joy, we will learn through pain. The sad truth, however, is that most people do not even learn through pain. Pain makes them incapable of learning.

The third group has experienced both of these extremes and has come to the realization that Life is about the search for balance. What is balance? It is lucidity. It is sanity. It is soundness. It is staying away from extremes. It is the balance between the titillation of the senses and suffering. Above all else, it is a Life in which we hurt nothing, no one … not even ourselves.

The fourth group of seekers says, "Is not the goal of Life the attainment of perfection?" They seem to feel that suffering is unimportant and that happiness is also unimportant. To them the only thing of importance is reaching a state of perfection.

I accept that this world is a world of imperfection. If it is a world of imperfection, then all beings existing herein are imperfect. The yogis and mystics are not concerned with perfection. They are concerned with the idea of completion. The concept of completion is quite different from that of perfection. Each of us should reflect and meditate upon the concepts of completion and perfection.

What is perfection? For a square, perfection is four nice, neat, pointed corners. However, the perfection of a circle is quite different. In order for a form to be a circle, it must be without corners.

Completion, on the other hand, simply means the fulfillment of what something is. It is dangerous to think that you are (symbolically) a circle or a triangle or a square because if you do, you will judge yourself by your understanding of the symbol that you believe yourself to be. Everything you do will be done according to your understanding of the symbol that you think you are.

It is not wise to conceive that you are any one thing because it will lead you to judge your entire life by that one concept. If a man thinks he is a banker, he will begin to think like a banker to the exclusion of everything else, thus endangering his love life, his family, etc.

Do not assume who or what you are. Do not strive for perfection because perfection is only a concept conceived by limited consciousness. Simply move to the completion of your consciousness: the awareness of awareness. Move to the awareness of awareness, rather than to the awareness of thoughts and things.

Seeking perfection is not what Life is about. Life has only one purpose and one goal, and that is to know Reality. It is Reality that brings us happiness, goodness, understanding and wisdom. It brings non-violence to our mind, tongue and body. Every struggle, every battle, every thought, deed, action, yantra, mantra, tantra or kriya is performed in order to move us a step closer to that Reality. This is the goal. This is why we practice techniques. This is why we meditate.

How do we know when someone is reaching toward this Reality? Mystically speaking, there are 13 ways to recognize this person:

We can definitely recognize a person who is *not* reaching toward that Reality. This person has no joy in their soul. This person is always bitching, moaning, crying and complaining.

We know when a person is moving toward the Reality by the way that person speaks. Their speech is simple. It is not complicated. It is not devious. It is straightforward.

We know when a person is not on the path toward Reality because that person is bombastic, egotistical, full of pride, ambitious, ostentatious, pompous, pretentious and boring.

We know when a person is on the path toward Reality because that person radiates warmth; there is a genuine caring for others. Thus, this person has a clear aura.

What is Reality? There are two answers:

First, he who meditates knows Reality. And even though this Reality may be inexpressible, it can be communicated.

Second, you are the Reality (Aham-Brahmasmi). I think there is an even better way to express this concept: You are Reality. You are Life. Life is you.

THE GOAL OF MEDITATION

Some people think the goal of Life is the attainment of perfection, whereas others say that it is to know God. So what is the goal of meditation? If there is a goal or function of meditation, it is to put your body to sleep while your mind remains awake. Thus, you gain a deeper and broader awareness of what lies within ... and it is Heaven that lies within.

With a deeper and broader delving into consciousness, you can more clearly see the meaning and purpose of Life as well as of your own life. Thus, you will be better able to adjust, adapt and acclimate to the flow of both personal and collective history.

Most of the time, the body is awake while the mind is asleep. This is how difficulties and problems arise. We have not understood two basic earth practices on the spiritual path:

We should read the signs of Life.

We should follow their directions.

Most people do not or cannot read the signs of Life, or when they do read them, they do not follow their directions. What is the key sign of Life? It reads thusly: Put your mind in gear before putting your tongue or body into action.

Meditation is really a way of putting the body to sleep while at the same time awakening the deeper levels of the mind: the subconscious, the unconscious and the super-conscious. The challenge is to keep the mind awake while one moves back into the world of the body.

Awakening the mind and putting the body to sleep is a very simplistic way of saying that we have produced a state of consciousness that exists on the outer fringes of samadhi. It sounds so much grander to say that the goal of meditation is to attain samadhi. However, the former definition is much more revealing and directive.

In the modern world, we refer to this as conscious trance. This establishes a state of focused attention without tension. It leads toward a conscious, lucid dream state and encourages a turning inward of our consciousness. This turning inward leads toward an automatic state of introspection. This automatic introspection with a conscious rebalancing of states of consciousness *is* the path. All else is preparation for *beginning* to walk the path.

In the earlier stages of walking the path, a key question arises in most seekers' minds: "What is real?" In order to answer to this question, we must first overcome the social conditioning that tells us that that which is real is external to us. This is just not the case.

The next stage of this search is to realize that Reality is an attitude. Attitude is not an intellectual concept. It is a state of consciousness. Thus, in some sense, what we are doing is attempting to produce a state of consciousness that allows us to become attitudinally aware of Life. There must be a realization that it is not what comes to us that is significant. It is not the karma that comes into our lives that is most important. It is, rather, our attitude and thus our reactions that are critical.

An example might be helpful to clarify this point. A woman named Jonnie once dove into a swimming pool that had no water in it. She was totally paralyzed from this accident. She lost the use of her hands and legs and has been in a wheelchair ever since. This is certainly a piece of adverse karma. Most people would have become more and more depressed with each passing day. But what did Jonnie do? She became a very famous artist by putting a pen and brush in her mouth and drawing. She is leading a very good life and is happy to have many talented friends.

The events that manifest in our life sometimes make us and sometimes break us. However, it is not the events that make or break us. It is only one thing: our attitude. It is not the events that come to us that are significant. Rather, it is our attitude toward these events that is all-important.

The attitude that all life is sacred is the pathway to the feeling state of consciousness. There exists in each person a primordial state of consciousness that is called feeling. It is from this feeling that various feelings—not emotions—arise. This primordial feeling produces a state of consciousness that produces thoughts. These thoughts produce words. These words produce actions. These actions produce reactions. And this is the cycle of one's karmic life.

Dr. Kreyche, a psychiatrist, once said to me, "I wonder if it is true that everything is logical even though it may not seem to be. Perhaps by "logical" we mean our ability to understand something. If we look at dreams and understand their language and symbols, they really are logical, especially in the light of astrological symbolism. Dreams do make sense even though they can appear illogical or irrational to us at the time. And we actually can trace our emotions and feelings back to a point where they do make sense at some level. There is some sequence we can use to understand which chakra, which unconscious factors, are contributing to those seemingly erratic emotions and imbalanced feelings."

Historically, the term "logical" means being consistent. You could say that many people are very logical in the consistency of their illogical behavior.

The entire system of Euclidean geometry is based on the concept that two parallel lines never intersect. We have built buildings, cities and many other structures using this system. However, after using this Euclidean geometry for hundreds of years, a new system of geometry was developed. This new system, non-Euclidean geometry, is based on the concept that two parallel lines *do* intersect in infinity. It is with this system that we have traveled to Jupiter, built the atomic bomb and accomplished things of this nature.

Where is the logic in the fact that two parallel lines intersect in one system yet do not intersect in another? Is it contradictory? Perchance. Is it alogical? (Remember that *alogical* does not mean *illogical).* The answer is yes. It is alogical because both systems have been proven to be true. We have Chicago and New York, which are nicely laid out in grid lines (Euclidean geometry). Yet we also have atomic bombs, and we have traveled to the moon, Mars and Jupiter (non-Euclidean geometry).

Expanding this idea a little further, the ancient Greeks agreed with Aristotle's logic, which was built on an either/or system. For roughly 2,500 years, Western thought has used this system. Philosophers, mathematicians and scientists have always liked it. Why? Because it supports the concept that if you're wrong, I'm right or I'm right; therefore you're wrong.

The blessing of modern technology, with all of its problems, has revealed the Light of the ancient mystics who have always said that Life is a threefold system. The ancient mystics and the modern computer technologists agree that it is an either/or/neither system.

With the development of modern-day computers, technologists have realized that Aristotle's "either/or" logic can no longer be used in advanced thinking. It is too immature; the advancement of machinery and technology have necessitated that man advance his thinking. Today, computer science is based on this threefold system of either/or/neither. With this, Aristotle's system has died. It is dead, although it has not yet been buried. It is just a matter of time before this new system moves more deeply into modern culture. The more computers take over a culture, the more that culture's thinking will change and improve.

I agree with Dr. Kreyche's concept. Once we know Reality, everything is logical. At least it is logical to those who have realized and experienced that Reality. In discussing the concept of Reality, we might ask whether or not meditation can be used to bring about past-life remembrances.

There is a gathering of gray matter at each chakric level. In yoga we call these gatherings of gray matter *small brains*. Some people refer to them as pre-cranial brains. One of the functions of these brains, together with the cranial brain, is memory storage. The moon chakra stores memories from our most recent past lifetime. For most of us, these emotional force-fields are all that is left from that past life and most of it is unconscious.

Memories from other past lives are stored in the lower chakras. Below the moon center, memories from two lifetimes ago are stored at the Mercury center. At the Venus chakra you will find the memories from three lifetimes back. The Mars chakra, at the solar plexus, stores data from four lifetimes ago.

There is always a strain between the forces of our present lifetime and those from four lifetimes ago. In mystical language, if you wish to see and/or understand this conflict, check the relationship between the ruler of your Ascendant and the planet Mars. If this configuration are harmonious, there will be no conflict between this life and your fourth pastlife. Thus, you will have the capacity to move ahead in the evolution of your earth life.

Moving further down the spine, Jupiter is the next chakra. It contains memories of the fifth pastlife. Lastly, the Saturn chakra contains memories of the sixth pastlife. Beyond these lifetimes, all other memories seem to move from subconscious memories to deeper level unconscious memories. These are much more difficult to reach consciously.

We have a total of six sub-brains, each containing data from a past lifetime. We are talking about the five lower chakras and the moon chakra. These symbolize the karmic patterns of the past six lives. These six astral chakras can be used to reveal your subconscious memory patterns, which are the basic samskaras of your subconscious personality patterns. The seventh chakra, the sun chakra, is the totality of the samskaras of the past six lifetimes. The sun chakra is symbolic of the karma of this lifetime and contains the greatest amount of free will.

Each brain is fighting to have its memories live again. The ghosts and specters of the past want to live again. Subconsciously and sometimes unconsciously, they drive us into areas of experience that make no sense at all to us consciously. However, they do make sense when we realize that the smaller brains are working to relive their past. Thus, be aware. Beware!

Meditation is one way to balance out the negative forces from the past that are lying in these hindbrains. When all of these force-fields are working and functioning together harmoniously, we become balanced in mind and soul. Once balanced, the cerebral brain can function beyond its former limits. The energy of the main brain can move up to and enter into the thousand-petalled lotus, producing cosmic consciousness.

According to yoga, we can do anything that we can conceive except conceive that which we cannot conceive. This is an extremely important concept, so allow me to repeat it: We can do anything we can conceive we can do, except conceive of that which we cannot conceive; we can will anything, except that which we cannot conceive of willing.

What does this mean? It means that if you watch a bird fly, only if you can grasp the concept of flying and can conceive that you too can fly will you be able to fly. If you are unable to grasp the concept of flying and that you too can fly, you will be unable to fly. You may not be able to fly like a bird, but you will be able to fly in some way—whether by balloon, by plane or by levitation. In other words, as long as you limit your thinking to the thought: "I am a body; I am not a bird," you will lose the key concept of flying and thus be unable to create the concept of a balloon or an airplane.

Like most of mankind's problems, the key problem stems from forgetfulness. We forget that we are a part of nature, not apart from nature. Thus, we find it difficult to conceive what lies beyond our own subjective lives. The mystics are continually saying that until we can conceive that there is something beyond this earth life, we are doomed to its confinement and its constrictions.

The word *Brahman* is an all-important word in Eastern thought. It means the Reality. It is this Reality that is standing just beyond our everyday limited consciousness. What is Reality? It is unconditioned, unbounded, unfettered, unborn, undying, unmolded Life.

As long as we can sustain a concept of reality, no matter what we conceive, there will always be something just beyond that concept. As long as we can hold that concept, we will always be able to move one step further into the exploration of Life. We will be able to get from here to there, no matter where "here" or "there" is.

If we do not expand into greater awareness by means of this concept of the Reality, we will tend to take on the outdated attitude that science knows everything about everything. We will sit back and accept that there is nothing left to do, nothing left to explore, nothing left to discover, nothing left to know. However, science has not yet even tapped the head of the pin stuck into the map of Life. Scientists will soon find that gravity is more than the primal force of the physical universe. They will discover that the universe is not slowing down; it is speeding up. They will discover that we are not at the center of our galaxy cluster and that the big bang theory is incorrect. But let us bless the scientists because they are continually seeking to find and understand. This is more than we can say for most religious and/or spiritual seekers.

Om Shanti.

CHAPTER TEN
The Eight Steps to Samadhi

When students ask me which meditation technique I recommend for attaining samadhi, I point out that samadhi is not a single-step process. It is an eight-step process, and the best method depends on the personality of the student. Here is a summary of this multi-step process of meditation.

Step 1: The first step is to attain a sense of peacefulness. This is best accomplished by meditating on beauty. Why beauty? Because meditating on beauty creates a feeling state that moves the mind away from superficial emotions and desires. It creates the awareness that Life is beautiful. It helps one realize, "I can be peaceful."

One of the best methods to move through this first step is to use the object of beauty meditation technique or a similar method. (This method is discussed in both *Beginner's Guide to Meditation* and *Intermediate Guide to Meditation*. For the sake of continuity, I will offer a short explanation of it here.)

When practicing the object of beauty meditation technique, sit in any comfortable position. Ask yourself, "What is the most beautiful thing I can think of at this moment?" Just answer the question for yourself. You may decide that it is a woman with a moon-shaped face. You may think of a man with a hairy chest. Do not be judgmental with yourself or with the object that you choose. Just visualize the most beautiful object you can conceive of at this point in your life. You may think of a red rose, the Grand Canyon, or a rainbow. However, let me give you three vital suggestions regarding your choice:

1. Try to stay from abstract concepts of beauty. That is why I said a beautiful thing and not a beautiful thought or concept. In other words, stay away from concepts such as "God" or "goodness."

2. Stay away from overly expansive concepts such as "Life." Find the beauty of a single, physical object. Keep it simple. Make it fun.

3. Distinguish between beauty and emotion. Beauty induces a feeling state whereas emotion induces an emotional state. For example, if a man thinks of a woman's body while practicing this technique, he may begin to move from beauty to emotion. The object should be beautiful but should not produce emotionality, sexual or otherwise.

With your eyes closed, mentally hold this object of beauty in front of the single eye at the ajna chakra. Using your visualization powers, concentrate on it. The key to this or any other meditation technique is that each and every time your mind wanders away from the object of beauty, you must gently bring it back to that object. It must be brought back without any emotionality whatsoever. If anything other than gentle pressure is used, you will interrupt the development of the meditation state. If your mind wanders away from the object 57 times, you must gently bring it back to that object 57 times without any vexation or irritation. If you get upset or impatient, you will lose your state of meditation.

I repeat, the secret of this meditation method is to continually bring the mind back to the object of meditation without any emotionality whatsoever. Eventually the mind will catch on and realize that it is far easier to fix upon the object than to continue wandering. When the mind settles down, you can begin your meditation. Remember that if you get upset, the emotional energy produced will feed the mind and the mind will wander forever.

Next shift your awareness from the object back into your consciousness so that you can become more aware of the feeling of beauty produced by the object and less aware of the object itself. This shift in your awareness from the object to the feeling produced by the object is the key step in this meditation. You now become more aware of the feeling produced by the beautiful object than of the object itself. Ultimately, and relatively rapidly, the object itself will fade into the background of your mind and you will experience a pure feeling.

Please do not overlook the fact that it does not matter what the object is. You will hold in your consciousness the same singular feeling state whether the object is a rose, a tree or a mountain. One person might start with a ten-karat diamond ring, another with a 50-kilogram gold ingot, and another with an animal. After the object fades into the background of the mind, all three of these people will have the exact same awareness: a pure feeling state. There is a great secret here.

Step 2: The second step is stillness of the body. Most yogis would say that if your mind is not somewhat peaceful, body stillness is impossible. Linked and vital to body stillness is relaxation of the body. The body must be at full attention without tension.

Step 3: The third step is to attain a state of quietness of the body. This is quite different from stillness of the body in Step Two. To attain this quietness, a breathing technique can be used. This third step is best accomplished by simple, deep, rhythmic breathing followed by the alternate breathing technique. (For a description of this and other breathing techniques, see my text, *The Spiritual Science of Kriya Yoga*.)

Step 4: The fourth step is to attain a state of quietness of the mind. This is best attained by the practice of the hong-sau technique, in which cosmic sounds are used in connection with unforced, automatic breathing.

Step 5: The fifth step is to attain a state of concentration. One of the best methods is through visualization. The ajna chakra, at the root of the nose between the eyebrows, is an actual astral golden disk. The golden disk has a dark blue dot in its center. You simply close your eyes and effortlessly visualize this golden disk. In the center of this golden disk, visualize the dark blue dot, which is so dark it appears black at first. In the center of this dot, visualize a pinpoint of white light. This three-fold visualization should be practiced until you can see this yantra quite clearly:
- The golden disk
- The dot
- The pinpoint of white light

Step 6: The sixth step is to attain a state of meditation. This is accomplished by creating a feeling state. This is a feeling of total contentment. To create this feeling state, visualize the pinpoint of white light unfolding into a five-pointed star. As this star opens up, feel contentment being transmitted to you. Bathe within this contentment. Sup upon this contentment. Breathe in this contentment. Allow this feeling of contentment to expand throughout your entire body, mind and being. Allow this contentment to flow

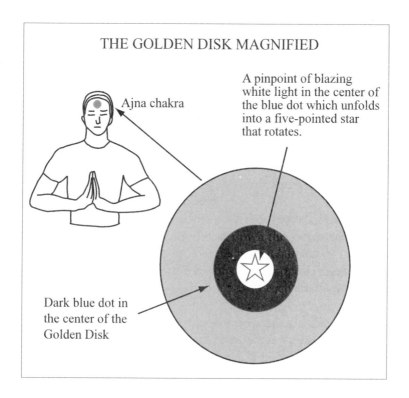

THE GOLDEN DISK MAGNIFIED

Ajna chakra

A pinpoint of blazing white light in the center of the blue dot which unfolds into a five-pointed star that rotates.

Dark blue dot in the center of the Golden Disk

into each cell of your body and every petal of your mind. Become content. Become filled with contentment. Become contentment itself.

Step 7: The final step for achieving a perfect state of meditation, and thus being able to enter into the very center of the outer fringes of samadhi, is to bring the quietude, the concentration and the meditative feeling states together. These states merge into a special state called *samyama,* in which you are no longer sitting on the outer fringes of samadhi. You are in samadhi; you are samadhi! You have stepped from the outer fringes into the inner circle.

At this point, you are moving toward something rather than running away from something. In this state of perfected peacefulness-stillness-quietude-bliss, there is nothing else you need or want. If you were trying to attain or obtain something, at this stage your mind lets go of it. This perfected contentment is not unconsciousness. It is not a point of weakness. It is a full realization that you can have whatever you wish. In this state of perfected contentment, there is nothing you want, there is nothing you need.

If we stop here, this perfected contentment will turn into what many mystics would call a wonderful prison. They refer to it as being wonderful because it is perfect contentment. Yet they also refer to it as a prison because one is unable to break out of this wonderful prison or perfect contentment to seek or attain that which lies beyond.

Step 8: So there must be an eighth step, which functions through compassion, through unselfish love. We realize that, although we are totally content, the vast majority of souls in the various universes are experiencing pain, anguish, suffering and lack. This awareness will cause us to take action on their behalf.

This eighth stage is called kriya or action. We now have work to do on the inner planes. This work on the inner planes produces an abundance of good karma, enabling us to pass through the open gate. It *is* open. It has always been open. It is only selfishness that kept us from passing through the gate before.

A kriya is performed when we take the inner light of perfected contentment and refocus that light upon the needs of other beings in the inner as well as the outer universes. We have spent years, even decades, turning inward and mastering our inner universe. Now it is time to refocus our awareness and break out of our perfected contentment. We must move our consciousness into the external worlds in order to serve others.

Help is always given first on the inner planes. Then help is given on the external planes. For example, if you try to help a person break a bad habit by hiding a substance or taking it away from him, you will probably not do a very good job. However, if you can get into the inner planes and remove this person's square to Neptune, for example, it might be possible to help him on the external planes to overcome his destructive habit. In other words, the true value of help on the inner plane is to soften other people's karma so that they can give themselves, or someone else can give them the external help they need to accomplish that which needs to be accomplished.

Yet keep in mind that we should not interfere in the lives of others.

Beloved seeker, truly help and assist other beings via the inner planes. Yet do not forget to help them on the outer planes.

According to tradition, there is a kriya ritual that, if done from the depths of one's soul in the inner planes, will soften another person's negative karma, open up their good karma, and transfer merit to them. Then we can truly help that person in this lifetime as well as in future lifetimes.

It is often easier to help others on the inner planes, because they have more good karma on the inner planes than on the outer plane. It is much more difficult to help them on the outer plane, because they do not have as much good karma there. They are merely having problems with their ability to manifest their inner good karma onto the outer plane. The way we really help people is not by changing their karma but by helping them to precipitate or crystallize the karma that already exists within them on the outer plane. Techniques to accomplish this will be described in my forthcoming text, *Spiritual Work on the Inner Planes.*

Om Shanti

CHAPTER ELEVEN
Balancing Your Mind Forces

It is not so much our karma that creates our problems but rather our attitudes about the events that come into our lives. Yes, karma is very important. However, when a karmic event begins to manifest, it is relatively weak and controllable. With insight, we can confine it to this stage. It is usually our inability, our incompetence, our ineptitude, our lack of skill and our unwillingness to do this that cause our problems. We fail to deal with these karmic events at the very beginning. It is only when they have grown totally out of control that we begin to pay attention to them. By then, it is too late, and the karma must run its course. In other words, what creates the real problem is our recalcitrant and reluctant disposition to contain one piece of karma at the very beginning, just at it begins to manifest. Because we fail to do this, before we know it the karma is manifesting forcefully. One piece of karma then mutates into three virtually different pieces of karma.

Many people can remain in the tropics without contracting any tropical diseases whereas other people travel there for just a week and immediately become sick. Psychologists and psychiatrists are beginning to understand that certain personality types are more mentally resistant to disease than others. They are not denying that germs cause sickness; they have not come that far yet. They are simply saying that it is our attitude toward events that is the key factor in our resistance or lack of resistance to disease.

In short, an unhealthy attitude toward events constitutes a negative attitude. Meditation is a method for attaining a positive, constructive attitude. A spiritual education is another way to develop a positive attitude. What is this attitude I am speaking about? Is it a sense of fearlessness? Definitely. Is it a sense of security? Absolutely. Is it a sense of personal competence? Yes.

It has been shown time and time again that if fear is induced in a human being, no matter what the cause, he or she will become more susceptible to various types of respiratory problems and other diseases. Just look at the many things that cause us to experience fear.

You may think that fear is too strong a word. It is a strong word. So let me convey to you some of the other stages of fear that are not as strong but which have the same effect on the body over a longer period of time. These stages can be symbolized by the following words: anxiety, apprehension, distress, consternation, dismay, trial, agony, concern, pain, sadness, trouble, suffering, apprehension, doubt, irritation, restlessness and uneasiness. Other word symbols for this milder state of fear consciousness include: disturbing, upsetting, brooding, fretting, fussing, stewing, bothersome, bugging, hassled, annoyance, antagonize, argue, inconvenient, irksome, perturbed or just plain old worrying.

Meditation is the art and science of removing all these negative states of consciousness. In yoga, they are classified under one group heading: negative attitudes. Meditation is the method of transcending these negative states of consciousness. It is the art and science of attaining and sustaining a positive life attitude. Therefore, meditate, meditate, meditate.

One of the important goals of living the life of an active meditator is to understand that the word *karma* expresses a series of unconscious, subconscious and semiconscious patterns. These patterns are known by the Western term *mental proclivities*. As most of us walk through everyday life, situations and opportunities often arise quite suddenly. When this happens, we usually have only a few short moments to make a decision regarding the situation, event or opportunity—just a few short moments to decide what to do and how to do it. However, this decision is rarely ever conscious. It is almost always unconscious and automatic. If we make a wise decision, our life often becomes more harmonious. However, if we make an unwise decision, our life may become more difficult.

Meditation is the method for overcoming negative subconscious proclivities. Thus, it is the key for overcoming confining karma. This reminds me of a story told to me by my guru about Yoganandaji. Yoganandaji used to tell his close disciples that when he was descending from the astral planes into the earth plane to be reborn, he had a difficult time deciding whether to become an American or an East Indian. His students did not take him seriously because they thought he was joking. However, one day my guru asked him, "Yoganandaji, why did you decide to become an Indian and not an American?"

"Oh," he answered, "I looked down there and saw that in America they have these things called taverns."

Shelliji answered, "Yes, people do drink a lot."

"Oh! No, no. My decision had nothing to do with drinking," Yoganandaji retorted. Then he continued to explain: "It was because of the cowboys. You see, a cowboy would walk into a saloon and say something like, 'Bartender, give me a drink!' Then a stranger would walk into the saloon, and the cowboy would say to the bartender, 'And give that fellow a drink on me!' However, the stranger, for whatever reason would say, 'I don't drink with strangers.' Then the first cowboy would slam his drink down and say, 'Smile, when you say that, stranger!' One thing would lead to another, and before you know it, they were both ready to 'slap leather' over a stupid attitude. Now, the first cowboy could pull his gun and kill the other one. Or the other cowboy could kill him. In either case, neither person would win."

Why did this happen? It happened because of an attitude of the mind. In that one instant, the personalities were challenged. Once these two cowboys faced each other, their pride would not allow them to back off. If either one of them backed off, that cowboy would have been considered a coward. Because the self-awareness of these two cowboys was quite weak, each of them would have thought it better to kill someone or be killed than to be called a coward. I am sure you understand how ignorant it is to shoot or be shot at over an insignificant attitude.

People continue to be violent over the most trivial things. Just the other day, two cars were at a stoplight, one behind the other. The driver in the second car wanted the first driver to hurry through an amber light, so he started honking his horn. The driver of the first car jumped out of his car and yelled, "What the blankety-blank is the matter with you?! Can't you see there's a red light?" With this, the second driver shot him.

Was this man violent to the first driver? Yes, indeed! However, he was far more violent to himself. When our personalities are offended, we do violent things. Yes, we do violence to other people, but we do far greater violence to ourselves.

Advanced meditation is one of the key mystical ways to neutralize these negative mental proclivities. It is important to attain and retain a balanced state of consciousness, because it brings about a very positive and strong feeling state of self-dependency. When we meditate, the world, its people, and its events do not threaten us. If we are not threatened by the world, we will not manifest stress or respond with violence.

THE HONG-SAU KRIYA TECHNIQUE

The Kriya Yoga technique uses two types of mantric patterns. The first is the dual mantric sound *hong-sau,* which sounds like "hong-saw." (The second is the 12-lettered mantra, which I discussed earlier.) Most Sanskrit texts do not use the term *hong-sau;* they use the term *hamsa,* which means "wild gander." These are two different mantras. *Hamsa* is an exoteric mantra whereas *hong-sau* is an esoteric mantra. Only the esoteric texts talk about *hong-sau.*

Both mantras refer to the wild ganders that always remember that there is a season to migrate home. This migration is a return to the spiritual stream of self-awareness. (The word *param-hansa* means "the great gander" and refers to the soul who has migrated a great distance and is on the final lap of completing his earth incarnations. The word *param-hansa* is often spelled *parama-hamsa.*)

In India and in many parts of Asia, there are wild geese that migrate from eight to ten thousand miles. The esoteric symbolism of the hong-sau mantra is that if you chant it long enough, fixing the symbol in your consciousness, you will symbolically become a spiritual hamsa. You will know that your soul must migrate back to your spiritual home. You will remember that you are on a journey—not on a mission. You will not only realize the need to migrate, but you will migrate home. Your soul will instinctively fly back to your spiritual home at the right season.

This mantra, like all dual mantras, is linked to the breath. It is chanted mentally. In Kriya Yoga, the *hong* is mentally chanted with the inhalation, and the *sau* is mentally chanted with the exhalation. In the exoteric mantra *hamsa,* the mantric sounds are reversed: *ham* is produced on the exhalation.

Preparation for Hong-Sau. Preparation is required before practicing the hong-sau method. While sitting in a meditative posture, take a deep breath. Relax. Take another deep breath and relax even more. Be at full attention but without tension. Your spine should be straight, the stomach muscles in, shoulders back. This technique begins by turning your head to the left and exhaling through the open mouth with a double exhalation, "ha-haaa."

You then bring your head forward, and with your eyes closed and focused at the ajna chakra, just watch the breath. Do not try to breathe. Do not try not to breathe. Allow the breath to breathe its own pattern. Simply observe the breath flowing in and out.

I repeat, do not try to breathe in; do not try to breathe out. Simply observe the breath as it flows in and out of its own volition. Do not try to affect the breathing. Just watch the breath as it breathes itself. Let the breath flow as it wishes. Let the breath breathe you. Become more and more aware of your breathing pattern, but do not attempt to influence it in any way.

The preparation for the hong-sau technique is directed at softening the impulse of the mind to control and interfere with everything. If this method is practiced long enough, the mind will let go of its impulse to control everything and everyone. Thus, it is a great technique. The success of this preparation depends on one's ability to break the mind's insistence on controlling everything. With the mastery of this method, one attains detachment ... and detachment is the "royal road" to freedom and ultimately to enlightenment.

After a little practice, shift your attention from your breathing to your mind. At this stage, you will bring into play the silent dual mantra, *hong-sau*. With each breath that flows in, and as long as the breath flows in, mentally chant *honggg*. With each breath that flows out, and as long as the breath flows out, mentally chant *sauuu*. Do not mentally chant when the breath is naturally suspended. (Do not make an effort to suspend the breath.) During the hold, do not chant or visualize. There is no imagery. There is no thinking. While the breath is suspended, just feel the bliss of being—total contentment.

In other words, if you inhale for three seconds, you would mentally chant one long *hong* mantric sound for three seconds. If you inhale for five seconds, you would mentally chant one long *hong* mantric sound for five seconds. If you exhale for ten seconds, you would mentally chant one long continuous *sau* mantric sound for ten seconds. The length of the breath should be equal to the length of a single mantric sound. The length of one mantra is linked to the length of the breathing pattern. However, the length of the inhalation and exhalation are rarely of the same duration in the beginning. Remember: Simply let the breath breathe you. Just observe your breathing. Link the proper mantric sound to the inhalation and the exhalation.

If any confusion or problems arise while practicing this method, you might find it helpful to begin the technique again. Turn your head to the left and exhale through the open mouth making the "ha-haaa" sound. Then close the mouth, return your head to its normal position, and begin again.

When you first begin to practice, the hong-sau mantra is mentally chanted five minutes in the morning before doing anything else, and again for five minutes as the last thing in the evening. If you do not have five minutes, chant it for whatever amount of time you have. In time, you will be able to extend the mantra meditation time without putting any psychic or mental pressure on yourself. The key concept is that you should not rush or worry about the time factor. If you can extend the time up to 30 minutes without any stress or strain, this will produce wonderful results.

This mantra affects the ida and pingala channels, and thus, in time, it will produce a state of samadhi. As you know by now, the ida is the lunar force, and the pingala is the solar force. As you breathe hong-sau for a period of time, the breath of its own nature will become shallower and shallower. Then, a little later, the breath will suspend itself for a few seconds, and your consciousness will enter into the outer fringes of samadhi. Your physical mechanism will literally suspend itself. However, you will not feel a sense of suffocation because your consciousness and your body will be sustained by the hong-sau technique.

I personally experienced this state of consciousness many years ago in my meditation. I had my clock in front of me. When I looked at it, it was three minutes to eight. I began to meditate. Suddenly I realized that my breath had been suspended right from the beginning. I did not feel any stress, and I did not think anything of it because it seemed like the time lapse was probably about four or five seconds. I did not feel any pressure to breathe. When I looked at the clock it was four minutes after the hour. The breath had been suspended for many minutes. At that moment I realized that we breathe not by air alone but by mantric sounds as well.

Some people will say that you should chant *hong* on the out-breath and *sau* on the in-breath. Others will say that you should chant *hong* on the in-breath and *sau* on the out-breath. Neither one is correct or incorrect. The in-breath is linked to the ida currents of the astral body. The out-breath is linked to the pingala currents of the astral body. The ida currents nourish and nurture the mind whereas the pingala currents nourish and nurture the physical body. How you use this mantra depends upon what you are trying to nourish. In Kriya Yoga, we start by nourishing the mind. We then use this as a springboard to reach higher states of consciousness.

One of the key purposes for breathing is to absorb the life force, prana. You can live quite some time without oxygen, but you cannot live without prana. If prana leaves the physical body, even for a very short period, the soul cannot remain in that body. One cannot live without the flow of the ida and pingala currents. I am referring not only to living in the physical body but also to living in the astral body. If the ida and pingala currents were to cease in the astral, there would be no astral body. It is a general principle that the ida and pingala, the waxing and waning, and all of these dualities are necessary to life. The key is in how one interprets my use of the word "live."

Not everyone can feel these currents rotating around their spine. However, with a little meditation, one will be able to do so. It just takes turning inward and attuning.

Two or three other levels of meditation lead to samadhi. I have already discussed one. We meditate to bring our soul together, to feel secure, to attain balance and to sustain that balance. We meditate to bring an expansion of a new horizon of awareness. In so doing, we no longer respond negatively to Life, internally or externally. We no longer respond to emotionality.

LOST OBJECT MEDITATION

There is another level of meditation—one that does not directly lead to samadhi. This level refers to the use of meditation to find a lost object. Because meditation reveals insights into the Self and into Life, we can use meditation as a technique to become aware of things. For example, if you lose an object and cannot find it, you can do the following:

First, center your energy by mentally drawing the energy from your legs into the trunk of your body. Next draw the energy from your hands and arms and bring it into the trunk of your body. Then take this energy in the trunk of your body and bring it to the center of your spine.

Now draw in the breath with a slow sipping movement, that is, sip in the breath as if you were sipping through a straw. As you do this sipping breath, let the energy of your mind project out to meet the lost object, which is somewhere in external space. You do not have to know the location of the object; you do not have to think of it being in the bedroom or garage or anywhere else. As you sip in, feel that the object is being drawn back from all directions into your being.

As you inhale, feel the energies being pulled back into your body and down the spine. Visualize that you are bringing the lost object back into your consciousness with awareness of the location of the object. This is called awakening the mystical memory or jogging the subconscious memory. When you come out of your meditative state, you will know where you can locate the object. You are using the feeling state of your meditation to attune to the object. This is a very good method for finding physical objects.

The second level of this technique is used to find lost knowledge. This technique can be used for answering questions like:

• What was the lesson I learned in my past lifetime?

• What was the secret formula my guru taught me fifty years ago?

• What is the confining piece of karma that a certain student of mine has?

The more you use this technique, the more effective it will become. It is very effective for bringing into awareness things and thoughts you have lost or forgotten. It is like Plato's statement, "All learning is but a remembering." I use this method to remember dream content that has been lost.

SAMYAMA, THE CLEAR GEM TECHNIQUE

There is a final level of meditation, which includes a very powerful technique called *samyama* or the clear gem technique. It begins by bringing your mind into a meditative state. Your mind should be balanced and free from worry and anxiety as you begin this technique. Remove all emotions and preconceived ideas. There should be only a cloudless mind, a mind that has become a clear gem. You now hold this clear feeling state, knowing that you can place this clear, colorless mind state on whatever object you choose.

Here is an example of how this clear gem technique works: If you place the clear gem on a red object, the clear gem becomes red. More important, when you remove it, there is no red stain left on the clear gem; it is no longer red. It is still pure and colorless. In the same way, if you now take this clear gem and put it on a blue object, it becomes blue. However, as soon as you take it off of that object, the clear gem again becomes colorless.

In the same manner, if you place the clear gem on an emotion like jealousy, it will reflect jealousy. When the clear gem is lifted off this emotion, it will become clear again. It will remain unstained. It is still the colorless, adamantine diamond.

Someone may ask why anyone would want to place the gem on a negative emotion. The answer is to be able to more fully understand the deeper ramifications of negative states of consciousness, in order to see the causational forces behind them.

In short, wherever or whenever you put this priceless clear gem in contact with an object, it will take on the color, the odor, the emotions, etc., of that object. Yet the object that it touches never stains it. The clear gem is not contaminated by the object when it is lifted off the object.

If you have a problem and you want to use this technique to solve it, just clear your mind. Center your mind. Now literally take the clear gem out of your head and mentally put it on your problem (or someone else's problem). You now see the problem, but at the same time you see the solution to the problem. You see the solution because your mind is in a clear, unclouded state of consciousness. Insight manifests, revealing the solution.

When you pick up the clear gem and put it back in your head, there is no contamination, only a remembrance of the solution to the problem. The words "no contamination" are important because they tell us that the clear gem can be used over and over again without end. There is no accumulation, no exhaustion and no fatigue factor in or with that clear gem.

There is a need to be careful when practicing this technique. You must become detached. You must remain detached. Remember the goal: detachment, detachment, detachment. Without attaining and sustaining detachment, you will not be able to use the clear gem technique. Until you can momentarily hold a state of non-emotionality, samyama will not be attainable. It is important to practice detachment daily *before* major problems develop. Then they can be solved when they do arise. This is the key reason that yogis and mystics place so much importance on living with detachment.

As you place your clear gem on a problem, you will see (feel) what the appropriate action should be. Sometimes the answer may be to take no action at all. However, negative action should never be taken. You must only take positive action. In seeing what is to be done, the next step is to accept the condition, realizing that you are not the first (and unfortunately, not the last) to experience this affliction.

In practicing this technique be sure that you do not pressure yourself to find an answer. Realize that your spiritual Self is not interested in whether the answer is yes or no. It just wants to know the correct action. So let go. The wisest way to perform this technique is to generate effortless effort. Effortless effort means putting your mind in an absolutely quiet place.

The key is to watch your feelings as you see (or think you see) what the correct action should be. Allow time for these feelings to come back into your consciousness with the correct and appropriate action. Then and only then, take action.

Om Shanti

CHAPTER TWELVE
The Holy Object Meditation

There is a series of psychological stages that one goes through in reaching the advanced meditation state. I will use the holy object meditation technique to point out these stages.

First, a meditative posture is established. You place your body in a comfortable posture so that you can be at full attention without tension. In this way, you can totally forget your body and leave your body awareness behind as you ascend to higher states of consciousness. After you are in the meditative posture, always take a few deep breaths to help relax your body and mind.

Now visualize a holy object that invokes a deep feeling within you. It can be the face of God, the face of your guru, the face of glory, etc. (You can even try visualizing your holy object as three-dimensional, although this is not necessary.) With this visualization process, you activate your key sense, vision, and that part of the mind related to seeing. These are also linked to the pineal gland, which is the all-seeing eye of Lord Shiva. This visualization stage of the meditative process will help intensify your concentration.

When you can clearly see your holy object, you should move to the next step, which is to bring this object closer to you via visualization. One of the ways you can do this is to mentally walk toward your holy object. In any event, bring it closer and closer until you begin to merge with it. Merge into it literally, figuratively and symbolically. Place your full consciousness within it so that you are right there with it, and it with you. The two have become one.

You may wish to activate another one of your senses. As you begin to come closer to your object, you can begin to smell it. Everything has a scent. There is the scent of flowers, the fragrance of perfumes, the saltiness of the sea, the aroma of food, and so forth. You bring this sense into play by becoming aware of the scent of your object. As you begin to perceive its fragrance, it will become more real to you. Thus, you will step closer to it psychically.

Next try to bring another one of your senses into play. Try to mentally touch the object. As you mentally draw closer and closer to it, slowly begin to touch or embrace your object to experience the feeling emanating from it.

Seek to bring into play as many of the senses as possible. Almost all knowledge comes via seeing. The second most vital sense is that of hearing. Perchance you are close enough to hear your holy object. Isn't it a joy to be so close to it and so united with it? What is it saying to you?

As you continue to visualize your holy object, very gently and without effort, be aware that at this very moment nothing else matters. You do not have to worry about anything. At this moment, the only thing that matters is that you focus on your holy object in meditation.

How pleasant it is just to take a few moments and immerse yourself in this experience. Surround yourself with this beautiful experience. Let go of all the stress and strain of your everyday life. For now, just visualize your object and sense it as fully as you can. Simply take the time to enjoy it.

Perchance you can hear cars or people. Do not allow this to distract you. It is the nature of life and the way things are. Soon these sounds will fade away. Do not try to shut them out. Just refocus on your holy object and become absorbed within it. It is amazing how quickly the noises will fade. In fact, when you grasp your object with your senses and surround yourself with it, you will rapidly lose awareness of your physical body and will enter into the outer fringes of samadhi.

Earth life has existed for thousands of trillions of years, and it will continue to exist for thousands of trillions of years. Truly, it will never end, only change. If happiness is your destiny, you need not be in a hurry. If spiritual wisdom is your destiny, you need not be in a hurry. There is no future. There is no past. There is only this eternal present moment. This moment is the only moment that exists. There only this moment, and when the next moment comes, *it* will become this moment. Therefore, hold to the awareness of this lovely experience of your holy object at this moment.

This particular technique is especially suited for people who are more imaginative or intuitive. (Imagination and intuition are two different modalities.) These generally include individuals born under the astrological signs of Pisces, Scorpio and Cancer or people who have a large number of planets in the water signs. Water signs tend to be more emotional, and thus intellectual meditations are best for them. They need to grasp the intellectual meaning of the holy object technique, not the emotionality of it.

The air signs—Gemini, Libra, and Aquarius—generally include people who are more verbal and/or mental. They are often more mentally active in their thinking processes. Therefore, techniques that quiet the mind are best suited for them. They will find greater benefit from concentration techniques than from meditation techniques. This does not mean that air signs should not meditate. It simply means that they will find meditation easier and more effective after they have mastered basic concentration techniques. We can all benefit from mastering concentration techniques before we enter into serious meditation. However, this is truer for the air signs.

The fire signs—Aries, Leo, and Sagittarius—tend to be more enthusiastic about life. These souls generally work better with mantra techniques that tend to balance out their enthusiasm.

Lastly, the earth signs—Capricorn, Taurus, and Virgo—tend to have more inertia than the other signs. Their minds tend to be directed toward practicality. Thus, the use of a straightforward mantra followed by a visualization technique would be most helpful in stimulating their inert nature. Meditations that inspire are also very good for these people. They should verbally rather than mentally chant their mantras.

One way to select or direct your meditation is based on basic personality types. This clarification may be helpful to some readers in choosing their meditation practice.

Om Shanti

CHAPTER THIRTEEN
Universal Concepts Underlying Meditation

I would like to elaborate on the more advanced concepts underlying meditation. To point out the deeper concepts and stages that underlie all meditation, I refer back to the object of beauty meditation technique, a universal primary technique of meditation used by mystics around the world in ancient times as well as today. Although different philosophies and cultures often modify the object of beauty meditation technique, the primary methodology remains the same:

Relaxation – Simply relax. Get into a comfortable position. You may sit in an advanced or beginning yoga posture or just recline on your back.

Deep breathing – Breathe deeply. Take a few deep breaths and relax your body and mind.

Closed Eyes – Close your eyes and begin to focus your awareness on your inner life.

Focused Attention – Focus your eyes and your attention on the root of the nose between the eyebrows. This must be a focused attention, not staring. There must not be any stress or strain whatsoever.

Visualization – Visualize whatever object you consider to be the most beautiful at this moment in your life.

Concentration – Concentrate. This is not meditation but concentration. Perfected concentration is the basis of all meditation.

Meditation – The last step is to meditate. This major step has a few stages to it.

In effect, you have: relaxation + deep breathing + closed eyes. This is followed by: focused attention + visualization + concentration + meditation.

Let us look a little closer at the concepts behind this seven-step process:

1. In the relaxation phase, it is essential that both your body and mind be completely relaxed so that your awareness can enter

into your subconscious mind. This is necessary because the "lever" that opens your consciousness to the super-conscious mind is found here. If your body is tense, your mind will remain, or become, tense. You will remain stuck on the surface of your conscious mind, unable to enter into deeper levels of consciousness. In order to reach a deep level of relaxation before you begin your meditation practice, you must control your attitude and your reactions to the events in your everyday life. In short, we all need to begin living a saner lifestyle.

2. In the practice of meditation, deep breathing is indispensable because it brings more life force, prana, into the mind. Without this added life force, the mind is not able to remain conscious as it enters into the deeper levels of the unconscious or super-conscious minds. If you do not remain conscious, it will be very difficult to press the lever that opens the door to the super-conscious realms. Furthermore, if you do not remain conscious, any experience or data that is gained will be lost to your conscious mind. Thus, it is necessary to practice breath control, *pranayama,* for some time before trying to enter into deep meditation.

3. When your eyes are closed, it is much easier to enter into your inner life, because it dynamically helps close off the outside world and its noise, experiences and emotions. Also, when your eyes are open, the kriya currents tend to move toward the right channel, pingala, increasing awareness of the physical world. When your eyes are closed, the kriya currents tend to move toward the left channel, ida. This makes you more aware of the dream state, which is one of the levers that opens up the astral to other inner planes of consciousness.

4. There are three main concepts behind the focused attention phase of meditation:
   • You intensify your awareness.
   • Different effects of intensification manifest, depending on which area of the body you focus. For example:
   By focusing on the sun center, you become more aware of the astral creative forces that are manifesting downward into the earth plane of consciousness.
   By focusing on the tip of the nose, you become more aware of the individual life force that holds your physical body together.

By focusing on the very top of the head, the door of God, you become more aware of the Divine Dream of God (in this sector of time and space).

By focusing on the solar plexus area, you become more aware of your personal karma.

By focusing on the heart area, you become more aware of the compassion and unselfish love surrounding your personal universe.

By focusing on the throat area, you become more aware of the forces that form your past lives.

• The day and the time of day that you focus are vital to the types of karmic forces that are working at that moment. This focusing time has powerful effects on softening your karma. An easy way to select a time is simply to focus at sunrise each morning. Focusing at this time will help to soften the karma that is going to precipitate on that day into the physical world as well as into the astral worlds.

5. Visualization is a very important part of this primary meditation technique because visualization of a form produces a given type of energy and arranges it into a given pattern. The visualized form that you use converts pranic and kriyic energies into specific types of energies. This is why it is preferable to visualize either something that is near to your heart or something that produces a definite holy feeling within you.

On a deeper level, any symbol you visualize has three basic levels of meaning: universal, cultural and individual. Every symbol contains three levels of energy. An example of a universal symbol is an *archetype*. An elderly bearded man is an archetypal symbol of wisdom.

In the process of visualization, independent of the form, color is vital. The color of your object has deep meaning to your subconscious and unconscious minds. A red triangle has a very different meaning than a blue triangle. Most mystics make this problem easier by simply making everything colorless or a radiant white.

6. Concentration is crucial to meditation. It is at this stage that almost all students encounter a major block. Concentration is an effortful action of the focused mind that is performed to hold the mind to its object of visualization. The techniques of concentration must be practiced correctly. If concentration is not done properly, the state of meditation will not be attained. Perfected concentration is basic to attaining and sustaining a meditative state.

Begin the state of concentration by fixing the mind on your object of meditation and holding it there. In a very short period of time, your mind most likely will wander off to another thought or thing. It may suddenly think, "I have to write a letter to my aunt." When this happens, do not get upset. Just bring your mind effortlessly back to your object of concentration. If you get upset or if you jerk the mind back to your object of concentration, you will energize your mind. This is not what you want to do. The worst thing you can do is to become upset because you were distracted.

When you have effortlessly brought your attention back to your object, it will stay there for a little while. In a very short period of time, the mind will again wander off and grab hold of another thought. Each time the mind wanders, just bring it back to your object of concentration with fixed intent but without any emotion. After a while, the mind will find it easier and easier to remain focused. When it does stay focused, you have attained a state of concentration. Bringing your mind back again and again to your object of concentration is imperative because in this way you burn off the excessive energy that produces angularity of consciousness. This angular energy keeps your mind flitting back and forth and thus holds your awareness to the surface of the mind. By working off this excessive mind energy, you are able to enter into a balanced state of consciousness. This allows you to attain knowledge from your meditative state.

When the mind jumps back and forth to various thoughts, its energy is primarily in the ida and pingala channels. As the mind enters concentration, the energy moves away from the ida and the pingala channels and toward the sushumna channel. When you enter meditation, the energy moves into the sushumna. When the mind no longer wanders, the energy ascends into the sushumna, and you enter into a meditative state.

If you lose the feeling state, just refocus on your object of beauty. Repeat the whole process again: Become completely relaxed, visualize, and return to your concentrated state. Then enter meditation when you have reestablished the feeling. Keep recentering on your object of beauty.

7. Meditation is the final stage in this technique. It is best expressed as "full attention but without tension." Once you have attained and sustained the state of concentration, you can slip into

meditation effortlessly. This is essential because only if the object is held effortlessly in the mind can deeper knowledge flow from the unconscious and super-conscious minds. In deep meditation, you can apply the clear gem to various objects and thoughts, both material and immaterial.

Historically the chief aim of meditation is to access a state of consciousness called *Ananda*. It is a Sanskrit word that is truly impossible to translate, although the word *bliss* is often used. Ananda ... ananda ... ananda. It is, they say, the primary state of consciousness of the earthling.

• Ananda is greater than love.
• Ananda is more exalted than compassion.
• Ananda is higher than happiness.
• Ananda is dearer than knowledge.
• Only wisdom is higher!

Ananda is superior to every other state of consciousness except wisdom. However, it is said that ananda is "living wisdom." The ananda state, the bliss state, is the most balanced state that a human being can experience, yet most people never experience it. Because most people tend to confuse bliss with emotions, it is wiser to say that contentment is greater than bliss.

In the concentration stage, each time you bring the mind back to its chosen object without becoming upset or angry or producing a strong mental reaction, you are learning to meditate. The secret of reaching the meditative stage is to non-emotionally concentrate the mind back to your object. By learning to attain and sustain a state of concentration, you learn to enter and remain in a state of advanced meditation.

After practicing this technique for a while, your mind will no longer become upset each time you refocus it. The mind will always go where it is easiest to go, that is, it follows the path of least resistance. When you continue to bring the mind back to your chosen object without emotionality, it quickly learns to fix upon the object of concentration. At this point, you are ready to enter into the next stage and begin to meditate.

The next stage in this meditation technique is to effortlessly shift your attention away from your object toward the feeling state evoked when your consciousness comes in contact with that object. The object can be a material or an immaterial object. It can be a gross thought or a super-subtle thought. As you shift your awareness from the object to the feeling within you, the object will fade into the background of your consciousness, and your awareness will become more and more fixed on the feeling produced by that object.

The next step is to find the quiescent point within your meditation. When you find it, you meditate upon the feeling existing within the center of that feeling state.

The final stage is to meditate upon the meditator. You turn from the object of the meditation to the feeling in the meditation to the center of the feeling and from that centered feeling to the meditator. In this stage, you meditate upon the feeler of that feeling. You meditate upon the seer of what is seen. In this state, you become more aware of the meditator than of anything else. Even the feeling itself slides into the background of your consciousness. Cosmic consciousness enters and centers itself in the forefront of your consciousness.

When I tell students to close their eyes and visualize something, many of them immediately say, "I can't visualize. I don't have visualization powers." Visualizing simply means that you draw your mind to your object and get a sense of it. Mentally look at it. If you feel you cannot visualize your object, just think about it. Like everything else you do, this will become easier with practice. When I explain this, many students say to me: "Are you telling me to use my wild imagination?" That's right. Use your imagination. It is not as wild as you think. And it does have great powers when it is trained and directed.

Learn to draw your mind to your chosen object. Initially it is important to realize that it does not matter whether you see the object in as detailed a way as you would a photograph. With a little practice, you will train your mind to rapidly become absorbed within your chosen object.

When you reach the stage where you begin to feel the object, you can bring the breath into play. As the breath flows in of its own nature, feel the feeling (not emotion) that has been evoked from the object of beauty flowing into the innermost center of your consciousness. As the breath flows out of its own nature, feel the feeling flowing out of your total being into the cosmos.

The flowing of this feeling throughout your being has a flushing action. There is a double flushing effect when you draw in this feeling with the in-breath to the center of your awareness, and then feel it flowing throughout your total being as you exhale. This flushing effect regenerates your physical body and your mind. As you saturate each cell of your being and each petal of your mind with this feeling, you will:

- Reduce the force of your confining karma,
- Dissolve away other pieces of confining karma,
- Make your mind more peaceful and less crabby,
- Attune your being to higher states of consciousness,
- Soften your personality,
- Eliminate many of your fears,
- Improve your ability to communicate with Self, others and higher states of consciousness,
- Develop your creativity,
- Vitalize your mental and thus your physical health,
- Enlarge your philosophical disposition,
- Expand your power base,
- Bring new friends into your life,
- Increase your occult knowledge,
- Harmonize yourself with your inner and outer worlds and the beings dwelling therein.

In a very short time, all of these positive forces will have unbelievably positive effects on your body, your mind and your life. They will also have a direct effect upon you, the meditator. As you practice this meditation method, the one factor that is clearly seen is that your personality truly softens and you become less upset when the unexpected occurs. This is substantial progress. The softening of your personality, no matter how balanced it was prior to beginning your practice, is proof of your unfolding spiritual evolution. This is important, so I will say it again in another way: An imbalanced, negative, emotional personality is proof of an unevolved mind; it reveals an underdeveloped soul. Spiritual unfoldment begins with the softening of the personality, or it does not begin at all.

As I mentioned earlier, emotions exist within the solar and lunar channels, which exist on the surface of the mind. Emotions create, intensify and release confining karma. Living on the surface of the mind weakens the mind and its powers. A centered mind is a concentrated mind. A concentrated mind has the power to do anything … in time.

If you got upset once a day, or once a week, you may now find that you get upset less frequently, maybe once every other day or only once a month. This may offend those of you who are "more advanced." To you I say that if you find yourself getting upset only once a year or once a decade, perchance you should look more closely at the intensity of your temper. Perchance what you conceived to be no reaction to an experience is a horrendous reaction in the mind of the guru. Do you understand?

It is not only a question of the duration of one's agitation but also of the intensity of it. Some seekers need to work on removing the duration; others need to work on softening the intensity; still others need to work on lessening the frequency. Some need to work on all of these aspects.

When the personality softens, certain things and events that once threw you off balance no longer negatively affect you because you are now more balanced. You are more self-aware, more mindful, and thus more centered. When you are in this state, most karmic impulses cannot manifest strongly.

The mind-stuff, the *chitta,* contains your personality. It is your personality that holds the karmic forces that bring negativity such as pain, suffering and lack into your individual life. As you begin to balance your personality, your life begins to balance. As you balance your personality, the experience of pain, suffering and lack dissolve, revealing a wondrous, glorious new life—here and now.

From month to month or year to year, your chosen object of beauty most likely will change. Each time you sit down to use this meditation, ask yourself, "What object might I choose today? What is the most beautiful object I can think of today?" You will select the object according to your moods, attitudes, and aspects. Do not be concerned when the object changes. The important thing is to feel an attunement to it at the moment of meditation. The only time it is wise not to change your object of beauty is if you determine to hold your object of beauty from the new moon to the full moon. Then the object should not be changed during that period.

As you open your eyes and come out of your meditation, sit and remain aware for a minute or so. This quiet period is called the aftereffect stage. After a few moments of stillness, move into the second stage: reflect and examine all that has happened within you. See if you have missed anything of vital importance that may have been on the edge of your consciousness. Next try to grasp the feeling stage and seek to sustain it throughout the day or night. Determine to hold this balanced feeling state throughout the entire cycle until your next meditation.

Slowly move to your desk and record all valuable data in your spiritual journal. Write down the complete date, time and the city where you did your meditation. You also may want to give the feeling state of your meditation a one-word label. I recommend using a single word label because this will give you words like fear, hatred, love or jealousy, rather than more complex descriptions such as "a multi-legged pink elephant with two trunks." If you give your feeling states more than a one-word label, it will tend to confuse the mind about what the feeling was. You may want to narrow down the feeling state by using five or six words, then trim it to three or four words and finally reduce it to a one-word description that most clearly defines the feeling.

Seek to retain the balanced state as you move out into the world. Remember that the goal is to not react to Life but to act on Life with a balanced state of consciousness. Yes, you should act to soften your karma before it manifests. Yes, you should improve your personality before it needs to be challenged.

It is also important to remember that even though meditation must be effortless, it is not a passive activity. Meditation is a very conscious activity, yet it is an effortless discipline. Even though meditation is effortless, it always has a direction; it is a consciously directed mental activity. You direct your meditation toward a given end. After you do this, you should allow the thoughts in your meditation to flow freely without any preconceived controlling pattern. The mind is very active in its perceptive forces. It is enlivening but not emotional. You are always actively moving towards your goal: merging with the inner feeling of beauty within yourself and finally with the macrocosm, which is pure beauty.

The object of beauty meditation technique is not the only visual technique. There are many others. If the stages are followed properly, one technique will be just as effective as any other. They are all good methods. It is important to recognize that the inner nature of the meditator must blend with the outer pattern of the technique being used. In other words, the technique that you use should somewhat reflect your mind and inner personality. Because of the fact that there are so many different personalities, there must be many different techniques.

Using an incompatible technique is like taking an Evangelist and putting him at a Catholic high mass or taking a Roman Catholic and putting him at an Evangelical service. Each of these individuals will be very uncomfortable and will want to leave these conflicting environments. The inner nature of one's mind and the outer technique need to be compatible. All techniques work, but some work better for certain personalities.

Many psychologists tell us that our difficulties are caused primarily by negative attitudes. Meditation is a way of attaining and sustaining a positive attitude. It is one of the best ways to balance your life so that you can daily enter the world and not be threatened or hassled by it. If you are not threatened or hassled by the world, you will respond to it positively and without violence.

As you use this object of beauty technique or any other meditation technique to attain advanced meditation, you will rapidly become more and more secure. You will become less and less fearful. As you regain your self-control, you will regain control over your life.

Om Shanti.

CHAPTER FOURTEEN
Techniques for Peace and Contentment

Give the gift of contentment to yourself through meditation, and you will be able to give it to others. No matter how stress-filled your life might be and no matter how many demands are placed upon you, the gift of contentment, peace, tranquility and serenity can be attained through the practice of meditation. Through the gift of meditation, you can attain joy—which is wisdom.

Meditation is a specific and very effective method for attaining happiness and greater self-confidence. Through meditation you can achieve life's most important goals: happiness and success. Yes, success. Success is a most important concept, even though it is one of the most abused words. I am using the word success to mean the attainment of your life's goal.

You should understand that meditation is not just a relaxation technique. It is a multistage process that begins with relaxation but goes far beyond it. Meditation not only improves your spiritual life, but it can help you achieve more in your everyday life as well. Most of all, meditation is a mystical method for softening and removing confining karma.

Yoga teaches that we meditate to regain something that we have lost, to recover something of ourselves. Some call it enthusiasm; some call it zest; others call it the bliss of being. The world has seemingly lost its capacity to experience joy. We have lost our capacity to enjoy life. We have lost our capacity to do what we do without worrying and fretting. We have lost the capacity to be in the here and now. The ancient sages said, "If you are going to walk, walk. If you are going to sit, sit. However, whichever you are going to do, don't wobble!" We must learn to do one thing with the full force of our mind and being.

Meditation allows us to work, play, love, create – and to do all of these things much more effectively and much more completely. Meditation allows us to be content now—in whatever we are doing or in whatever we are not doing. An old Sanskrit poem puts it this way:

Yesterday is but a memory,
Tomorrow is but a hope,
Today and today alone is the eternal now.

The practice of meditation gives us that special state of awareness that enables us to live effectively and harmoniously in the eternal now. Thus, let go of your fears, let go of your hopes, let go of your aspirations for tomorrow. Live now. Be happy now. Be content now. Be peaceful now. Be serene in the eternal now.

Whatever you are seeking, it should be sought harmoniously and effectively while still maintaining the peace and harmony of this present moment. Be peaceful now and harmoniously strive to attain noble goals.

Meditation will enable you to become more direct and forthright with yourself and with other people. It will enable you to be more whole. Meditation will help your life to be more complete. Finally, meditation will enable you to rejoin the universal stream of life consciousness from which we have become disconnected. Meditation brings the following key awareness, "You are now, and have always been, a part of Life, not apart from Life."

Let us continue our discussion on meditation by exploring the following eight techniques:

1. THE BREATH CONTROL MEDITATION TECHNIQUE

The breath control meditation technique is also known as the breathing meditation technique. It is much like the preparatory hong sau technique discussed in an earlier chapter. This technique begins by finding a comfortable posture. The spine should be straight but not tense. The shoulder blades should be gently pushed back and the stomach muscles slightly in and up. Close your eyes and focus your attention at the root of the nose between the eyebrows at the ajna chakra. As with all techniques, you should be at full attention without tension.

This technique consists of simply being aware of your breathing. You do nothing else. This may sound simple but it is difficult to do, because as soon as you focus your attention on the breath, you change it. By focusing on the breath, you influence it and subconsciously and unconsciously change it. The aim of this practice is to be aware of the breath and yet allow it to "do its own thing." As you learn to do this successfully, you will be able to perceive people without your subconscious mind wanting to influence them. Even more importantly, you will become more aware of your own inner universe without trying to change it. (There is a reason that your inner universe is as it is. Any adjustments that take place should be done wisely and carefully.) One of the aims of meditation is to become aware of what is within you without trying to influence it in any way.

Remember that meditation is a way of becoming fully awake. It is a way of becoming fully aware and fully alert. In your life, BE ... and become fully awake in your consciousness. BE ... and become fully aware of your spiritual Self, of the Reality within you. BE ... and become alert to the thoughts and emotions within you. Be peaceful in this awareness. Be awake and aware of your inner universe.

As you practice this technique, you will rapidly discover that there are many inner distractions in your consciousness. The way in which you handle these distractions will determine whether you attain meditation or remain in a state of concentration. Remember that concentration is the effortful control of the mind, whereas meditation is the effortless control of the mind.

As you watch the breath, relax and let the breath breathe you. As you relax more and more, focus effortlessly upon the inhalation and the exhalation. At this point, more mental distractions will most likely occur. You might remember that you were supposed to call someone or that you forgot to buy something from the store. As you enter into this second stage of effortless meditation, many other thoughts, emotions, needs, demands and suppressed energies will rise up to the surface of your mind.

I want to emphasize again it is neither good nor bad that thoughts come into your mind. They are *not* an indication of a faulty meditation. They are an indication of a good meditation. The secret of going deeper into your meditation is learning to deal with these distractions by remaining undisturbed by them. You are balancing the excessive energy from the surface of your mind. As you do this, the energy that has been suppressed will flow up into your consciousness. The goal is to move beyond the stage of these distractions.

Controlling these mental distractions is the first stage toward advanced meditation. There are a number of ways to do this:

• The most essential thing is not to become upset or emotional when distractions arise. Do not allow them to cause you to energize your mind more than it is already. When distractions occur, quietly and peacefully tell yourself, "Yes, yes, I will think about this later, after my meditation. The important thing right now is that I meditate." When you come out of your meditation, you can reflect about the thoughts that arose. You can analyze them and ask yourself why they came to the surface of your mind during your meditation. You can now take action wisely. This process allows you to balance the energies that exist in your unconscious and/or subconscious minds.

• Continue centering your mind again and again. Center your mind more and more on your breathing and the awareness of the breath. Focus more on this than on anything else. Find more joy in observing the breath than in observing and getting caught up in the mental streams of agitated thoughts.

• Follow one of these streams of distraction for a short period of time and let its energy run out while not totally losing the awareness of the breath. Once the energy is dissipated, bring your full awareness back to the breath.

You might practice each of these methods to find out which one is the easiest or most comfortable for you. In any event, the key thing is not to put energy into the mind-force by becoming agitated. Put the energy into the awareness of your breathing pattern. This will enable you to begin to bring the mind back to one thing—the object of your meditation. With this method, you use the observation of the breath as your object or focus point. This technique will help you release energy from within yourself, enabling you to have greater control over your mind. It will allow you to gain what we all need, but have lost and forgotten—the enthusiasm, the zest and the joy that is in Life. Because you have linked the meditation to the breath, this technique also becomes a karma-softening technique.

2. THE AFFIRMATION TECHNIQUE

In the West, we are familiar with the use of affirmation. Affirmation, a process also referred to as autosuggestion, consists of taking a powerful word or phrase and continually repeating it, in order to influence the subconscious mind. Affirmation can be very effective. I want to emphasize, however, that mantra will have a much deeper effect on your subconscious mind than affirmation or autosuggestion, because mantra reaches into the unconscious levels of the mind.

If you wish to use the affirmation technique, I suggest you use the following one: "Every day in every way, I am becoming more and more content." As with most affirmations, I suggest the use of this powerful affirmation each night while you are falling asleep and again the first thing in the morning. It is most effective at these times.

You will notice that the affirmation does not say, "Every day in every way I *am* content." Why? Because you may not be content at this moment and you need to acknowledge this. Thus the affirmation says, "Every day in every way I am *becoming* more and more content." This reaffirms that, even though you may not be content at this moment, you will be more content shortly and with each passing hour.

This fundamental affirmation can be modified to suit your various needs. For example:

Every day in every way, I am becoming healthier and healthier.

Every day in every way, I am becoming wiser and wiser.

Every day in every way, I am becoming more and more conscious.

Every day in every way, I am becoming *more and more aware of my dreams.*

These affirmations can be made more powerful by changing their duration factor. You can intensify the affirmation by saying, "*With each breath I breathe,* I am becoming happier and happier." This pattern points out that with each passing breath you will become happier and happier. Thus, even if you are unhappy at any given moment, as long as you continue to breathe you will automatically become happier!

The secret of affirmation is to take only one thought or concept and hold onto it. Too many thoughts confuse the subconscious mind. Use only one thought. If you cannot decide on a single thought, just affirm, "Every day in every way, I am becoming more and more peaceful." As the mind becomes more peaceful, it will reveal to you what it needs.

3. THE OM SHANTI MANTRA MEDITATION TECHNIQUE

The word *mantra* is a Sanskrit term that means thought form or thought pattern. It conveys the meaning of thought energy. Mantra is not a word but a vibration. Repeated over and over, it vibrates in a given chakra and releases positive forces in a given area of your mind and external life. It is this vibration that sets up a positive mindset.

This technique consists of chanting the OM shanti mantra. It sounds like this: Ommmmmm, shannnnti, shannnnti, shannnnti-he. Each shanti vibration becomes softer and softer. The first *shanti* is the most robust and symbolizes peace, tranquility and serenity to your body. The second *shanti* is pronounced more softly and symbolizes peace, tranquility and serenity to your mind. The third *shanti* is the softest and symbolizes peace, tranquility and serenity to your astral body. This mantra, like many mantras, should be recited aloud.

The third repetition of the *shanti* sound has a slight change in its vibration. The first sound is *shanti*. The second sound is *shanti*. However, the third vibration is *shanti-he*. It sounds like *shan-tihe*. Although it is not implied in Sanskrit, I like to think that the *ti-he* means, "Keep smiling … keep laughing." Thus, I could say that the mantra *Om, shanti, shanti, shanti-he* means: "Keep smiling … Keep laughing … Be happy with Life, whether you have what you want or not." Or as the wise sages would say, "If you do not have what you want, at least be happy!"

At this point, you should have a clearer understanding of the difference between the breath control meditation and mantra meditation. Each leads to the same goal but because of individual personality traits, different lifestyles and the period of time in our lives, one method will be more harmonious and easier to attune to than another.

4. THE AURA MEDITATION TECHNIQUE

The mystics theorized that a massive energy field called an *aura* surrounds the body. This aura extends outward from the body two and one-half to three feet. You and your body live inside this mantle of colored lights. By observing your mind and consciousness with the previous two types of meditation techniques, you will become aware that many things are happening in your inner life. Many thoughts and emotions flow through your consciousness at the same time. Many of these thoughts and emotions jangle and clash together. Thus, it is often difficult to separate them.

So that we can clearly observe our thoughts, we need to be able to separate them by slowing down the speed of our mind. Meditation enables us to do this. Another approach is to lower one's blood pressure. This is one reason why yogis sit on the floor. There are two other methods: inducing rhythmic breathing and practicing the aura meditation technique.

The value of the aura meditation technique is that it helps slow down the mind, enabling us to break down the forces and thoughts that rapidly flow through it. This technique allows us to separate the streams of thought and emotions that happen simultaneously. We do this to see, analyze and understand each pattern more fully and clearly.

The aura meditation technique is best practiced in the evening when the day is behind you and your subconscious mind is more relaxed. This technique is more difficult than the first two that were discussed in this chapter.

This is how the aura technique is performed: Imagine your aura as a giant balloon, and see yourself inside this balloon. This giant balloon is filled with astral water, which has the properties of regular water except that you can breathe in it quite freely.

As each thought or emotion manifests, imagine it flowing out of your big toe. Each thought you think is released as a small encapsulated bubble. You will find that there are many of these bubbles coming out of your big toe. As this occurs, just grab hold of one and fix your attention on it. As each thought flows out of your toe as a tiny bubble, visualize it rising and flowing past your eyes. However, because this astral water is thicker than normal water, the bubble will flow upward at a much slower rate. As it flows upward and moves past you, see it becoming larger and larger so that you see it more clearly. In effect, you are observing the thought form slowly ascending to the surface of the astral water. If you have seen underwater scuba films, you may recall seeing the water bubbles expand and become larger as they ascend to the surface in this manner.

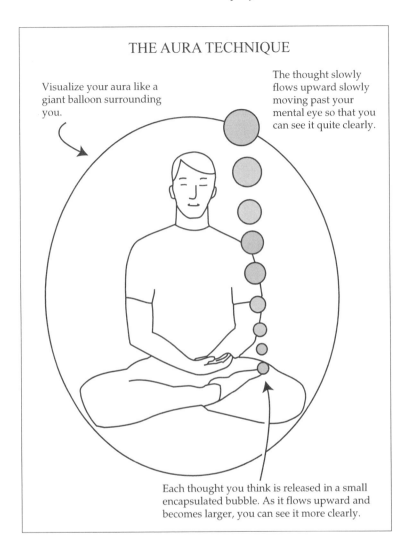

THE AURA TECHNIQUE

Visualize your aura like a giant balloon surrounding you.

The thought slowly flows upward slowly moving past your mental eye so that you can see it quite clearly.

Each thought you think is released in a small encapsulated bubble. As it flows upward and becomes larger, you can see it more clearly.

As you watch the thought forms rise through your aura, you will see them very clearly because you have separated them, divided them and enlarged them. Do not try to analyze them at this moment. Just observe them. Do not judge them. Just look at them. Just perceive and remember them. After your meditation is finished, jot down something about them in your journal. Then you may analyze them and their meanings.

With this method, you amplify the thought or emotion as if you were looking at it through a microscope. As it ascends slowly, you can see this thought or emotion quite clearly for an extended period. You can slow down these bubbles, so they may take as long as 10 to 30 seconds to ascend from the bottom to the top of the water balloon.

You can add to the technique after you have had some practice. See the emotions exit through your left toe and the thoughts through your right toe. Thus, you will see a set of bubbles ascending upward: the thought and its emotion (or is it the emotion and its thought?).

The aura meditation technique is a process that separates your many states of consciousness into one, the one that you choose. This technique should be done to find the most essential thoughts in your consciousness. Generally 5 to 10 minutes should be dedicated to this practice. This process is really much more actual than symbolic, although most people assume that it is symbolic. However you conceive of it, it is a great method and it works. Use it!

After a little practice, this extraordinary and crucial technique will enable you to see what is happening deep within your mind. It will enable you to effectively slow down your entire thinking process to the degree that you can separate a single thought from all other thoughts in your flow of consciousness.

The aura meditation technique is a visualization technique that can be linked to the *neti, neti, neti* mantra affirmation. "Neti, neti, neti" means "I am not this thought. I am not that thought. I am not this thought saying that I am not that thought. I am not thought. I am pure unbounded and unhampered consciousness."

As you perform the aura meditation technique, when you see a thought or emotion, say to yourself, "Isn't that interesting?" However, if a thought becomes too distracting, it may be wise to use the neti, neti, neti technique in order to remind yourself that you are not your thoughts. You are not your emotions. You are not the stuff in your mind. You are not the mind. You are spirit moving through time and space.

Mankind seems bent on assuming that if we have an ugly thought, we ourselves are ugly. However, when a hideous thought flows through your consciousness, it is important to realize that this does not mean *you* are hideous. If an ugly thought flows through your mind, it means that somehow you have walked into a force-field of negative, ugly thoughts. So what is needed? You simply need to walk out of that negative force-field as directly and quickly as possible.

This technique helps to disengage the entanglement of the thoughts and emotions from the mind. It teaches you to become detached from your thoughts and also to become detached from the thoughts of others. In short, the power of negative thoughts will no longer bind and confine your mind or spiritual being.

This method is a very important technique because it contains the beginning stages of a more advanced technique called the replay meditation technique that is discussed at the end of this chapter. We must be able to see what is happening in our mind in order to control our thoughts.

The problem is that most humans are too judgmental. They need to let the mind, "mind." They need to just let the eyes, "eye," the ears, "ear," and the stomach, "stomach." We must learn to accept these functions. At the same time, we must accept the fact that we are to train the mind to transcend them. We must always seek to gain greater control over the instruments of our earth life body. The problem with most human beings is that they are unaware that their minds are such busy mechanisms.

5. THE CONTEMPLATION TECHNIQUE

The contemplation meditation technique is a simple process. You simply count from 1 to 5: 1 ... 2 ... 3 ... 4 ... 5 ... and as you are counting, think of nothing but the number you are counting, and then the next number.

Next try to count from 1 to 5 but a bit slower. Count the number 1, then the number 2, then the number 3, then the number 4 and then the number 5. As you count very slowly, the mind will begin to fill in the blank spaces between the numbers with thoughts. The goal is to count very slowly from 1 to 5 without thinking of anything else except the number you are on, and then the next number. Especially in the beginning stages, you will find this extremely difficult unless you count very fast. The key to advancement with this technique is to make the numbers farther apart in time duration. When practicing this technique, your mind and being must be totally relaxed; otherwise it will not be a meditation technique.

The secret is not to allow your mind to think of anything between the numbers. It is amazing how many thoughts can emerge.

The slower you count, the more time there will be for the mind to release other thoughts and emotions. The slower you go, the more difficult it is to maintain your focus. Obviously, if you count from 1 to 5 very rapidly, no thoughts will enter the mind in between the numbers. This is why you have to count quite slowly to make the technique more and more effective as a means of spiritual advancement.

At first, the best way to do this is to count quickly. Then begin to slow down, holding your mind meditatively only to the numbers. When you have had some success attaining pure space between the numbers, begin counting even more slowly. Then stretch out the time even more. As you do this, try to be aware of the pure consciousness that exists between them. In short, be aware of only the numbers and not of any random thoughts that interject themselves between the numbers. This is the contemplative phase of this meditation technique.

Each time you encounter any thoughts between the numbers, recenter yourself, refocus the mind and, with fuller contemplative powers, begin the process over again slowly. Begin again with the number 1. (It took me a number of weeks to get to the number 1 in my earlier stages of learning this method.)

At some point, your mind will be so concentrated at number 1 that you might forget that number 2 is next. When practicing this technique, you will become aware of how the mind resists what you are trying to do. Obviously the mind wants to go its own way.

6. THE ADVANCED CONTEMPLATION TECHNIQUE I

This is a variation of the previous contemplation meditation technique. By introducing the breath, the technique becomes even more powerful. As you count from number 1 to number 5, focus your mind on your breathing pattern. It should be natural and quiet; do not force the breath to do anything. Simply allow the breath to breathe itself. You are focusing on the breath and counting.

As the breath naturally and gently flows in, mentally repeat the number 1. As the breath naturally and gently flows out, mentally repeat the number 1 again. As the breath flows in again, mentally repeat the number 2. As the breath flows out, mentally repeat the number 2 again. Repeat this pattern up to the number 5.

Again, you are not forcing the breath in or out. You are focusing on the breath and counting. If you lose your concentration and begin to think of something else, start all over again with the number 1. You most likely will have to restart at number 1 several times. Just keep returning to the number 1 until you can count without losing your focus on the numbers.

Most students find it quite difficult to get to the number 5. If you can reach the number 5 without the intrusion of thoughts, continue the technique by starting with number 1 and counting up to 8 or 10. This cycle can be repeated as often as comfortable. This is an excellent technique for gaining control over a restless mind and for quieting the mind.

7. ADVANCED CONTEMPLATION MEDITATION TECHNIQUE II

This is another variation of the contemplation meditation technique. This technique focuses your mind to such a degree that you forget everything else. Close your eyes and draw your full attention to an object. Even an abstract symbol can be used. Do this with full attention but without tension. See the object. Mentally touch the object. Perceive only the object and nothing else. Clearly hold the object in your mind, and at the same time, hold the awareness of the being that is doing the perceiving. The technique is as simple as that. It is important to recognize that this is done with a state of contemplation rather than a state of will power. This contemplation method is a deeper and more profound state of meditation. It is an excellent technique. Artists and other creative people find it very meaningful.

8. THE REPLAY MEDITATION TECHNIQUE

The final technique in this chapter is called the replay meditation technique. It has many similar characteristics to the reversal technique given in the *Intermediate Guide to Meditation*. This is a very important technique for people actively engaged in the workday world, including busy householders. The replay meditation technique is psychological and philosophical in nature because it deals with what some psychologists call the "fantasizing process" of the mind. Although most people are unaware of it, their minds are constantly generating a series of pictures or thought plays. When we sit down for a meal or drive along the road, our mind plays funny mind games. The mind suddenly begins to fantasize all sorts of things. Most of the time, these fantasies are negative: we hurt ourselves, limit ourselves, or lose something.

The replay meditation technique is done by continuously observing your mind throughout the day while you are studying, playing, driving, eating, working, loving, etc. However, as soon as you become aware that your mind is fantasizing, back up the flow of these negative thoughts and make them more positive. When negative fantasies enter your mind, stop them. Back up your mind and replay these fantasies with a positive pattern. Whatever type of fantasy your mind creates, back it up again and neutralize the negative forces by replaying the fantasy, making it more positive. Then replay the fantasy a third time, making it still more positive. In time you will learn how to easily modify these fantasies through positive imagery. This technique will teach you to respond to your mind much more positively, constructively and effectively.

Replaying negative fantasies in a positive mode will tend to release you from triggering various pieces of negative karma. It also washes out and neutralizes negative thought patterns from your past lives. Replaying these negative fantasies again and again, each time in a more positive manner, will affirm to your mind that it should, and will, think more constructively and fruitfully in the future.

Watch your mind. Think about your negative fantasies. You can even allow them to continue but make them more constructive and less limiting with the use of meditation. Fantasies go by very quickly in the mind. Some of them are very subtle, but they are there. Most people, most of the time, are not only unaware that they exist, but they are also unaware of how destructive they are.

Negative fantasies not only create negative suggestions, but they act as triggering mechanisms for limiting karma. They clearly indicate that we have not learned to accept life and that we are frustrated with life. They suggest an ego personality that needs approval from other people. Nothing, nothing, is more destructive to our life or to our spiritual search than the need for approval from the crowd. Why? Because this invites group karma into our lives, and group karma is always more negative than individual karma.

Some people do have positive fantasies. If you feel that you have positive fantasies, then this technique should be used to make them even more positive. Mystically, however, we would say that they are negative because they are mechanisms by which we escape the so-called harsh reality of earth existence. When we fantasize, we tend to put the energy into the fantasy and deny the flow of energy to the process of solving the real problems of our earth life.

The replay meditation technique is not something that is done for a few minutes. It needs to be practiced continuously throughout the day; it is a technique that requires constant awareness 24 hours a day, day in and day out. This is the goal. Therefore, get into the habit of practicing it. At first, practice it in the morning and in the evening for a short time. Then get into the habit of practicing it three times a day, then four times a day, then five times a day, etc. With each passing day, try to comfortably extend the period of time you practice so that eventually you are observing the mind and stopping the flow of negative thoughts and replaying them in a much more positive mode.

The secret of this technique is to catch the negative patterns earlier and earlier, before they acquire a strong foothold in your mind. Later this method automatically stops the mind from generating negative fantasies. Use this method to acquire new and more positive ways of thinking.

In short, be aware of what is happening in your mind and immediately stop the negative fantasies as soon as you become aware of them. Replay them and make them more positive. Wipe out the negative mental tape that is playing. Back it up. Start recording all over again. Realize that, at first, you may have to back it up and replay almost everything that is happening in your mind. However, in time, the fantasies will become less negative. Later make them positive. Then make them even more positive until there is no need for negative fantasies whatsoever.

It is vital to remember that you are not your brain. You are not your mind. You are not the thoughts and emotions that are occurring inside your consciousness. With this concept in mind, we will discuss the spiritual psychology by which samadhi can be attained.

Om Shanti

CHAPTER FIFTEEN
The Spiritual Psychology of Samadhi, Part I

As you reach the level of advanced meditation, reading and contemplating the aphorisms in the next few chapters will be most helpful in attaining samadhi, the deepest and most expanded level of balanced self-conscious awareness. These chapters may seem somewhat unusual to some readers because of their form. Nonetheless, I assure you that they are the most important chapters in this text because they deal with the spiritual psychology for awakening samadhi.

The reader needs to study these aphorisms and practice the methods inherent in them. Meditating on these aphorisms is one method of attaining supreme happiness, peace, joy and ageless wisdom. If you put these aphorisms into practice, you will attain samadhi and thus awaken your higher consciousness.

As you read through these chapters, meditate on each major aphorism in order to build up your own personal inventory of wisdom. After meditating on each one, begin to meditate on the sub-thoughts inferred within each aphorism.

Let us begin with the first kriya aphorism in the spiritual psychology for awakening samadhi.

1. The spiritual psychology of awakening the mind consists of:
    • Understanding the preliminary practices that are given in this chapter.
    • Comprehending the main practices that are given in the next chapter.
    • Ascending the path of kriya by transforming adverse life events.
    • Measuring your spiritual progress upon the path.
    • Committing your Self to subtler, internal accomplishments.
    • Maintaining an avoidance of the obstacles on your internal path.
    • Practicing thought transformation through kriya thought alchemy.

2. Notice that all seven of the above concepts are in the progressive tense. What do you think this means? Do you think it has anything to do with the eternal now?

3. The spiritual psychology of samadhi is a transformational psychology for awakening to higher states of consciousness and a broader horizon of awareness of one's being. It does this by activating and generating a state of samadhi and applying that samadhi.

4. One of the first steps in this transformational psychology is to strive to become free, to be free, and to remain free. This means striving to always be free from ignorance and forgetfulness. It means to be free from pain, agony, anguish, concern, distress, misery, sadness, sorrow, suffering, torment, trouble, woe, worry and affliction of any kind. This is accomplished through skillful thoughts and skillful actions.

Skillful thoughts and skillful actions working together are called kriya. In the performance of these skillful thoughts and skillful actions, you are not to be dispassionate, impersonal, disinterested, inhibited, unconcerned, unfriendly, jaded, apathetic, cold, unfriendly, calloused, heartless, hardhearted, unkind or unsympathetic. In essence, you are not to be indifferent.

5. Reflect on the extensive instructions given by your guru and your lineage for activating and awakening samadhi. Once you understand these instructions, you should:

- Put them into practice.
- Seek inner enrichment of your mind and soul.
- Attain spiritual accomplishment.

6. You should understand the oral tradition of the guru and his lineage. It is also important to understand the enormous difference between the oral tradition of the guru and his lineage and any of their literature written for general dissemination. What is their oral tradition? Where is it directing you? Where is it leading you? Reflect on these concepts.

7. Obtain a firm understanding of the fundamentals of your guru's pathway by meditating on the essence of his teachings. If you do not accomplish this, you will not grasp the basis of mind training and thus you will attain greater ego-hood rather than sage-hood.

8. Do not seek mere intellectual stimulation from these aphorisms, but seek to integrate them into your daily life through kriya and kriya meditation.

9. The value of any method lies in its value to your everyday life, both externally and internally. The worth of any method lies in the benefits it brings to others, as well as to the environment in which you practice. He who feeds is fed. He who teaches is taught. He who seeks to enlighten ...

10. Here are the key aphorisms and concepts regarding thought transformation:

• Find ways to transform your mind so that you move from unconscious, negative, destructive, unskilled thoughts and actions to conscious, positive, constructive, skillful thoughts and actions.

• Find ways to transform your mind so that you move from self-centered attitudes to an awareness of the needs of others and of Life.

• Find ways to transform your mind from ego centeredness to celestial centeredness.

Gain a deep experience of full consciousness by attaining samadhi. Thus, you will remove confusion and it will never return.

11. The key question you should ask and continually reflect upon is this: What is the single most important achievement I can accomplish in this lifetime?

12. Always and continuously examine your subconscious thoughts and your mental stream of consciousness. Find the link between your words, deeds and the subconscious impulses.

13. When an emotional affliction begins to arise, face it fully. Fully avert it. Fully transform it.

Free yourself from illusion and thus gain detachment. Be no longer in bondage.

Do all preliminary practices.

Gain stability on all levels of your being.

Impress upon your mind that it should examine the nature of the as yet unborn subconscious emotions and thus of the as yet unborn negative thoughts.

14. In the early years on the path, meditate on the essence of the path. Establish a foundation in all things. Move from unawareness to awareness. Transform all that is negative into that which is positive. Remove your lightest afflictions first and then remove the heavier ones. Improve your attitude, yet remain natural.

15. Remove the attitude of wanting and/or needing recognition, rewards and/or gratitude.

Do not inflict pain or misery in order to gain any possessions. Do not depend on others or upon external circumstances. Be self-sufficient.

16. In the middle years on the path, seek instructions for controlling the imbalanced needs of the mind to grasp at things. Seek to gain control over the mind's eternal grasping. Have you not noticed this? Have you not noticed this in others? Have you not noticed this in your own mind?

17. In the later years on the path, meditate, meditate, meditate ... and then contemplate.

THE PRELIMINARY PRACTICES

18. The following five meditations give you the ability to establish a firm foundation for walking the path and for living the spiritual life:

• Meditate upon and correctly understand the occult human form.

• Meditate upon and correctly understand that all is change.

• Meditate upon and correctly understand karmic actions and the fruits of these karmic actions. All actions are karmic.

• Meditate upon and correctly understand the nature of cyclical events in a cyclical existence. What meaning is revealed here?

• Meditate upon and correctly understand that there is no true death. There is only unconsciousness and changing forms.

19. To ensure success in your meditation, establish your own meditation practice. This is done by:

• Attuning to the internal Reality.

• Mastering the adept asana.

• Quieting the mind.

All of the extraneous thoughts and emotions that force themselves upon your mind drive your awareness to the surface of the mind. Soften or eliminate these emotions and extraneous thoughts with the practice of meditation. Then you will move from the surface mind to the interior mind.

20. The following mystical technique will help quiet your mind and bring clarity to your consciousness. It will also neutralize confining karma, helping you to prepare to reach a deeper state of meditation.

As you inhale, visualize very fine white smoke entering and descending into your heart area. As you exhale, visualize very fine dark smoke coming up and out from your heart through your nasal passages and out into the air around your body. Visualize this dark smoke immediately turning colorless as soon as it reaches the outside air.

As you inhale again, visualize very fine white smoke re-entering and descending into your heart area. Again, as you exhale, visualize very fine dark smoke coming up and out from your heart, exiting through your nasal passages and turning colorless as it reaches the outside air. As you visualize this total process, be sure that the breath is even and gradual. Practice this from 11 to 22 rounds.

As you practice this technique, breathe softly so that you do not hear the in and out breaths. Be sure to breathe effortlessly.

Inhale slowly and do not exhale for an extended period of time. This will force in the in-breath. Stay centered and remain undistracted while practicing this technique.

21. When you have determined that the extraneous emotions and thoughts have become somewhat quiet, move to the next level of this technique, which is hong sau with mindfulness. Hong sau with mindfulness is the state of consciousness that is produced after practicing hong sau long enough to induce a more balanced state of consciousness. This more balanced state allows the mind to be more aware and more mindful, thus the phrase "hong sau with mindfulness." After hong sau with mindfulness, you will reach the next stage called the after-effect phase. At this level, sit with a quiet mind and feel the stillness while remaining mindful. With stillness of mind and with mindfulness, unemotionally vow to remain undistracted by worldly forces or by internal forces.

22. Trying to memorize something without motivation can be quite difficult. Likewise, the total process of hong sau needs quiet motivation, or it will be quite difficult to achieve the goal. By attaining a mindful state with the stillness of breath, you can use this fullness of consciousness, this fullness of awareness and this mindfulness to take the vow not to be distracted by worldly forces or internal forces.

23. As you move further along the spiritual path, greater skillfulness is needed to remain undistracted by worldly forces. Later upon the path, you will learn not to be distracted by internal forces.

24. It will help you to know that:
   • In the occult human form, there is the wish cow.
   • In the occult human form, there is Aladdin's magic lamp.
   • In the occult human form, there is the all-seeing eye.
   • In the occult human form, there is the genie's magic lamp.
   These are the things by which everything can be accomplished.
However, to the unskilled practitioner these are the very things that
distract the mind from its spiritual goal.

25. As you move through the earth life, as you move through
the inner life, move further and further away from mundane goals.
The last mundane action to be given up is teaching via words. At
this level, the person is on the inner planes helping others via astral
rituals. Move more and more toward the trans-mundane life.

26. We all have an "other mind." Not everyone is aware that we
have or possess it and not all of us can use it.

27. This other mind is like a treasure that is buried in your own
backyard. You must first realize where it is. Then you must become
aware that it is, in fact, a treasure to be sought, otherwise you will
not seek it. Once you discover this treasure, you must use it to help
others. You must use it to find the greater treasure.

28. To remove pain and suffering from yourself and others, you
must follow the principles of the inner path, of your inner path.
You need to realize how extremely fortunate you are to have taken
on human form. You need to understand how extremely fortunate
you are to have come in contact with the kriya dharma.

29. The ultimate goal of the human form is to obtain time for
spiritual unfoldment through spiritual practice, that is, helping others on the inner planes.

30. The impermanence, the ephemeral nature and the transitory nature of all things are not an intellectual secret. Yet it is not
emotionally evident to most people. Is it evident to you?

31. Having gained basic insight into your mind, the path and
Life, use that insight to achieve deeper growth on inner levels. It
wise to use your environment as a powerful learning tool.

32. Practice yoga in order to soften and overcome confining
karma. Follow the kriya dharma in order to reach a state of enlightenment.

As you gain a foothold here on the earth plane, move forward
to gain a foothold on the astral.

What you gain on the astral while living on the earth plane will be carried over into your next earth life.

33. Human birth is not an accident. It is not a punishment. Human birth is serendipitous. It comes about because of specific karmic causes coming together.

Only *you* will taste the fruits of your actions, those that you, yourself have created.

Understanding the laws of karma is a vital and profound task. Karma is primarily produced by the actions of your body, speech and thoughts.

In order to avoid confusion and future pain and suffering, cease creating confinement in others through any type of injurious actions of your body, tongue or mind.

With full awareness and by skillful means, create favorable, freeing and unconfining actions for others.

34. The unskilled actions of your body include:
    • Physical body imbalances
    • Taking what you have not earned
    • Wounding others physically

35. The unskilled actions of your tongue include:
    • Lying
    • Slandering
    • Wounding others mentally

36. The unskilled actions of your mind include:
    • Greed … subtler greed … still subtler greed
    • Ill-will
    • Wounding other souls
    • Clutching illusions, delusions, erroneous and imprecise beliefs, notions, ideas and concepts. In short, having incorrect views regarding Life.

Realize that performing any of the above actions has hurt you more than any other being. Until you understand this, you will be your own worst enemy.

37. When negative impulses arise:
    • Stop the impulses as soon as they manifest.
    • Look at them clearly. See them clearly.
    • Analyze these negative impulses and recognize their misleading nature.

• Understand that all negative actions bind and limit you now and in the future.

38. With thought transformation to awaken samadhi, you gain greater insight into Life, and thus you can see what most likely will manifest tomorrow. Remember that if you know what will manifest in the future, you can change it.

39. The nature of Life is cold, then hot, and then cold again. For most souls, Life is an ever-returning wheel. For the sage, however, Life is an ever-expanding cycle.

40. With this knowledge, you will comprehend the need to break the wheel and move onto the ever-expanding cycles within the Cycle. If you are unaware of the need to break free from your limitations, you will more than likely never try to gain release.

41. Examine the suffering and pain people experience. Understand that each person's pain and suffering is caused by that person and by that person alone. Examine the suffering of all sentient life-forms with the awareness that this pain can be stopped. Life can be happy and joy-filled. Life is joy-filled. However, only the person in pain can stop his pain. Only that person can erase the cause of his own pain. No God, no other soul, no other person can sustain or remove that suffering because it is self-created. Therefore, it has to be removed by that same person, although we can truly help other souls by showing them the sky path.

42. Through the awakening of samadhi, you can examine this self-created pain and self-created suffering, as well as the reasons people cling to these states of consciousness. You can also clearly see how these states can be softened, dissolved, and removed from your life and from the lives of others.

Om Shanti

CHAPTER SIXTEEN
The Spiritual Psychology of Samadhi, Part II

43. Other practices for awakening super-conscious samadhi include meditating on greed in its subtlest forms. In doing this, you can soften and/or totally eradicate greed. Greed is the key emotion binding us to our egocentric, limited world.

44. It is important to understand how greed functions and limits our cosmic-consciousness. However, it is not as important to understand how greed functions as it is to eradicate it. Often in psychology, we spend too much energy trying to explain a bad habit rather than correcting that habit. There is the story of the man who was wounded by an arrow. Before pulling it out, he began wondering whether it was manmade, what type of poison was used, whether it was made at the full or new moon, whether the archer was standing or kneeling when he released the arrow, etc. The vital factor is to first remove the arrow and only then to ponder over other questions. If he reflects too long before taking action, the poison will kill the man.

Turn your mind away from worldly fame and gain. Turn your mind away from admiration, glory and praise.

Practice the internal union with your guru, spiritual master or your inner spiritual symbol. Come to understand the teachings.

In your daily life, apply the insights that you have gained from the teachings and from insightful meditation.

45. Become more aware of yourself, of what is happening within your inner universe, and become aware of the world. Always look around and understand what is happening in your external environment. Become more aware of what has not yet happened but which will shortly manifest. Forever seek to comprehend and appreciate the relationship between internal and external forces.

46. Use this awareness in your meditation to develop intuition and a deep conviction of which teachings are most true. Exert yourself to experience the validity of Life, Self, and the teachings through insight meditation and intuitional action, kriya. Put the teachings into practice.

THE MAIN PRACTICES

47. The main practices for awakening super-conscious samadhi consist of first understanding what meditation is and what it is not. When this has been done, develop the recognition of what samadhi is.

48. Next aspire to attain and cultivate full samadhi and use it wisely. After being intellectually well prepared, correctly practice your yoga of advanced meditation. Gain emotional stability through your preliminary exercises. Become fully confident of your chosen path.

49. Understand the fundamentals of karma, of cyclical existence and the transitory nature of everything except spirit, atma.

50. Establish a firm physical meditation pose in order to practice and reach advanced meditation. Practice transformational psychology to train and awaken samadhi.

51. In this present Kali-yuga cycle, which is the lowest of the four stages of the universe's evolution, there is much self-inflicted pain and suffering. This is a result of the entities in this cycle using up almost all of their good karma. At the same time, because of greed, they are working off very little of their confining karma. Thus, the entities in this cycle carry within themselves the seeds of countless emotional afflictions from the past and the present. These afflictions are caused by greed and grasping. These seeds of pain and suffering are caused by non-skillful thoughts and non-skillful actions, by non-wisdom. In ignorance, these entities grasp at everything and anything. The karmic seeds, which bring about a grasping attitude, need to be softened and then dissolved.

52. The first concept to be explored in advanced meditation is that pain and suffering are not an inherent part of Life. They are manmade. That is to say, they are produced by mankind's attitudes of need, greed, desire, expectation and aversion. Pain and suffering are not a part of the macrocosm. Rather, they are part of the microcosmic structure of life due to the ego personality. As the great Eastern sage said, "If I had no ego, what pain and suffering would there be?"

53. Life is not suffering! Life is what you choose to make it. Soften and remove the concept that all Life is suffering. Do this by creating positive states of consciousness within your deeper stages of meditation. That which you create in your deeper meditation will manifest in your so-called external earth life.

54. When the mind of the average person is calm, it cannot easily see the ego or how the ego functions. It is only when a strong emotion arises that this mind becomes aware of the ego and how it functions. Nonetheless, this is only possible with self-awareness.

55. Strong emotions give the average mind an excellent chance to observe the ego personality and its self-made identity as it relates to individuals, the so-called external world and itself.

56. In the early years on the path, spend time seeking to recognize the seeds of non-wisdom. See how they function. See how they cause a person to grasp onto the concept of and identity with the ego self and with the objects that give value to the ego identity.

57. Come to know that there is a true Self, the atma, which carries its soul—its memory banks of all self-produced karma—from lifetime to lifetime.

58. Examine how you perceive with your five senses. With ever-increased awareness, see how the ego and non-wisdom function together as a unit.

59. Recognize that what you perceive does not exist as you see it. External objects are not independent of your own consciousness. Neither are they independent of your mind or your emotions.

60. With your advanced meditation practice, examine how outer phenomena appear to exist in the forms that they do. Learn to see how external objects appear to exist independent of your mind without any relationship to your perceptions, senses or the mental/emotional labels you attach to them. They seem to be independent from your existence. But you can never know phenomena independent of the ego's mind, which is part of that experience. Thus, the knowable self-existing phenomena, in this manner, do not exist.

61. All phenomena, outer and inner, are dependent on the various factors of your mind-stuff. Mind observes by desire. It observes by hate, by pride and by a host of other emotions. This afflicts and affects your mind and ego, giving you erroneous answers. In this sense, nothing has independent existence. All is connected with the macro-micro glue of consciousness. In modern terms, this is the morphogenic force-field.

62. What is Truth? The Truth is that internal and external phenomena do not exist independent of your mind. For most people, this concept is extremely difficult to understand, and it has been

poorly and incorrectly discussed in most books that address it.

63. Even your mind does not exist in the way you conceive that it does, because your mind is part of the mechanism of seeing. Do not let your mind become dark and dull. Make it bright, clear, alert and radiant. Illuminate it. Make it calm and tranquil. Make your mind concentrated and unwavering. Intensely examine your mind and the ego-Self that dwells therein.

64. Be aware and watch your emotions as you enter and leave your meditations. Be careful how you handle strong emotions, desires and thoughts. The excessive crushing of a strong emotion or thought can lead to complications, whereas the suppression of stray thoughts can lead to confusion.

65. Learn to transcend the mind processes. Go beyond confusion. Go beyond suppression. Wisely and gently, balance all the energies in your mind. Discipline your mind with a deep and continuous meditative mindset. Be vigilant. Guard against disturbing thoughts and emotional afflictions that cause fantasies. Do not expend your energy uselessly; do not dissipate your energy with the five senses. In this way, your understanding of life will become clearer as you attain pre-conceptional realization, that is, intuition. Move to a state of direct perception so that your mind-stuff does not become part of the process of knowing. With attainment of this state, intuition is born and wisdom is attained. Intuition can arise only after the mind-stuff, the ego-personality, has been balanced. If the mind-stuff becomes a part of the process of knowing, that knowing will be colored or distorted by the emotionality of the mind-stuff.

66. Keep your mind directed toward the recognition of intuition. Hold this awareness in your post-conceptional periods. The clearer the realization of intuition, the weaker the force of non-wisdom.

67. Earthlings consider themselves important. This attitude leads to thinking unskillful thoughts and committing unskillful deeds.

68. In this Kali Yuga, most souls have accumulated much confining karma. They have so many negative imprints on the stream of their consciousness that they have copious karmic debts to repay. They have many lessons to be relearned. They have many things that need to be rebalanced.

69. Awareness that our faults and problems are actually within us is the beginning of the removal of the root cause of non-wisdom.

70. The accumulated karmic debt we owe others can be terminated by intense meditation, by occult means, and by our acceptance of the fruits of those debts.

71. You need to regard the person who appears to be harming you or who appears to be causing you pain and difficulty as a person who has come to free you from the karma that you, yourself, have created and that you, yourself, are manifesting. That person is only the bringer of your karma. If that karma were to manifest later, it would be more difficult to soften because of the added "interest" caused by the karma replicating itself into stronger karmic sub-forces. View that person as a soul coming to free you from that karma. Nonetheless, protect yourself from it and from this person.

72. You have drawn this person into your life. This person is helpless in the face of your powerful karma. Everyone is powerless in the face of another's powerful karma. Constantly remember this person's kindness in showing you that your pain and difficulty are actually the result of your own past unskillful thoughts, attitudes and actions.

73. Realize that your self-cherishing attitude should be removed from your mind. All sentient beings are your true friends. Love them and benefit from them as much as possible. Trying is essential. Helping is an added blessing.

74. All sentient beings desire happiness and wish to avoid pain and suffering. Strive to override their strong confining karma by being a bringer of good karma. Be a bearer of blessings to them. Do everything possible to remove and/or dissolve their limitations and misery so that they can enjoy happiness. Strive to override your own confining karma before it manifests. If a person is bringing you difficult karma that is manifesting, use skillful thought and skillful action to soften it.

75. In a state of advanced meditation, reflect upon the fact that during your countless past-lives, every sentient being you know has been, at one time or another, your mother, father, spouse, lover or your dear friend at least once.

76. Remember their love and caring. Aspire to repay this kindness to each of them. The aspiration to repay the kindness must be generated in the depths of your heart. Generate a strong wish to

replace their suffering and pain with all of the happiness you can conceive.

77. This aspiration should be united with a prayer to your guru, to your Ishta Devata or to the Supreme One that exists in the jewel that lies above the head of God. To accomplish this aspiration, the prayer should be offered again and again. Attain and sustain this accomplishment by sending bliss, happiness and blessings to them at lease twice a day, upon awakening and upon entering sleep.

78. This blessing is sent to them in the form of a visualized radiant light blazing forth from your venus chakra into vast space. At the same time, it should also be blazing forth from your mercury chakra into the ether, where all beings live. This blazing radiant light directed toward the three beings of Light will illuminate all sentient beings and thus fulfill their wishes for happiness.

79. Repeat this technique several times a day in order to transform the lives of those in need and to transform your own thoughts, making them more skillful and effective.

80. Another technique that you can use to generate pure white light is to visualize spiritual light as you exhale. Visualize this spiritual light expanding in all directions throughout the ether, giving peace and happiness to all sentient beings on all planes of existence.

81. These practices may not appear to change anything immediately. Even though they may not appear to change anything external, you will be changed. You will be transformed. You will transform your consciousness and your mind and you will soften your karma. These practices will release all latent positive karma existing within you. People pray to God to change the world, but they have forgotten that the mystical process of meditation and prayer is for one purpose—to change themselves. We meditate to change ourselves.

82. If confining karma that should manifest now does not manifest at this time, it will never ripen. It is over. Appropriate metaphysical motivation in each and every action is the essential art of spiritual unfoldment.

83. In this Kali Yuga, inhabitants in this plane of consciousness are filled with the effects of unskillful past-life actions. Many problems and dangers in this lifetime stem from past-life greed, hatred and aggression. Many of tomorrow's problems and dangers will

stem from today's greed, hatred and aggression. These are the root causes of all pain, suffering and ignorance.

84. Accordingly, the path can be rapidly traversed through the proper use of adverse circumstances. Use these circumstances to help you become stronger, wiser and more aware of your ego personality, other people's egos and the laws of this plane of consciousness. This will assist you in understanding the nature of the universe.

85. Difficult circumstances can be favorable for spiritual unfoldment when you handle them wisely by performing such spiritual practices as self-inquiry and self-discipline. However, these negative circumstances should not be encouraged.

86. Your main spiritual effort should be directed toward softening and removing contrary karma. Remove all difficult circumstances in your everyday life. However, if and when these difficult circumstances do arise, use them as a means for emotional and metaphysical unfoldment. Be aware that the difficulties you are now experiencing have not arisen without cause, nor were they caused by someone else. They are rooted in greed and forgetfulness. In your grasping, you produced forgetfulness. No matter how subtle these difficulties might be, they are rooted in an ego attitude that emotes, causing you to believe that you are the most important being in the universe.

87. Understand that it is this very attitude or viewpoint that has caused us to commit many unskillful thoughts and actions in the past. These unskillful thoughts and actions have created attachments and aversions, which have caused us to experience what we are now reaping.

88. When a person assails you for no apparent reason, do not respond in anger. Do not blame that person. Know that this soul is trying to help you fulfill your karma. This is the fruit of your own past unskillful triple actions. This realization should cause you to become more careful and more skillful, metaphysically. In this way, you will not create any more confining karma for the future.

89. From this experience you should realize that your enemy could be your greatest source of enlightenment.

90. Despite your own difficulties and pain, you should come to understand that many other souls have experienced and are experi-

encing deeper pain and anguish. It is for them that you should unleash the "lightning bolt of goodness and bliss."

91. Karma that you did not deal with wisely in the past does not have to manifest in this lifetime. This karma can and should be neutralized before it manifests. This karma can and should be put off until a later date, if done wisely.

92. It is in your initial response to adverse karmic conditions that you need to practice occult wisdom and enlightenment.

93. Always continue self-analysis on all levels and in all streams of consciousness. If you meditate correctly on these streams of consciousness, you will always be content yet filled with energy. By meditating upon these things, you will attain occult wisdom. You will change the negative circumstances in your everyday life and thus progress on the path. You will purge yourself of all obstacles. You will eliminate the reseeding of unskillful past thoughts and actions and you will accumulate merit.

94. You must be fully prepared at all times. You must fully prepare yourself by gaining a disciplined mind through living a simple, orderly lifestyle, by meditating, and by performing a karma-softening ritual. Four preparations are needed in this area. They must be performed with the strongest and highest of altruistic aspiration. They include:

• The preparation and planning for accumulating merit.
• The preparation for cultivating the awakening of samadhi.
• The preparation for meditating on occult wisdom, and
• The preparation for performing the kriya karma-softening rituals.

95. Perform ritual meditations to the protectors of the path. Do this often. Direct these meditations to your Ishta Devata, to your guru and to the kriya dharma protectors. Always request their blessings and their protection.

96. After you have done this, ask for smooth and rapid progress on the spiritual path. Remind them that your fundamental objective is to attain enlightenment, so that you can benefit other beings more effectively than you are able to at this moment.

Om Shanti

CHAPTER SEVENTEEN
The Spiritual Psychology of Samadhi, Part III

97. It should be your lifetime practice to be well prepared for heavy karma and also to be well prepared for the time of the death of your physical body. This death is the transference of your consciousness from your physical body and from this material plane to your astral body and the astral planes. We will all leave our physical bodily existence. Therefore, remove all external attachments now. In this regard, there are five disciplines that should be practiced throughout your entire lifetime.

Be motivated. Be vigilant. Stop all emotionality as soon as it begins.

Become accustomed to awakening samadhi. Acquaint yourself with it. Always be aware of your elevated goal.

Cultivate the seeds of kriya samadhi that have not yet manifested within.

Destroy the cause of confusion and thus misdirection in your life—which is the veneration and cultivation of the ego self.

Meditate for aspiration and inspiration, in order to skillfully walk the path. See the path clearly. See clearly. Learn from this seeing, in order to help others.

98. Remember that all is caused. Karma is the principle of cause and effect, beyond time and space. The goal is to soften confining karma. The following technique will help you to remove confining karma, gain positive karma and move your consciousness into a higher realm.

Lay your body on its right side. Support your head with your right arm and palm. With your right ring finger, close the right nostril. Center your mind in this mystical pose and practice the hong sau technique. This technique will rapidly move you into the astral worlds, one of the doorways to samadhi. It should be understood that closing off the right nostril activates the ida channel, stimulating the astral worlds. This will produce clearer dream states and, in time, other mystical states.

99. If possible, die without others' tears, sadness and their sense of loss. Forget about what will happen to your body and how others might treat it. It is not important whether they bury your body or cremate it. Far more important is the mindset in which you leave your physical body. You should be in a state of peaceful forgiveness, understanding and contentment. This will allow you to reincarnate with a stronger body and mind and in a more highly evolved form. Consequently, you will have a more advantageous rebirth and in a more advantageous setting.

100. All is cause and effect. All methods and all techniques must be directed toward the expulsion of greed and grasping. In short, you should remove non-wisdom. Non-wisdom means having the ego Self at the center of your life. Instead, place wisdom at the center of your life.

101. If you are not attaining these two goals—the removal of greed and the removal of grasping—in your daily life, there is something wrong with your method or the way you are practicing it, or your lifestyle is not harmonious with your mystical search. If your lifestyle and technique are appropriate and correct, your emotional afflictions will decrease and your outward behavior will improve. Your guru, both internal and external, will become more exacting and demanding.

102. All actions and impulses should move you toward meditation. Everything should move you toward awakening samadhi. This needs to be done with correct lifestyle, meditation, karma-softening methods and contemplation.

103. The kriya dharma is spiritual food. No energy is gained by merely gazing at food. You must ingest and digest it. Digest it with meditation. Integrate it with contemplation. Bring it into your daily life to serve others.

104. You should not need a guru to show you whether or not your spiritual practices are effective because there are definite signs of attainment.

105. If you experience happy, joyous, and blissful feelings even under adverse conditions and situations, this is a sign of attainment. If you manifest a positive change in your attitude toward other sentient beings, this is a sign of attainment. If you realize others are as important as you are, this is a sign of attainment.

106. There are five levels of advancement:

The Great Mind: This refers to the soul who is always dedicated and steadfast in the development and cultivation of awakening samadhi.

The Great Restrainer: This refers to the soul who is always aware of the law of karma. He continually protects himself with self-discipline, which is awareness of awareness and also of the Self. This soul is ever mindful of self-discipline.

The Great Ascetic: This refers to the soul who fearlessly prepares to undergo all difficulties and hardships, in order to remove all limiting karmic inclinations from himself and his environment.

The Great Soul: This refers to the soul whose triple actions of body, speech and mind are always one with the goal of awakening samadhi.

Th*e Great Sage:* This refers to the soul who increases that which has already been awakened. This soul never regresses.

107. Maintain your commitment to your spiritual precepts. Use these precepts as your guide when physically away from the external guru. They will clarify and assist you in your spiritual transformation. They will clarify that which hinders you from further transformation and unfoldment.

108. Understand that all incorrect ideas and concepts reinforce your mind's greed and grasping. In order to remove these negative forces, encourage positive ideas to flow into your consciousness. Cherish and hold onto positive ideas, ideals and spiritual concepts.

109. Work constantly to transform incorrect attitudes and to progressively change your negative motivations. Always strive to blend yourself and your behavior with your environment. Remember that you do not need to prove your spiritual transformation or unfoldment with external habits. Indeed this action is often an indication that you have not progressed very far along the path.

110. Never allow your spiritual transformation to cause the development of any ego emotions such as pride or arrogance.

111. Do not exclude from your practice those techniques that you do not like. Rather, these are the practices I strongly suggest you do.

112. Do not break any spiritual pledge that you have made regarding your transformation, no matter how small it may be. If

you break even the smallest spiritual commitment, you open a door that can allow major commitments to be broken.

113. All souls have emotional imbalances, and thus all souls suffer. Different souls have different afflictions with different time spans and different intensities.

114. The outstanding afflictions of the mind include ignorance, desire, aggression, arrogance, jealousy, attachment, hatred, indifference, pride, greed and subtler greed and still subtler greed. Look within for your major affliction and then strive to balance it. Remember this affliction is within you. You created it, and thus it can only be balanced by you.

115. All mystical techniques are performed to assist in balancing the state of consciousness that is out of balance in a given chakra. Work constantly to awaken samadhi and your intuition. Awaken these for the benefit of all sentient life forms.

116. My guru, Sri Shelliji, often said that we should be lenient, kind and thoughtful regarding the faults of others. However, we should not be lenient toward our own emotional afflictions. It is due to the indulgence in our own afflictions of greed, arrogance and aggression that we remain caught up in the web of non-wisdom.

117. Help others so that they do not get caught up in, or remain in, the negative magnetic force-field of their own mind. Help them:

By not giving anyone more responsibility than he or she can handle.

By not inflicting pain on anyone in order to obtain possessions or to satisfy your own desires.

By not seeking to gain credit for work that has been accomplished. Give the credit to others.

118. All methods and techniques used for destroying negative thought patterns should be integrated with the essentials of thought transformation. Therefore:

• Always keep in mind higher motivations.
• Always respond with loving kindness and compassion.

When strong negative emotions start to develop, recall what you have done in the past. Do not repeat that error. Stop the flow of negative, destructive thoughts. Create and release positive, constructive thoughts.

119. Every morning, plan your spiritual day. Resolve to awaken and cultivate samadhi this very day.

120. At the end of the day, recollect if you have benefited others. If you have, pass the good karma to another worthy soul or to an unworthy soul. In so doing, you break the mind's need to grasp and be greedy. You also transform the good karma that you have given away into merit. If you benefited no one that day, be aware, beware. Be aware so as not to repeat this pattern. Move into the next day with more self-conscious awareness and wisdom. Benefit others. Benefit your environment.

121. Make the following rule your guide: Do not depend on the mundane. Do not depend on others. Do not depend on the world. Become self-dependent.

122. When you meet with misfortune, do not become depressed. Use this experience to learn about your mind, your attitudes, your ego Self and the laws of Life. When you meet with good fortune, remember that all is change. Learn from experience and share good fortune. In either case, learn to awaken your self-awareness and balance it into balanced self-conscious awareness.

123. Refrain from doing unskillful thought, speech and action. Gain knowledge and understanding of your mind, of your world and of the path. Obtain guidance from a guru who will reveal to you the undistorted and total path to freedom.

124. Realize that without right effort all else is meaningless.

125. Experience ever-greater joy in walking the path and in awakening your self-awareness. Have ever-greater reverence toward the teachings.

126. Learn to apply the skills that you have created while in the state of awakening samadhi. Seek opportunities to reinforce the essential concepts of kriya practice.

127. Negative emotions can easily arise within you about those who have done you a favor. This occurs because it is the nature of the mind to direct its emotions against those with whom it has had close contact. It is also the nature of the subconscious mind to feel that a person who has done you a favor is superior. The subconscious mind always attacks authoritarian figures. Be aware. Beware. Correct the imbalances of your own mind.

128. Negative emotions and lack of respect for those with whom you have close contact can easily arise within you. Do not allow this negativity to develop.

129. When in the presence of others, control your tongue. When alone, control your mind.

130. Gain greater awareness, and exercise it. Be ever aware of your emotions and instinctive reactions toward those souls for whom you feel any type of aversion or love. Know that there is karma between you and that person. Do not allow that karma to manifest in an uncontrolled manner.

131. Do not wait for the time when all your needs are satisfied before you begin your spiritual practices. Begin and continue to cultivate awakening samadhi at all times, in all circumstances, in all situations, and under all conditions.

132. Meeting the guru, receiving the teachings, having contact with the path, having the freedom to practice the dharma and having the ability to awaken samadhi: these are all very rare and positive karmic conditions. If you experience them, do not waste time ... do not lose that moment ... do not lose that opportunity!

133. To make progress on the path, be like a steady flowing river. With erratic practice, you will not attain enlightenment. Relate to the path like a young, ardent lover. Relate to the path like a successful business executive. Relate to the path like a true seeker.

134. Do not underestimate your own ability to prompt and stir spiritual unfoldment and thus to be extremely helpful to the universe.

135. Use self-examination and self-reflection to discern which mental afflictions arise most frequently and most strongly. Soften them within yourself. Use awareness, analysis and recall to recognize the physical or mental objects that activate these afflictions.

136. When you benefit others, do so with a celestial and metaphysical attitude. Do not entertain the thought of receiving acknowledgment. Do not expect praise. Do not expect thanks. Do not expect appreciation for what you have done or are trying to accomplish.

137. Remember the goal. The goal is contentment. Remember the goal. The goal is peace of mind. Remember the goal. The goal is to awaken samadhi and to go beyond.

Om Shanti

CHAPTER EIGHTEEN
The Mystical Psychology of the Soul

In this chapter and the next, I will emphasize some of the general principles of Kriya Yoga that are contained in the *Intermediate Guide to Meditation*. I am doing this for two reasons. First, some readers may not have read the book. Second, these principles and concepts are vital for creating a basis for progress in advanced meditation. You will benefit by regularly reflecting on these aphorisms.

1. Kriya Yoga deals directly with the mystical psychology of the soul. Kriya Yoga is the spiritual psychology of the soul.

2. Kriya Yoga living is a methodology by which you learn to remove your karmic limitations.

3. In Kriya Yoga, you begin almost all the techniques by watching the flow of your thoughts and the mind's stream of moods and patterns. At first, you watch for negative daydreams and negative thinking patterns. Later you watch for negative dreams and nightmares. As soon as you see them, stop them immediately. Then reverse them by reliving positive psychological patterns with the replay meditation technique.

4. This watching is done in a state of acute attention and internal reflection, called tarka. After some time, you will become more comfortable doing tarka. With continual practice, you will realize that there is not just a single negative thought pattern but groups of negative thought patterns.

5. When this awareness develops, you need to ask yourself the following essential questions:
   - Why am I thinking these detrimental thoughts?
   - What caused them to manifest within my mind?
   - What was the precipitating cause?
   - Was the precipitating cause primarily external or internal?

6. In determining the precipitating cause, you need to ask yourself whether it was a specific person, a specific object, a specific action, a specific word, a cultural patterning or simply bad training or no training at all.

7. As soon as you become aware of these group thought patterns, ask yourself a few more questions:

• Am I thinking these thoughts because I subconsciously want to punish myself mentally, physically and/or spiritually?

• Am I thinking these thoughts because I want to hurt my mind and/or my body in some way?

• Am I thinking these thoughts because they make me feel brave or because I want people to feel sorry for me?

• Am I thinking these thoughts because I think they make me holier?

8. It is also essential to determine which chakra is the driving astral force of these negative subconscious energies. In order to balance that chakra, do the following:

Override the negative force-field with a stronger positive suggestion. Continue doing this until the positive force is stronger than the negative force within the chakra where the problem exists. (See the technique in the next chapter for this method.)

Redefine any concept linked to the negative force. For example, if you are reckless in your thinking (the actions of the mercury and mars chakras) sooner or later recklessness will occur in your external life. The reason for this reckless thinking may be a subconscious thought pattern equating recklessness with bravery. By redefining your concept of bravery, you can override this negative force-field. You could redefine the word "brave" as a state of positive thinking that enables you to help other people. In this way, your actions can be directed toward more positive goals. When negative thoughts manifest, you can replace them by visualizing yourself helping others.

Mystics point out that these negative thought patterns are very damaging to us because they cause us to become unaware of both our internal and external environments. When we lack awareness, our environment has the ability to control us. Why do these negative thoughts make us unaware of our internal and external environments? Because negative thoughts are emotional thoughts, and emotions distract us from our ability to be focused and perceptive. Meditation brings about self-awareness. This awareness gives us control over our environment and the circumstances within that environment.

In the spiritual psychology of the soul, it is wise to locate the most negative and constricted area of your consciousness. In Kriya

Yoga, you can do this with meditation and intuition while practicing the following technique:

Put a small golden ball of consciousness inside your spine and rotate that ball. Visualize the rotation of that ball of light producing a stream of light. The stream of light first flows upward, inside the spine. It then flows downward, over the back of the spine. Then it ascends again, through the center of the spine.

Next visualize control areas called chakras at specific locations along the spine. Each chakra has a meshing of a different size. These meshes act like fish nets that collect different size thought forms. In observing your stream of light, locate the most negative or constricted chakric force-field. These chakras are indicated in the diagram below.

As you rotate the light up and down the spine using your creative imagination, visualize the chakric areas along the spine and feel if there are any chakras that are warm or cold or that have a resistance to energy flowing through them. With this technique, you are looking for subtle psychological feelings as you visualize the light current flowing around the spine.

Specifically, you are looking for chakras that feel warm or cold. Specifically, you are looking for chakras that seem to resist the flow of energy. This technique is a process for sensitizing the mind so that you can feel these subtle astral force-fields. This technique is repeated three to five times.

If you find that two force-fields (two chakras) are active, work with the chakra that is lower on the spine. Correct and balance that one and then correct and balance the second chakra. This balancing is done by softening the subconscious negative input of this force-field. You do this by overriding any subconscious negative force-field with conscious, stronger, more positive suggestions. By using positive visualizations, negative thoughts become weaker, and in time, they dissolve. This positive visualization pattern neutralizes the active chakra so that it releases only positive thought patterns.

(You can also determine which chakra is most out of balance with symbolic math or by studying your esoteric horoscope.)

9. As you gain control over the psychological flow of your consciousness, you release your limited living, which means two things:

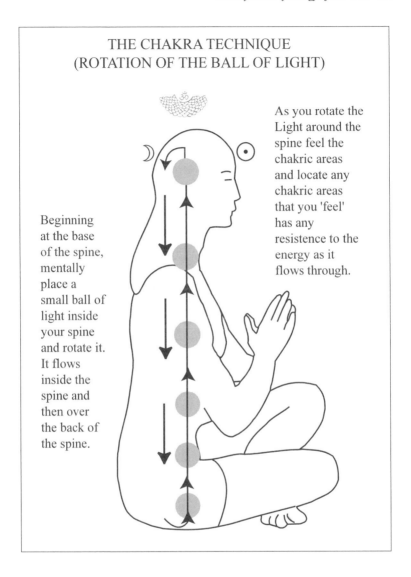

THE CHAKRA TECHNIQUE
(ROTATION OF THE BALL OF LIGHT)

As you rotate the Light around the spine feel the chakric areas and locate any chakric areas that you 'feel' has any resistence to the energy as it flows through.

Beginning at the base of the spine, mentally place a small ball of light inside your spine and rotate it. It flows inside the spine and then over the back of the spine.

• You gain control of your mind's negative thinking patterns.

• You gain control over the imbalanced chakra and the flow of consciousness entering and leaving it.

You can now draw more positive, creative thoughts into your mind, making it relatively easy to create positive circumstances in your life. The secret is not so much learning how to bring these positive events into your life. The secret is learning how to *keep* them in your life.

Sooner or later most of us find love or what we consider to be love. The tragedy is that most of us lose that love shortly after we find it. The force-field of our negative thought patterns releases confining karma from the subconscious mind. The confining karma and our self-serving impulses from the subconscious mind negate the very goal we value. Thus, our dreams tend to disintegrate because of the force of our subconscious negative thought patterns. Consequently, it becomes difficult to sustain our goals with harmony, and that which is not harmonious will die.

10. The process of keeping the good things in your life is very simple. One of the best ways of doing this is to practice the replay meditation technique. Several times each day, for a very short time, go into meditation and be aware of your negative thought patterns. Spend more time visualizing the opposite positive forces. Do this in a quiet, unemotional, relaxed manner.

Repeat this over and over again until the negative forces dissolve. For a few minutes each day, visualize positive thoughts and feelings in the areas where the negative forces once were. Through the repetition of this technique, you will be able to hold onto the positive psychological forces. Soon they will become automatic, positive habits. In time, this will bring into your life people and events that will be more positive and satisfying.

The secret is to stop the stream of consciousness each time your mind thinks a negative thought and to back it up and replay a more positive version. Then replay it again, making it even more positive. Feed positive thoughts into the chakra that is causing the negative thoughts to arise. It is as simple as that.

An example might be helpful. Let us say that your daydream reveals that you wish to be a hero. You daydream of a young girl walking into the street with a car rushing toward her. You wish to save her so you run into the street and push her to safety. However, in the daydream, the car hits you. You feel this makes you a hero. Some people would consider this act of heroism to be great, but it is actually a very self-destructive thought pattern. Therefore, stop this flow of negative thinking by replaying and reversing the daydream. Visualize once again the young girl running into the street and see yourself rushing to save her. This time, though, do not visualize being hit by the car. Next replay the daydream again but on a higher level. It is vital to recognize that the daydream is revealing that you want to be hero. Replay and lift the daydream to a level that will elevate your mind and value system. You could visualize the young girl trying to solve a problem. You know the answer to her problem and you give it to her. Thus, you become a hero.

The purpose of this exercise is to remove all self-destructiveness by redefining the key words in your emotional vocabulary. In this case, the word is "hero." Your original concept of a hero was defined as someone being hurt or dying in the place of another being hurt or dying. You have now elevated your definition of hero from someone being hurt or dying to someone who has the answer to a problem. Replay the daydream again, but this time replace the girl with all of mankind and give everyone the solution to their pain and suffering. Then you become a superhero in a far more positive way.

After you have replayed the daydream in a more positive way, return to the thought that triggered the idea of the young girl running into the street. You want to remove this triggering thought. If you cannot grab hold of the triggering thought, try to see which chakras are involved. The venus chakra contains the symbol of young girls as well as many other symbols of beauty. The mars chakra contains the symbol of cars. Thus, you would send positive thoughts to the venus chakra, but because the mars chakra is lower on the spine, you would send energy to the mars chakra first. As you practice this technique, be aware of other new thoughts and emotions that are manifesting in your mars and venus chakras, and take the proper psychological action.

In the evening, when you perform your nightly tarka, ask yourself this question, "Why did I think that negative thought? Why did I not daydream the thought of lying on a beach in sunny Hawaii?"

I am sure you realize that in and of itself, one such reversal of a negative thinking pattern is basically meaningless. These negative thought patterns must be removed again and again, and the positive thinking patterns must be repeated again and again until the subconscious mind establishes a new and positive patterning. This will bring about powerful self-improvement.

THE SIX STAGES OF SELF-IMPROVEMENT

There are six stages to self-improvement with meditative awareness. These are as follows:

Stage One is the awareness that you can only improve your life by improving your karma. To do this, you must remove greed and all negative thought patterns that lead to greed. As you improve yourself, you will improve Life. In this stage, there is also the realization that to improve your karma, you need to soften your negative thought patterns. You must work to remove anger, greed and boredom. By removing all negative thought patterns and replacing them with positive ones, you keep negative karma from activating strongly.

Stage Two is the realization that to open your karmic sphere, you need to remove jealousy. Replace jealous thoughts with positive thought patterns and remove all thought patterns that lead to jealousy. It does not take much reflection to realize that jealousy is a reaction to greed. It may be very subtle greed, but it is greed nonetheless. Jealousy tends to develop in the following ways:

• When a strong craving or desire is not fulfilled when you feel it should be.

• When a strong craving or desire is not fulfilled to the degree that you feel it should be.

• When you see other people with things you desire.

• When you remember seeing other people with the things you desire.

In relation to your earth life, these inner experiences may be inconsequential. However, in relation to your psychological stream of consciousness, they are negative forces that need to be balanced. You need to break into the astral world by renouncing your attachment to earth consciousness. Later, as you evolve, you need to break into the causal world by renouncing your attachment to astral consciousness.

By reflecting on anger and jealousy, you will soon understand that anger is a reaction to fear and that it is based on fear. Thus,

Stage Three is the elimination of fear and all the negative thoughts that cause your mind to create fear. This especially includes the removal of the fear of the unknown.

If you lack something but know that in the near future you will obtain it, there will be little or no fear regarding that lack. However, not knowing what tomorrow will bring can create fear of the unknown. You might think, "Perchance I will never have it. Or perchance I will lose what I already have." This type of thinking produces fear.

Reflect actively on the concept of fear, as well as on the manifestation of your own fears. Understand that fear manifests from many levels of consciousness, from many subconscious patterns and imbalances in the astral plane. In the astral consciousness, there exist archetypal symbols that form patterns and affect earth consciousness and thus earth events.

We need to examine the causes of our fears no matter how subtle they are. We need to reflect on the most effective way to soften these negative forces and then remove them. Remove fear.

Stage Four is gaining happiness by moving into the higher astral realms and learning the laws of correspondence, which relate inner consciousness to external events. You need to learn these laws of correspondence in order to master your awareness and your life. Some people refer to this as the law of happiness, the law of joy, the law of contentment.

The word "happiness" does not mean doing what you want to do when you want to do it, nor the titillation of the senses. Some people refer to happiness as joy, whereas others call it contentment or bliss. You gain happiness by moving into the higher astral planes and learning the laws of self-conscious awareness, and thus becoming better able to master your inner life. Any type of fear constricts consciousness, whereas happiness only expands it.

Stage Five is attaining a meditative state that expands your consciousness. This expansion of consciousness allows you to enter into the causal planes that exist just above the astral plane. In these higher planes, you are able to gain even greater control over your earth life.

Stage Six is the process of moving from intermediate meditation to advanced meditation. Here you gain a masterful level of control with which you can bring your awareness into self-awareness. From this stage, you bring self-awareness into balanced self-awareness. Then you move into expanded consciousness.

In *Stage Seven*, you need to learn to die mystically. To die mystically means to die consciously and expansively. It means the ability to consciously take your consciousness out of your physical body and move out into the higher planes unembodied. This is the primary goal of mysticism for all earthlings.

Emotions lock us into earth consciousness. They lock us into physical body consciousness. Our fears and negative emotions stop us from expanding our consciousness. Without expansion of consciousness, it is impossible to become aware of the true Self.

Strive daily to do the great work, which is to die consciously and expansively. With advanced meditation, continue to die mystically and to ascend. Practice this until the technique of dying consciously becomes an automatic daily habit. Then when it is the time for the natural death of your physical body, you will be able to manifest a state of consciousness called *maha-samadhi*. You will immediately move into your astral body and continue your life without interruption. There will be no death for you, because in mysticism the word "death" means to become unconscious.

When the physical body of the average human being is about to die, that person tends to experience fear, guilt and regret. These forces constrict consciousness and cause the person to become unconscious. You can see why it is essential to remove these emotions beforehand.

Mastering the mystical technique of dying consciously is not that difficult. It does, however, require continual effort to become emotionally mature and to deepen meditation each and every day. Some of the mystical side effects of this practice include:

• The ability to reincarnate in a shorter period of time, speeding up your evolutionary process.

• The ability to return to the earth life with a less constrictive life pattern.

• The ability to return to the earth life with a higher soul vibration.

• The ability not to return to the earth but to migrate to a higher plane if one so wishes.

• The ability to go to another universe.

• The ability, here and now, to soften your personal karma. This is most important.

In short, because one is conscious at a deeper level, there is greater control over most personal future events.

You need to do everything you can to remove all emotionality. You especially need to root out fear. In this way, you can overcome the fear of the unknown and the fear of death. Thus, you can overcome constricted consciousness, which produces unconsciousness. With expanded consciousness, you can continually remove negative thinking patterns. You can then soften karma and improve your life here and now, as well as in the future.

We need to face the fact that at some time, we will lose our physical body. For some people this is not a problem. However, most people consider losing their ego personality very important. This is their major fear. The elimination of this fear is essential.

The fear of death and the fear of the unknown are two key fears that the mystic needs to overcome. If we cannot overcome our smaller fears, how will we be able to address these larger fears? We begin this process with the ancient technique of forgiveness.

Most earthlings die as the result of sickness. This sickness may be physical, but in most cases it is brought on by a negative mental attitude. Thus, in the practice of advanced meditation, you need to correct your past negative actions and learn to live wisely, skillfully and positively in the present. You need to remove all negativity that remains in your mind, allowing past negative karmic impulses to impact you.

Do everything you can to remove the negative forces of fear and guilt. Learn to forgive your mind and body.

Om Shanti

CHAPTER NINETEEN
Balancing the Unbalanced Chakra

Hopefully, you have practiced some of the techniques given in this advanced meditation text and are now ready to perform one of the major kriya ritual meditations for evolving into higher stages of unfoldment. This technique consists of becoming aware of the contents of your stream of consciousness.

1. For just two or three minutes each day, go into a state of reflection. Reflect on your life and write down the major difficulties that you have had. Begin with today and go backward as far as you can remember. For most people, this will be to around the age of three to five.

2. Next list only major problems that you have experienced directly or indirectly. Think about these events for some time. Then group these stressful experiences based on common denominators. Usually, there are five major categories, each linked to a specific chakra:

• Group 1 contains problems relating to communication, work and travel.

• Group 2 contains problems relating to money, love and partnerships.

• Group 3 contains problems relating to hate, anger, jealousy and health.

• Group 4 contains problems relating to knowledge, religion and foreign cultures.

• Group 5 contains problems relating to delays, confinements, fear and friends.

You will notice that in this system there are only five levels of chakric awareness, the five chakras existing below the sun-moon level of consciousness.

3. Examine these five groups and determine which ones have been most repeated or most critical in your life. Categorize your experiences into one of these five groups by reflecting on the types of experiences and types of daydreams you have had.

4. Link the key group of problems with its associated chakra and its area of influence in your life.

5. Enter deep meditation and symbolically pull out all of the energy from your arms and legs, placing the energy into the trunk of your body. Then take the energy from the trunk of your body and move it into your spine. Next take all of this energy and move it up your spine, holding it at the ajna chakra.

6. Simply watch the breath for a few moments. Then move your consciousness over the top of your head and down over your back. As you do this, stop at the chakric area that symbolically contains the imbalanced energy relating to the key group of problems in your past. Gently inhale fully and hold your breath and consciousness at this chakric area of imbalance for three seconds. Now release your breath through the open mouth gently but robustly.

7. Drop your mind to the base of the spine and, as you slowly inhale through the nose, slowly begin to lift your mind upward inside the spine. Stop the breath as you reach the key problem chakra. Hold your mind in this chakra for three seconds.

Listed below are the associated chakras and the chakric sounds used in this technique:

LOWER CHAKRAS – MANTRIC SOUNDS

		Non-Kriya Sound System			Kriya Sound System
Group 1	aaa	"a" as in "anna"	ga	"a" as in "aha"
Group 2	eee	"e" as in "me"	bha	"a" as in "aha"
Group 3	i	"i" as in "it"	mo	"mo" as in "oh"
Group 4	o	"o" as in "mow"	naw	"na" as in "not"
Group 5	u	"u" as in "you"	om	"o" as in "home"

8. Exhale the entire breath through your nasal passages. Do this as slowly and quietly as possible. As you exhale, mentally chant the proper mantra for that chakra. Chant the mantra only once. The mantric sound should last as long as you are exhaling. If it takes ten seconds to exhale, mentally chant the mantric sound for ten seconds. If it takes 25 seconds to exhale, the mantric sound

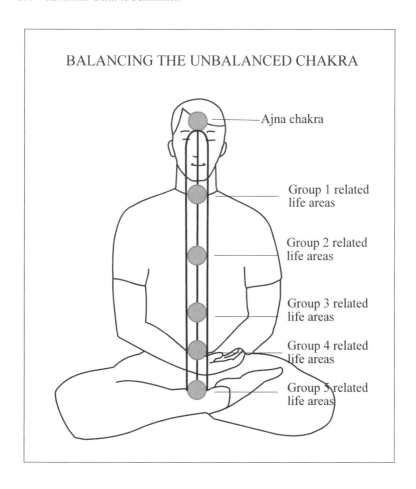

BALANCING THE UNBALANCED CHAKRA

— Ajna chakra

Group 1 related
life areas

Group 2 related
life areas

Group 3 related
life areas

Group 4 related
life areas

Group 5 related
life areas

should be extended for 25 seconds. This is the total mystical technique.

Now it might be helpful to sit in a quiet meditative state for a few minutes and reflect on the above thoughts.

Om Shanti

CHAPTER TWENTY
Sickness and Death

No advanced text of meditation would be complete if it did not address sickness, death and rebirth.

What happens when a person dies of a sickness? That soul goes into the fifth plane of the astral world and into its third sub-plane. This soul finds itself lying on a bed-like platform in the room of exaltation, which is an astral hospital. (In truth, the soul is suspended about three and a half feet above the ground.) Around the bed are always three beings of Light. One glows yellow. One burns green. One flames red. Occasionally other beings of Light come into the room. They are of different colors—silver, purple, etc. Rarely does a being of white Light ever enter into this room. There are never more then five beings of Light in the room at any one time.

These beings stand around the bed observing and gazing steadily at the departed soul, still encased in its denser and encrusted astral body. After gazing at the astral body for some time, minuscule sparks are emitted from their three "bodies." Later, lights flow out of their bodies and down over the astral spine of the departed soul. Still later, these lights flow into the center of the astral spine of the disincarnated humanoid and enflame that person's astral spine. This causes the soul to be vivified. Thus a few things manifest:

The darker spots in the dull astral body shrink in size and become lighter in color. Finally they disappear.

After this happens, the astral body becomes more brilliant. Then a brilliant flash of light is seen. The aura and the astral body begin to glow.

After these colored lights enflame the astral body, it begins to look much like the physical body just before death.

The astral body slowly begins to transform into a younger body. The aged astral body slowly begins to regress to an age when the person was happiest on earth; it takes on the form it was at that time. For most people, this is between the ages of 16 to 23 years.

I relate this from personal astral experiences that I had many decades ago. It is interesting to note that in my latest astral experiences, the age of greatest happiness for most people was much younger. And many modern souls are finding it almost impossible to find or locate a period of happiness.

On the average, this process of transformation and rejuvenation takes from 549 to 3,652 astral years. The length of time spent in the room of exaltation depends on the seriousness of the physical and/or mental sickness. Physical sickness is easier to cure than mental sickness.

When the astral body becomes revivified, it leaves the room of exaltation and moves out into a meadow. It wanders happily or just sits in that meadow for some time. When the soul is ready, it begins its reincarnation to the earth. The astral body moves into the cosmic theater to activate the desire force that will form its new physical body.

Om Shanti

CHAPTER TWENTY-ONE
Death, Dying and Rebirth

In the last chapter, we discussed what happens after a person's physical body dies. In this chapter, I would like to discuss the reincarnation process.

That which survives physical death is known as the mind-stuff, the *chitta*. It resides in the astral body. Whatever survives astral death is known as bliss, *ananda*. It resides in the causal body. We have three bodies: the physical, the astral and the causal. These are often called the dense body, the subtle body and the super-subtle body. Over and above these three bodies, we have five sheaths: the food sheath, the energy sheath, the mind sheath, the knowledge sheath and the bliss sheath.

At the time of death, the mind-stuff, which generally resides more in the astral body than in the physical body, pulls itself completely out of the physical body and enters into its astral vehicle. This mind-stuff contains within itself its own karmic seeds. Because of the power of these karmic seeds, the mind-stuff can and does project itself into a specific given form: a subtle body called the astral body. The astral body is primarily a temporary body. Although it is temporary compared to the time span of the physical body, it can be considered immortal.

The form that the astral body takes is limited by the karmic seeds within the mind-stuff of the person. These seeds give a particular form to the freed astral body, and thus to forming the new physical body that will be reincarnated back to earth.

It is with the forces of this astral body working in the astral plane that any and all processes of transformation ultimately occur on the physical plane. When the student is ready, it is the responsibility of the guru to give that student the knowledge and the techniques needed so he can use the spiritual tools of transformation in his state of advanced meditation. This kriya training requires that:

- The student learns self-discipline.
- The student learns to stabilize his or her everyday mind.
- The student learns to meditate.

• The student learns to enter into advanced meditation.

• The student learns to pull the mind-stuff out of his physical body while in this advanced meditation and while remaining conscious.

• The student learns to put the mind-stuff into his astral body.

• The student learns to move and explore the macrocosm while in this astral body. (This process is called *kriya projection*. When this kriya projection is performed the last time at the death of the physical body, it is called *maha-samadhi*).

The goal of any kriya technique is to attain greater awareness, greater self-awareness, greater balanced self-awareness, and thus a greater horizon of awareness. The benefits and the blessings are many: happiness, peace of mind, wisdom, compassion and unselfish love. These spring from understanding what Life is all about and your place in Life.

The attainment of kriya projection will remove all your fears regarding death and dying. It will remove the assault of anxiety in your last hours on earth. It gives the more advanced student the power to soften karma and to improve karma for himself and for others.

It is by peacefully making the transition from one plane of consciousness to another that you become mentally and spiritually prepared to see through the open door. Thus, you can quickly, easily, and safely pass through it into a pristine, bright, new, eternal life.

During advanced kriya meditation, the forces of your physical body are redissolved. This is not the redissolving of the physical body; it is the redissolving of the *forces* of your physical body.

It is during advanced kriya meditation that you can glimpse images of the negative forces that were in control during your careless and/or thoughtless years. Today in your advanced meditation, you reap the fruits of your mature and responsible years. All of this leads to finding a more auspicious path. It leads to a rebirth into this earth life on a higher plane of existence. This new incarnation will definitely have far superior circumstances—physically, mentally, and spiritually.

These karmic forces refashion the awareness of your astral body before it descends into the material plane. This gives your next incarnation a very positive, specific rebirth pattern. This rebirth pattern is only potential and does not have to manifest. However, for 97 to 99 percent of all souls, it does.

Of greater importance in this present incarnation is the realization and awareness that each and every time you come out of your advanced kriya meditation, you are reborn. Yes, each time you come out of your advanced kriya meditation, you will have caused your astral body to be reborn with less karmic limitation.

This "new you" may not be much of a change at first. However, it will be a movement in the right direction. Moreover, these changes that have taken place are seeds for unfoldment in the external world. These seeds are organic. Everyday in every way, they will spiritually mature and produce a divine garden of wisdom, compassion and happiness.

By the time your physical body is ready to die, these seeds will have produced a full garden of God-consciousness for you to enter into while you rest and refresh yourself. Over and above this, you will bring that garden of God, for the benefit of others, back down into this life when you return.

In short, you will come out of your kriya meditation as a new you. This new you will bring with it new and more marvelous states of consciousness that will manifest externally as unconfined events.

The laws of consciousness and their corresponding techniques are to be learned and used in your everyday life. No matter what type of body you inhabit (causal, astral, or physical), the present moment is the only moment to improve your present condition. Improve yourself now, during this day, during this hour. As you improve this moment, you improve tomorrow—not only for yourself but for those around you.

OM TAT SAT OM.

CHAPTER TWENTY-TWO
Conclusion

We have come to the end of our meditation journey. At this point, I send you my deepest Shanti. May your journey continue to be fruitful.

Stop judging. See correctly. Stop judging. Hone and discipline your mind. Seek deeper levels of awareness and deeper levels of joy. Remember that meditation is something that begins inward and remains inward. Meditation becomes automatic as you practice it daily. It brings a new creative enthusiasm for life. It brings a new zest for life. It brings new joy to life. It brings a new life.

The art of meditation helps you to accept yourself and therefore to accept others. Meditation helps you to accept Life as it is. You begin to see things as they really are, and you begin to understand the difference between seeing things as they are and seeing them colored by your ego thoughts. Meditation helps you to express yourself more easily and more fully in a harmonious way.

The major problem with the world is its people. Most of them grow old, but they do not grow up. They grow old at a very young age. They grow old because their dreams have been blocked. Thus, their fantasies become more negative, and they become more out of balance and more self-deprecating.

We fail to recognize that the battle we are fighting is a battle with our internal world and not with the external world. In our frustration and ignorance, we turn outward—blaming our mother, our father, our spouse, our children—blaming anyone. Some people even blame God. It seems that they need to blame something external. If we do not blame others, we will have to think the unbearable: that we ourselves are imperfect. We do not seem to know that in this wondrous, imperfect world, only wondrous, imperfect souls exist. Nonetheless, each of us is and must be accountable for our own actions.

It is my meditation and my hope that you do not blame others. It is my meditation and my hope that you do not blame yourself. I hope that this text reveals to you that which is blocking your dreams—the undisciplined and unhoned mind. It is my meditation that your meditation will remove your limitations.

You now have a great tool not only for spiritual success but also for earth life success. It is a great tool for attaining happiness. It can be used to improve your creativity, and with this, you can solve your life problems. You can even help others. It is a great tool for gaining confidence. All that remains is for you to use this tool. Practice your meditation daily.

We talked about meditation and its relationship to restructuring one's personality. Sooner or later we must understand that there are times when our personality needs to be made smoother, stronger and more flexible. At these times, our personality needs to be harmoniously disciplined with the gentle joys of meditation.

Modern psychology is concerned with the contents of the mind. It is concerned with why and how these contents were incorrectly placed within the personality. Some psychologies are concerned with how to rearrange these contents so that there is less strain and stress. As mystics, however, you and I are primarily concerned with consciousness, and secondarily, with the *content* of consciousness. It is consciousness and the laws of consciousness that produce thoughts, things and events.

I conclude this section by reminding you that

> *Yesterday is but a memory, and*
> *Tomorrow is but a hope.*
> *However, today is the "Eternal Now"*
> *In which all happens.*

Let go of all of your apprehensive and fearful hopes for tomorrow. Find joy now! Find happiness now! Sail on! Sail on and continue your exalted journey into the Eternal Now. Continue your journey with wisdom, peace, joy and harmony.

Know well that you are not alone. Daily, throughout the worlds, great Shanti sages send forth to you and all sentient beings the following meditative affirmation:

"Oh, Great Spirit, thou knowest better than I that which they need. Send that unto them now! Sent it to them swiftly, surely, and most, most harmoniously! Om Shanti, Shanti, Shanti."

What else can I say? Consume not Life and be not consumed by Life! Find within yourself noble thoughts. See those noble thoughts flowing to you from every side. Share those noble thoughts with your heart. Share them with your mind and soul so that you may become happy *now!* Share noble thoughts with everyone so they might become happy *now.*

Seek and find peace, tranquility and serenity. Seek them in your daily meditation. Seek them in your everyday activity. Seek now. Be happy now. Be wise now ... by being content now!

In short, *seek out your own enlightenment now with great diligence!*

Shanti, My Beloved.

INDEX

Learn Astrology....
The Language of the Soul

Goswami Kriyananda offers books and home study courses that explore Astrology from both the practical and spiritual levels. By understanding Astrology and learning to read charts, you can help yourself and others. Through Astrology you can learn the art of timing events--when and when not to begin them. Astrology is one of the finest tools for life-guidance and skillful living. By learning Astrology you can gain greater contol of your life.

Beginner's Guide to Natal Astrology
Home Study Program
Four audiotapes and an 84-page notebook

Learn the fascinating science of Natal Astrology. "Natal Astrology is the science and the key to character." To understand a person's character is to understand his destiny. This introductory Astrology program by Goswami Kriyananda takes you through the fundamentals of understanding and interpreting the natal chart. It includes lessons in the signs, houses, planets, aspects, and then how to blend these to meaningfully interpret any chart including your own.

This home study course includes four 60-minute audiotapes accompanied by an 84-page notebook which supports the tapes. It includes a set of flashcards, study guides, and study questions.

$49. (One-half of the cost of this program can later be applied to the Practicing Astrologer Course.)

Wisdom and Way of Astrology (Book)

Astrology is the language of the soul, a doorway to Self-Revelation. In this book, Goswami Kriyananda returns Astrology to its primary role as the mother science of the spiritual search. It is the science of proper timing, a tool for personal transformation, and a method for understanding oneself and the world.

The clear and understandable presentation of the signs, planets, houses, aspects and philosophy of chart interpretation makes this an excellent study guide for the beginner. It also includes an abundance of deeper mystical information for the more advanced astrologer. (*The Wisdom and Way of Astrology* is included free with the Practicing Astrologer Course.)

8-1/2 X 5-1/2, perfectbound, 420 pages....$17.95

TO ORDER:
Outside Illinois: (800) 248-0024 - Inside Illinois (773) 342-4600
www.yogakriya.org -- E-mail: kriya@yogakriya.org

In Just 14 Months You Can Become A
PRACTICING ASTROLOGER

Through the study and practice of Astrology you can reap innumerable benefits in your life socially, financially and spiritually. Astrology reveals where your strengths and weaknesses exist, and how to use them so they work for you. Astrology affirms your ability to use free will and thus helps you to more comfortably manage your life-patterns. It helps you to recognize ways for achieving greater success and happiness in your life and how to share these with others.

Whether you are new to Astrology or have studied it for years, our extensive at-home course can provide you with the special knowledge, training and understanding needed to practice Astrology professionally. Learn how to give astrological readings with depth and skill! In this 14-month all encompassing program, Goswami Kriyananda begins with a thorough study of the basics of Astrology, and then continues with how to interpret a chart. He includes esoteric studies and gives you all the information needed to start your own practice.

The Practicing Astrologer program includes extensive study of the signs, houses, aspects, natal astrology, transits, progressions, spiritual and past-life astrology, and more. Goswami Kriyananda puts into this course the best of his 50+ years of teaching and counseling in Astrology. He blends simplicity with depth.

The complete course includes more than 120 audiotapes (60-90 minutes in length), and three large volumes of printed astrology lessons which support these tapes, including study guides and transcripts. It also includes flashcards, self-help tests, and other essential books and information necessary to construct a chart and delineate it. We even provide the pencils and pens! It also includes a free copy of Goswami Kriyananda's 420-page classic text: *The Wisdom and Way of Astrology*.

The Practicing Astrologer home study program is divided into 3 individual parts at $595 each. (Or it can be purchased in its entirety for $1395 which includes a $400 discount). To order this all-encompassing program, complete and mail the order form on the last page, or write or call the Temple for more information:

Outside Illinois: (800) 248-0024 - Inside Illinois (773) 342-4600
www.yogakriya.org -- E-mail: kriya@yogakriya.org

Book Releases
by Goswami Kriyananda

The Laws of Karma:
Deeper Insight to the Esoteric Teachings of Kriya Yoga
Goswami Kriyananda's text on karma clearly and simply explains the laws of cause and effect. This unique book contains many yogic techniques used throughout the ages to remove pain and suffering. It is a must for all who wish to move toward greater happiness in life.
8-1/2 X 5-1/2 , perfectbound, 183 pages. ... $14.95

Intermediate Guide to Meditation
This book is a companion to Goswami Kriyananda's classic text, "Beginner's Guide to Meditation." It provides deep insights and techniques to expand your awareness and bring greater harmony and balance into your life through meditation practice. It is an easy to read text, excellent for the novice and advanced practitioner. *5-1-2 X 8-1/2, perfectbound, 145 pages ... $13.95*

A Yoga Dictionary of Basic Sanskrit Terms
In this book, Goswami Kriyananda has taken a further step to include some major English mystical terms. He feels this basic dictionary will help the student of Yoga gain a deeper understanding of many Sanskrit terms, meeting the needs of the contemporary student, and being helpful to the general reader of yoga literature. He has taken the liberty of dividing the Sanskrit terms to make it easier for the student to pronounce them. *5-1/2 X 8-1/2, perfectbound, 112 pages ... $8.95*

A Dictionary of Basic Astrological Terms
In this dictionary, Goswami Kriyananda has included the most basic astrological terms that will help the beginning or intermediate student gain a deeper insight into astrology. This book is a superb reference work. It is easy to read and one you should keep with you throughout your astrological studies. Goswami Kriyananda has taken complex astrological terms, not only simplifying them for easier understanding, but also adding deeper insight into their meaning.
5-1/2 X 8-1/2, perfectbound, 91 pages ... $8.95

Pathway to God-Consciousness
Goswami Kriyananda first wrote Pathway to God-Consciousness as a home study course for his disciples living far from his ashram. It is composed of 16 lessons or chapters, each with self-help questions, and reveals much of the esoteric science of Kriya Yoga. It gives guidelines and Yogic techniques for the fundamentals of the mystical search: the evolution from Awareness to God-Consciousness or Balanced Self-Awareness. *5-1/2 X 8-1/2, perfectbound, 130 pages ... $9.95*

TO ORDER:
Outside Illinois: (800) 248-0024 - Inside Illinois (773) 342-4600
www.yogakriya.org -- E-mail: kriya@yogakriya.org
SEE ORDER FORM ON BACK PAGE

Meditation

Books and Audiotapes by Goswami Kriyananda

The benefits of meditation are endless....Many of today's health and medical centers are suggesting meditation as a means to regain the ability to concentrate and reduce stress. Learn to improve your health and well-being, restore lost energies, and attain inner peace through meditation practice.

◆ Beginner's Guide to Meditation (Book)

This is Goswami Kriyananda's classic text on how, when and why to meditate. It is simple and clear and gives you a variety of meditation techniques to begin your own individual practice. It contains simple stories and analogies to bring ease and enjoyment to learning and practice. This book is an inspirational way to learn the joys and benefits of meditation. *5-1/2 X 8-1/2, perfectbound, 112 pages ... $13.95*

◆ Beginner's Guide to Meditation - A Talking Book

(Audiotapes and book) This talking book gives you the opportunity to listen to Goswami Kriyananda's recording of his classic text, *Beginner's Guide to Meditation*. It gives you the option to hear Goswami Kriyananda's voice as he teaches you a variety of simple and gentle meditation techniques. *Four 90-minute audiotapes (also includes the book). Introductory Offer ... $29.95*

◆ Beginner's Guide to Meditation - Book and 2-Audiotape Program

This program gives you the *Beginner's Guide to Meditation* book and two audio tapes: *Meditation Techniques for Inner Peace* which contains five classical meditation techniques, and *Corridors of Stillness*, a gentle 30-minute guided meditation (recorded on both sides of the tapes). *Two 60-minute audiotapes and the book ... $24.95*

◆ Intermediate Guide to Meditation (Book)

A continuation of *Beginner's Guide to Meditation*. This book includes added techniques and helps you train the mind to move from limited conceptualized thinking and negative emotions to more expanded awareness. It opens up practice to the deeper levels of inturning and meditation practice.
5-1/2 X 8-1/2 paperback, 151 pages ... $13.95

TO ORDER:
Outside Illinois: (800) 248-0024 - Inside Illinois (773) 342-4600
www.yogakriya.org -- E-mail: kriya@yogakriya.org
SEE ORDER FORM ON BACK PAGE

 **SEMINARS ON AUDIOTAPE**

Karma, Causation and the Laws of Balance

The law of karma is the law of balance. Join Goswami Kriyananda as he shares his insights into a doctrine whose roots lie in antiquity. Gain a clearer understanding of your unconscious mental patterns. Master the deep-seated conditioning of your past. This program includes four 90-minute audio tapes along with Goswami Kriyananda's 183 page text: *The Laws of Karma: Deeper Insight to the Esoteric Teachings of Kriya Yoga.*

Highlights of the course include:

♦ The three types of karma
♦ Why your karma is the way it is
♦ Techniques to soften and dissolve karma
♦ Historical development of the theory of karma

This seminar is an opportunity to enrich your future by transforming your past.

Four 90-minute audiotapes and book ... $54.95

Dreams, Your Magic Mirror

Dreams reveal your future and illuminate your past. Dream symbols are the language of the soul, the means of communication between your subconscious, conscious and superconscious minds. In this seminar, Goswami Kriyananda reveals the deeper significance and function of your dreams.

Learn how to:

♦ Increase your dream awareness
♦ Understand the language of dreams
♦ Improve your life by improving your dreams
♦ Interpret dream symbols
♦ Keep a dream journal
♦ Develop conscious dreaming

To understand your dreams is to understand yourself. To master your dreams is to hold the key to personal transformation.
Three 90-minute audiotapes ... $39.95

TO ORDER CALL:
Outside Illinois: (800) 248-0024 · Inside Illinois: (773) 342-4600
www.yogakriya.org ·· E-mail: kriya@yogakriya.org

SEMINARS ON AUDIOTAPE

The Chakras and Energy Transformation

Your chakras are energy converters which are unconsciously activating and controlling your body and mind. Goswami Kriyananda discusses the esoteric functions of the chakras and their activities, revealing techniques for utilizing and balancing chakric energy.

In this seminar you will discover:

♦ The anatomy of the chakric system
♦ The three worlds
♦ The dynamics of energy transformation
♦ The modifying principle of self-awareness

Learn to utilize the forces of your self-conscious awareness to speed up your spiritual unfoldment, soften your karma, and open hidden areas of your conciousnes

Three 90-minute audiotapes ... $39.95

Self-Improvement thru Self-Hypnosis

Self-hypnosis is a tool for releasing the creativity and hidden potential of your mind. Goswami Kriyananda will teach you safe and simple techniques designed to utilize the power of your mind to bring about permanent, positive changes in your life.

In this seminar you will learn how to:

♦ Remove unresolved conflicts
♦ Overcome self-imposed obstacles
♦ Eliminate negative habits
♦ Attain a deep, peaceful sleep state
♦ Gain self-knowledge to improve your life
♦ Increase your mind power
♦ Improve your attitudes and moods
♦ Overcome negative emotions

Through this seminar, you can learn to reprogram the negative mental patterns that block the fulfillment of your most cherished goals.

Four 90-minute audiotapes ... $54.95 (includes an accompanying 25-page booklet on self-hypnosis). **SEE ORDER FORM ON BACK PAGE**

The Awakening of Your Serpent Power

Learn the concepts and obstacles to awakening the Kriya Kundalini Fire.

In this seminar Goswami Kriyananda answers such questions as: What is the Kriya-Kundalini? What does awakening the Kundalini mean? What should one know about Kundalini awakening? How does one know when the Kundalini has awakened?

This long-awaited seminar reveals the secrets associated with awakening your serpent power so that you can speed up your evolutionary unfoldment. Goswami Kriyananda discusses the methods, means and concepts dealing with the sacred art of wisely and sanely awakening and directing the Kriya-Kundalini. He explores the use and procedures for using the Kriya-Kundalini to neutralize negative pieces of karma and to help soften blockages so that you can move to higher transformative states. He also discusses the common misconceptions about the Kundalini and how these need to be overcome through higher spiritual knowledge.

Other Highlights of this program include:

- ♦ How to measure the Kundalini release
- ♦ Positive effects of Kundalini awakening
- ♦ The blessings of Yoga-siddhi; the dangers of Yoga siddhi
- ♦ The proper utilization of a sacred mantra
- ♦ The conversion of Kriya to Kundalini

Three 90-minute audiotapes $39

An Overview of the Kundalini Upanishad

Includes 3 Audiotapes and a 37-page Notebook

Includes 3 Audiotapes and a 37-page Study Notebook The Kundalini Upanishad is found in the Yajur-Veda. Although this Upanishad is classified as a minor Upanishad, it is of major importance to the yogi for it deals with the fundamental and esoteric subject of Kundalini awakening as well as directing that cosmic Life-Force. In this program, Goswami Kriyananda reads and gives an enlightening commentary to his newly edited edition of this most valuable text. The great secret of this Upanishad relates to the average Earthling's breathing pattern. Thus, Goswami Kriyananda will explain how the Kriya-Kundalini awakening can be accomplished by key yogic practices. This program is an excellent adjunct to 'The Awakening of Your Serpent Power' program listed above.

Three 90-minute audiotapes and a 37-page notebook which includes Goswami Kriyananda's edited version of the Kundalini Upanishad $54

SEE ORDER FORM ON BACK PAGE

Goswami Kriyananda's
'How To'
Audiotape Series

This series of audiotapes will enable you to take a life improving concept and apply it positively to your life. Find new ways to solve many of the most common problems that we often face. Open your life to new ideas and new possibilities for success. Listed below are just a few audio tapes from this series:

How to Decide What You Want Out of Life gives you a step by step method to gain insights into your life and develop your goals.

How to Improve Your Life With Creative Visualization maps out an easy and systematic approach to materialize your dreams, plans and wishes, and transform your negative thoughts and emotions.

How Your Thoughts Materialize Into the Earth Plane defines what thought is, and how thoughts magnetize powerful astral forms that flow into your unconscious and manifest as your reality.

How to Understand the Yoga Diet teaches you that what you eat and the way you eat influences your mind, body and soul. A great tape filled with practical tips to help keep you healthy, peaceful, and focused on your life's goals.

How to Overcome Depression discusses the ingredients responsible for depression, the symptoms, and tools to overcome depression. You can attain a new life of happiness by refocusing the mind.

Other "How To" Tapes in the Series:
How to Attain a Peaceful Mind
How to Turn Your Obstacles Into Miracles
How to Manage Your Moods
How to Discover True Wealth
How to be Happy While Walking the Spiritual Path
How to Improve Self-Confidence
How to Understand Shamanism
How to Understand the Mystical Path
How to Become Aware of the Divinity in You and Be Happy Now
How to Begin to Recognize and Attain Your Spiritual Goals
How to Understand Yourself and Your Universe
How to Love, Remember and Serve
How to Solve All Your Problems
How to Understand Asceticism
How to Come Alive

60 minute audiotapes
Single tape:: $8.95
Any three: $19.95

SEE ORDER FORM ON BACK PAGE

Astral Projection Seminar

(A New Expanded Seminar
Containing Added Data and Techniques)

Astral Travel or "Out of Body Experience" is within your reach! Astral projection is the natural ability to withdraw your awareness from the outer universe into the inner universe, and then move from the lower inner universe, to the higher inner universe. It is natural to each one of us. Some find it easier than others, but everyone can accomplish this projection. All that is needed is a method and a great deal of practice.

This Astral Projection program is a unique opportunity to receive your training directly from Goswami Kriyananda. You, the mystical seeker, will find it of great value, for it will reveal the way that Life manifests from the invisible universes.

In this seminar you will learn about the four worlds and the seven planes, where, when and how to project, things that hinder projection, how to protect your physical and astral body while projecting, and how to create a safe platform in the astral for launching into Higher Planes of Consciousness.

Other Highlights of the course include:

♦ How to strengthen your aura
♦ The Ball of Light Projection technique
♦ The Mystical Sufi method of leaving your body
♦ Clues telling you which method is best for you
♦ The best method for "contacting" departed souls
♦ How your fears reveal what you need to overcome in order to project
♦ How to give greater elasticity to the Silver Cord
♦ How to tell the difference between a "thought-form" and a living entity

This extraordinary program gives you the opportunity to learn the ancient secrets which can give you freedom from the boundaries of your physical body!

8 hours of taped material (six 90-minute audiotapes) ... $79 (5/2002)

TO ORDER:
Outside Illinois: (800) 248-0024 - Inside Illinois (773) 342-4600
www.yogakriya.org -- E-mail: kriya@yogakriya.org

The Kriya Yoga Seminary
A 2-Year Home Study Training Program by Sri Goswami Kriyananda

"Give a man a fish, he will eat for a day; teach him to fish, he will eat forever."

Do you feel called to a life of spiritual service - a life dedicated to benefiting all living beings? Do you wish to make your work in the world something that aligns deeply with your spiritual values? If the answer is yes, then the Kriya Yoga Seminary can be a catalyst to the fulfillment of your aspirations.

The Kriya Yoga Seminary is a two-year home study program which ordains priests (swamis) capable of communicating the ancient wisdom in the form that is applicable in people's lives today. It is supported by audiotapes, printed lessons, and retreats. This intensive training program is for men and women who are called to be spiritual teachers, who will utilize their knowledge and experience to help, to heal, and to serve others.

The Kriya Yoga Seminary will provide you with a thorough understanding of the principles and practices of the mystical yogic tradition, as well as the study of yoga cosmology, philosophy and psychology, death and dying, the doctrine of karma, symbolism and ritual, the study of sacred texts, meditation and mantra, pastoral care, spiritual guidance, and Kriya Yoga.

The Kriya Yoga Seminary is not just a home study training course, it is a step toward making a lifelong commitment to assisting others. Compassionate engagement is a crucial part of the spiritual path and the priesthood. Therefore, in addition to the audiotapes and printed lessons you receive as a part of this program, a minimum of 48 hours of volunteer service work that benefits others is required during your two years of study.

It is not necessary to have prior experience in yoga or metaphysics in order to enroll. It IS necessary, however, to be dedicated to the awakening of your own spiritual potential and the impetus to sincerely help others along the path to greater earth happiness and Enlightenment.

$325/quarter (certain tuition discounts apply). For a complete course syllabus, brochure, and application call the Temple:

Outside Illinois: (800) 248-0024
Inside Illinois: (773) 342-4600
www.yogakriya.org -- E-mail: kriya@yogakriya.org

The Temple of Kriya Yoga's
Home Study Yoga Teacher Training & Certification

This course is designed for you to ...

♦ Increase your understanding of yoga

♦ Develop self-confidence as a teacher

♦ Discover how yoga can be integrated into the pattern of your daily life.

♦ Gain a practical understanding of how the asanas (postures) function to bring greater strength and flexibility of body, youthfulness, health and vitality.

♦ Make your life more meaningful by gaining teaching skills for sharing the joys and benefits of yoga with others.

The Temple of Kriya Yoga has successfully trained hundreds of students in the science of yoga. Many of them are using their knowledge to support themselves and help others to develop lives of greater health, happiness and wisdom. The Temple now offers this Yoga Teacher Training Home Study Program to those who wish to take the rewarding step from student to teacher. It is an extensive 12-month program providing over 200 hours of instruction including audiotapes, videos, books, study guides, lesson plans, and a personal advisor. It is a great opportunity to develop the skills you need to teach others while learning at your own pace. There are also two special weekend retreats to help lay the foundation for teaching, correcting postures, and providing you the opportunity to teach a series of classes and participate in reviewing other student teachers. The retreats will be held in a serene, beautiful retreat center located in the Midwest.

Course curriculum includes:
- Yoga Theory and Practice
- Anatomy and Physiology
- Theory and Practice of Pranayama
- How to Teach Meditation
- Communication Skills for Yoga Instructors
- How to Establish Yourself as a Yoga Teacher

For more detailed information and/or an application call **888-742-9642** or visit our website at **www.yogakriya.org**

The Yoga Sutras of Patanjali
The Science of Enlightenment
A course on how to attain Samadhi in this very lifetime.
A step-by-step guide by the Master of yoga.

Goswami Kriyananda has said that this is a basic and essential course for anyone seeking to understand and attain higher states of consciousness. It is a vital course for anyone not having a Guru. If one has a Guru, it is the Guru's textbook for teaching Yoga, and guiding souls upon the sacred Path.

Sri Patanjali in his four books entitled, *"The Kriya Yoga Sutras,"* gives the basics of all spiritual psychology. He shows the path for overcoming negative karma and for attaining happiness. In them he speaks of the causes of negative habits which lead to confinement, along with the methods to cure this confinement and thus attain Enlightenment. The emphasis in these great texts is the total step by step method for attaining Samadhi.

This home study course gives a detailed, step by step plan for moving from everyday earth consciousness to spiritual Enlightenment. It is a rare chance to tap the oral tradition of yoga. Goswami Kriyananda gives a new, deeper esoteric interpretation of each and every Sutra in the four books. He gives added insights into the more important Sutras and how to use them in your daily life to attain Samadhi.

Highlights of the program include:

♦ The nature and purpose of Kriya Yoga
♦ The key yogic techniques to overcome obstacles so that you can attain Samadhi and Enlightenment
♦ An exploration of the nature of karma and the things to do to avoid your karma from manifesting
♦ The means by which a dedicated soul can open the eye of wisdom and obtain, first hand, the occult, mystical secrets of the universe

This is truly a course which will guide you during your entire life. Each of the four books are conveniently divided into three parts for easier learning and remembering. Goswami Kriyananda lists each Sutra in the book, along with his deeper interpretation of its meaning.

This home study course contains fifteen 90-minute audiotapes, a 280-page notebook of printed text of the Sutras, along with Goswami Kriyananda's interpretation of them. It includes study questions to help you learn and retain the concepts and information.

Introductory offer ... $139

SEE ORDER FORM ON BACK PAGE

Chakras:
The Garden of God

Goswami Kriyananda's
Comprehensive Audio Tape
Home Study Course With Text

The Complete Set Contains:
- ♦ 15 Ninety Minute
  Audio Cassettes
- ♦ 620 Page Text and
  Study Guide
- ♦ 12 Full Color Illustrations
- ♦ Tape Case and
  3 Ring Binder

This extensive home study program is the most comprehensive course you can find on the esoteric philosophy of the Chakras. It contains a variety of very special mystical techniques given by Goswami Kriyananda for awakening and balancing the Chakras and bringing about higher states of consciousness. Kriyananda utilizes the Chakric Tree of Life to reveal the numerous ways in which we climb towards the apex of our spiritual maturity.

This program provides you with answers and insights into many of the most frequently asked questions about the Chakras, including:

- ♦ What are the Chakras?
- ♦ How do they affect your life?
- ♦ What is the value of this knowledge?
- ♦ How do you utilize them toward Enlightenment?
- ♦ How do you activate the Kriya currents within you?
- ♦ How do the Chakras relate to awakening Kundalini?
- ♦ What are some of the misconceptions about its awakening?
- ♦ What is the difference between Shakti, Kundalini and Kriya?

Chakras:
The Garden of God

You know that your physical body has a highly organized, elegantly designed anatomy. In this course you learn to understand and explore the equally wondrous anatomy of your subtle or astral body. The key structures of the subtle anatomy are the Chakras. These creative centers of consciousness are the inner keys to transforming and recreating our life at every level. A clear understanding of the Chakric system provides you with a map for understanding how you have created your current life conditions and how you can recreate those conditions in a more balanced, joyful, and harmonious form.

Goswami Kriyananda presents teachings that cannot be found in any other text. These are the techniques and insights that, in the past, were only transmitted orally from teacher to student.

You Will Discover:
- How you can tap into the tremendous energy and creative potential stored in the Chakras
- How Chakric energies manifest as health or disease
- The relationship of breath to awakening the Chakras
- The difference between balances and unbalanced energy in the subtle body
- How to awaken kundalini without pain or emotionality
- How Chakric energy manifests in our relationships.

Complete set including 15 audio tapes, text and study guide $169.00

TO ORDER:
Outside Illinois: (800) 248-0024 - Inside Illinois (773) 342-4600
www.yogakriya.org -- E-mail: kriya@yogakriya.org

SEE ORDER FORM ON BACK PAGE

Kriology®

THE STUDY AND PRACTICE OF THE
ESOTERIC TRADITION OF KRIYA YOGA
A New Home Study Program
by Sri Goswami Kriyananda

Kriology is the study and practice of the mystical tradition of Kriya Yoga. It is a pathway to wisdom, a mature, self-directed inquiry into the nature of you, your life, and the universe in which you dwell. It is a system for awakening a direct experience which expands the horizon of your awareness and cultivates greater joy and freedom.

The goal of this program is to share the oral tradition of Kriya Yoga and assist you in using the system to improve your life. Kriology offers you methods to nourish and heal your mind and body, develop greater clarity of purpose, soften your karma, and attain your spiritual dream. Through the study of universal principles and the use of specific spiritual techniques, Kriology offers you an opportunity to experience a transformation in consciousness, which can enrich your life on every level.

This course is designed to help you:
- Discover the Inner Rituals of Kriya Yoga
- Study Kriya Cosmology and Philosophy
- Learn the Laws of Self-conscious Awareness
- Quiet YourMind & Regenerate Your Physical Energy
- Transform Your Life & Become a Blessing to Others
- Break Free of Self-Imposed Limitations
- Deepen Your Practice Through Optional Retreats

Kriology offers you the unique opportunity to fully explore the Kriya tradition at your own pace and in the comfort of your own home. It is taught by Sri Goswami Kriyananda and features all new audio tapes created especially for this program. Kriology is offered in two parts or levels. Each level is comprised of 9 months of home study training including audiotapes and printed lessons, supported by an optional retreat led by Goswami Kriyananda to integrate the teachings more fully into your life. (All retreats will be held in serene, beautiful retreat centers.)

$325/quarter (9/2002). **For a complete course syllabus, brochure and application, call the Temple at: (773) 342-4600 OR e-mail:** kriya@yogakriya.org

ORDER FORM

PLEASE SEND ME THE FOLLOWING ITEMS:

Item	Quantity	Price

Please include these shipping and handling charges
for orders inside the Continental U.S.:

For orders:		$50-$100:	$6
Under $20:	$4	$100-$200:	$7
$20-$50:	$5	$200 or more:	$8

Subtotal $_____
Shipping $_____
Total $_____

For International orders, please call the Temple for shipping costs.

Enclosed is $_____   ☐ Check   ☐ Money Order
                          ☐ Visa   ☐ Mastercard

Credit Card #_____Exp Date_____

Signature:_____

SHIP TO:

Name _____

Address_____

City _____State_____Zip_____

Phone_____

☐ Yes, please send me a free catalogue of Goswami Kriyananda's
books, audiotapes and videos.

Phone Orders: Outside Illinois: (800) 248-0024
Inside Illinois: (773) 342-4600
FAX: (773) 342-4608

www.yogakriya.org -- E-mail: kriya@yogakriya.org

Send Your Orders to: TEMPLE OF KRIYA YOGA
2414 N. Kedzie Blvd. Dept. 03AGM
Chicago, IL 60647

♦NOTES♦

◆NOTES◆

◆NOTES◆